Praise for previous editions of this book:

"Absolutely the Social Security bible."
   Mary Beth Franklin, CFP, Contributing Editor, *InvestmentNews*

"Dive[s] into, and actually make[s] sense of, the maddening minutiae of Social Security."
   Glenn Ruffenach, *Wall Street Journal Encore*

"Everyone between 60 and 68 needs this book. This book allowed me to get $50,000 more in benefits that I did not know I could get!" ★ ★ ★ ★ ★ —top rating
   Amazon.com reader

"Out of six books that I've read about Social Security this is by far the best." ★ ★ ★ ★ ★ —top rating
   Amazon.com reader

"Worth every penny. This is the Bible of Social Security books." ★ ★ ★ ★ ★ —top rating
   Amazon.com reader

"…an excellent job … easy and enjoyable to read. I was impressed enough with it that I am switching to this book as required reading for two classes I am the instructor for." ★ ★ ★ ★ ★ —top rating
   Professor, College for Financial Planning

"Fantastic resource on all things Social Security!!! As a Certified Financial Planner®, I have referenced this book numerous times to help plan with my clients. The book is written in easy to understand language and covers pretty much anything you need to know. He uses great examples and provides many links to additional resources. This is a must-have for anyone in the financial services industry or anyone who wants to truly maximize and understand their benefits." ★ ★ ★ ★ ★ —top rating
   Tom Faley, CFP®, http://tomfaley.com/

"Great resource for professionals. This should be mandatory reading for rookie as well as veteran financial planners. The author lays out the often confusing "world" of Social Security in an understandable and entertaining fashion. The book's title says it all." ★ ★ ★ ★ ★ —top rating
   David Koch, CFP®

"Best explanation of Social Security I've ever seen in print. I'm a retired Social Security Claims Representative and I rate this book as the best explanation of Social Security benefits I've ever seen. The writer's style is great and he ha   ... It's not an easy subject, but he explains things in a simple, understandable fashio
   Amazon.com reader

"For anyone who is approachi   ...rce. Recommended."
   Midwest Book Review

"Absolutely fabulous!! My husband ordered this. This book gave information he had not found anywhere else and now that he's 62, we want to know exactly what our benefits are. We have an adult disabled son and this book explained some critical information that even our attorney did not know (or failed to tell us) that could affect SS benefits (in a positive way) if our son's disability is deemed severe enough for the special rules." ★ ★ ★ ★ ★ —top rating
   Amazon.com reader

"**Very useful book!** I've found Andy's book to be absolutely essential for anybody planning their retirement. Andy tells you how to get the most from Social Security, which can add many thousands of dollars to your lifetime payouts. And his info on Medicare helps you navigate the complex rules, so that you minimize your out-of-pocket medical expenses." ★ ★ ★ ★ ★—top rating

    Steve Vernon, FSA, President, Rest-of-Life Communications and author of *Money For Life* and *Recession-Proof Your Retirement Years*, http://restoflife.com

"**Good overview and a fairly easy read.** Social Security is complicated because there are many rules and even more personal situations. This book did a good job of giving you the basics so you have an understanding of the general terrain. It's also well written so most people should be able to understand the subject." ★ ★ ★ ★ ★—top rating

    Amazon.com reader

"**Social Security Demystified.** I use this book in our Retirement Planning Seminars. This is a fantastic resource on all things related to the Social Security System and how you can benefit from it. Andy Landis is both knowledgeable and concise. A must-own." ★ ★ ★ ★ ★—top rating

    Amazon.com reader

"**Absolutely the best on explaining when to take Social Security.** Excellent book for anyone trying to decide when to begin Social Security. A lot what he explains is not common knowledge. I highly recommend this book as a reference for retirement planning." ★ ★ ★ ★ ★—top rating

    Amazon.com reader

"**Excellent. Easy to read. Much helpful information.** Mr. Landis has succeeded in making a very complicated subject comprehensible to the average reader. I appreciated the fact that Mr. Landis was employed by the Social Security Administration for many years and was able to give an insider's account of procedures and benefits. Many thanks for this very helpful book!" ★ ★ ★ ★—Amazon.com rating

    Amazon.com reader

"**A Perfect 'Layman's' Guide To Social Security.** This book provides a very thorough, yet practical explanation of Social Security in an easy to read format. This is a great guide for almost anyone wanting a better understanding of not only how the program works, but how it will work for them as an individual participant." ★ ★ ★ ★ ★—top rating

    Matthew P. Jarvis, Chartered Financial Consultant, www.jarvisfinancial.com

"**Landis does for Social Security what J.K. Lasser and others have done for taxes**—provide reliable, understandable, and comprehensive guidance."

    Booklist

"In a market full of manuals on Social Security and Medicare, this new book is the first that provides a comprehensive review of the regulations and at the same time explains how the Social Security Administration works."

    Jon Robert Steinberg, *New Choices for Retirement Living*

"Your book will, no doubt, help numerous individuals as they plan for their future. *The Inside Story* is not only full of important information, but also easy to read. You have made a complex subject understandable."

    Horace Deets, former Executive Director, AARP

"**Andy Landis makes the complexities of Social Security easy to understand.** This well-organized book covers all of the important Social Security topics. The numerous real-life examples are especially helpful. I highly recommend this expertly guided tour of Social Security."

    Ray Eads, President, Wealth Management Northwest, http://wealth-nw.com/company/

SOCIAL SECURITY
THE INSIDE STORY

2018 Silver Anniversary Edition

Andy Landis
THINKING RETIREMENT
www.andylandis.biz

Social Security: The Inside Story
2018 Silver Anniversary Edition
By Andy Landis
THINKING RETIREMENT
www.andylandis.biz

Printed in the United States of America.

2018.1

Library of Congress Cataloging-in-Publication Data

Landis, Andrew S.
Social Security: The Inside Story, 2018 Silver Anniversary Edition
by Andy Landis. 2018 Edition. Includes index. 308 pages.
$19.95 Softcover
ISBN-10: **1981651837**
ISBN-13: **978-1981651832**

Library of Congress Control Number: **2017919811**
CreateSpace Independent Publishing Platform, North Charleston, SC

1. Social Security—United States—Popular works.
2. Medicare—Popular works. I. Title
HD7124.L36 2010   344.73/02

*To Ramona and Vera with love,
and with hope that Social Security will be even healthier for their generation
than it is for mine.*

☆ v

Acknowledgements

My primary debt is to the thousands of people I have met over the past 40 years, at SSA and after SSA. Your concerns, your tough questions, and your kind attention helped me to see both the details and the "big picture" better.

Tom Washington, you opened my eyes—and a door. Kaycee Krysty steered me by encouragement and example. Ray Larsen gave me an opportunity I will never forget. The fine people at SSA, especially the staffs at the Bellevue and Renton (now Kent) offices and the Auburn TSC, answered my questions and provided invaluable information and materials. Particular credit is due to Kirk Larson, Bill Beineke, Rod Smitkin, Michael Clement, and Kathy Cox for their extensive help and patience.

And to friends and contributors who have gone on, Dr. Ralph Richardson, Ray Larsen, Elwood Chapman, and Andrew Tartella, *adios. Vaya con Dios.*

This work was greatly improved by the tactful editing of Scott Provence, editor extraordinaire. Special thanks also to Kay Landis and Mary Lou Standerfer for additional editing assistance.

I'm very grateful to Marcia Mantell of Mantell Retirement Consulting for correcting a computation error (!) in an earlier edition.

Naturally, any lingering errors are mine.

Disclaimers

Every effort has been made to ensure accuracy at the time of publication. However, each individual case is unique, policies change, and space limitations prevent including every Social Security provision. Only the Social Security Administration can make official decisions. Always consult directly with SSA, Medicare, IRS, your employer, or private insurers for individual determinations on your case and your family's.

Examples used throughout this book are fictional. Any resemblance to actual persons, living or dead, is purely coincidental.

I am not affiliated with the Social Security Administration. The opinions expressed are my own. They do not represent the positions of the publisher or the Social Security Administration.

☆ CONTENTS ☆

Today a hope of many years' standing is fulfilled.... We can never insure one hundred percent of the population against one hundred percent of the hazards and vicissitudes of life, but we have tried to frame a law which will give some measure of protection to the average citizen and to his family against the loss of a job and against poverty-ridden old age.

Franklin Delano Roosevelt
Upon signing the Social Security Act
August 14, 1935
www.ssa.gov/history/fdrsignstate.html

☆ INTRODUCTION ☆

THIS BOOK IS FOR YOU

This book is valuable if you are:

- Retirement age or approaching retirement age.

- Any age and facing disability.

- Dealing with survivorship issues, either after a death or as part of advance planning for yourself or a family member.

- A taxpayer wanting to know what you're getting for your money.

- A financial advisor.

- An attorney who prepares estate plans.

- An insurance professional needing to know how your products can augment Social Security and Medicare.

- A social services provider needing to know when to refer clients to SSA.

- A human resources professional wanting to understand how Social Security benefits relate to your employer plans.

- Just a wonk or a student of public policy wanting in-depth understanding of the program.

In short, this book is for anyone with a stake in Social Security and Medicare, and for those who assist others with retirement, disability, death, or health insurance.

WHY THIS BOOK

There are good books out there on Social Security and Medicare.[1] And the Social Security website is exhaustive.[2]

This book intends to be the best resource available.

"Best" means the most up-to-date, the most comprehensive, the most accurate, the easiest to use, and the most readable.

- It's *up-to-date,* with every computation and numerical fact updated to 2018. The latest provisions are explained, including the Affordable Care Act of

2010 (Obamacare) and the Bipartisan Budget Act of 2015. *Reform Targets* describe recent or proposed changes that could affect your payments.

- It's *comprehensive,* covering many topics, like Medicare, overlooked by other books. Dozens of web links invite you to drill deeper into any topic, without endless searching. (Remember, weblinks are case-sensitive; you must use upper- and lower-case letters just as shown.)

- Its *accuracy* is ensured by my 40 years studying Social Security, 12 years inside SSA and 28 additional years as a speaker and consultant. Outside review by financial advisors have further honed accuracy.

- It's *easy to use,* quickly answering your specific questions like a reference book. A detailed table of contents, glossary, and index pinpoint the answers you need.

- It's highly *readable.* Realistic stories weave the facts together into an understandable whole. Plain English replaces technical jargon.

In short, it *makes sense* of Social Security and gives you the *inside story.* With this book you will understand what your hard-earned tax dollars are buying, and how to get the most from your stake in the system.

WHAT'S NEW

New in this edition:

- **New "Chapter in a Nutshell" summaries.** Each chapter starts with a snapshot of important points.

- **New Medicare cards.** New card design will eliminate the Social Security Number, starting in 2018 (page 142).

- **Medigap changes.** Medigap types C and F will be closed to new subscribers in 2020 (page 156).

- **Affordable Care Act repeal.** "Reform Target" notes pinpoint changes if Obamacare is repealed. Obamacare provisions that are still phasing in are described (pages 130, 163, and 167).

- **Updated "maximizing" chapter.** The maximizing chapter has been rewritten for clarity, with numerous examples of "Voluntary Suspension" and "Restricted Application" under both the old rules and new rules. (pages 241 and 248).

- **AERO.** A description of the Automated Earnings Reappraisal Operation (AERO) is added (page 211).

- **Disability solvency.** A re-allocation of payroll taxes to extend solvency of the disability trust fund is reported (pages 214-215).

- **"My Social Security."** The latest capabilities of the online service are detailed (page 177).

- **Same-sex marriage.** A second US Supreme Court ruling has extended spousal and survivor's payments to same-sex couples in every state (pages 61 and 87).

- **Editing.** The book is exhaustively re-edited for accuracy, brevity, and clarity. Information mapping is expanded.

- **New visual aids.** New charts and artwork clarify complex provisions.

- **Chapter endnotes.** Footnotes are updated and more complete than ever.

TOWARD FAIRNESS AND SIMPLICITY

I have spread examples among people of many backgrounds, a variety of ages, and both sexes. Any bias is unintentional.

I sometimes use the (improper but colloquial) "they" to indicate a third person singular of unknown gender, rather than the (correct but cumbersome) "him or her." For example, "Your spouse can file for their own Social Security when they file on your record."

I offer my apologies to grammarians, with whom I usually am allied.

FOR MORE INFORMATION...

Chapter Endnotes
1. See https://www.wsj.com/articles/where-to-get-clear-social-security-answers-1504275610 for some great Social Security books.
2. www.ssa.gov

☆ NOTES ☆

CHAPTER ONE

YOUR SOCIAL SECURITY: AN OVERVIEW

⬢ Chapter in a Nutshell

- Social Security is a complete package of worker benefits: retirement, disability, survivors and health insurance.

- It dates from the 1930s and has evolved over the decades.

- It is a social insurance program—an earned benefit based on work, not a handout.

- It is self-funded and financially sound in the near term.

Sally Smith has only ten years of part-time work scattered over the years of her life.
She will get Social Security payments.[1]

Bob Johnson had worked only a few years when he had a serious accident. The doctors think it will be years before he can return to work, if ever.
He will get Social Security payments.[2]

Marsha Jones, who worked as a homemaker and volunteer her whole life, has almost no paid work. Her husband John is retiring soon.
She will get Social Security payments.[3]

Frank and Karen Ferguson are in high school. Their father died last month from a sudden illness.
They will get Social Security payments.[4]

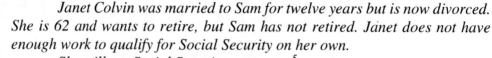

Janet Colvin was married to Sam for twelve years but is now divorced. She is 62 and wants to retire, but Sam has not retired. Janet does not have enough work to qualify for Social Security on her own.
She will get Social Security payments.[5]

Each of these people was surprised to learn that Social Security is more than just a retirement program for workers. It's much more, as you will learn from this book.

In coming chapters, you will visit each of these individuals, and many others, to discover *why* they are eligible for Social Security and *how much* they can expect. From them, you will learn what *you* can expect from Social Security for yourself and family members.

Social Security is a broad, complex program with a rich history. This chapter is an overview of the program and its background, with special attention to Social Security's strengths and weaknesses, and why Social Security is what it is today.

This chapter will also show you how Social Security works. It gives you a "big picture" perspective to apply to the following, more technical chapters, showing the forest before the trees.

If you can't wait to learn about the technical aspects of the program, skip ahead to Chapter 2 for retirement benefits, or another chapter that interests you. You can return to this chapter at any time to tie the details together.

SOCIAL SECURITY'S HISTORY

Franklin D. Roosevelt signed the Social Security Act into law in 1935. It was the product of several years of often bitter controversy, negotiation, lobbying, and compromise. The debate took place in the chambers of Congress, the editorial pages, the Supreme Court, and the streets and workplaces of America.[6]

On one hand, there were charges that the program would be socialist, that it would lead to social chaos, and that government could not be trusted to pay benefits properly, if at all.[7]

On the other hand was the desire to protect workers and their families against poverty after their work years—poverty which, in the midst of the Depression, was a real threat to millions of families.

How did today's program come from such turmoil? FDR envisioned Social Security as a new kind of government program, uniquely suited to its mission of protecting against poverty after a worker's retirement or death.

To accomplish its mission, Social Security would draw from two "big three's":

- The "big three" concepts: a powerful underlying philosophy, an independent method of funding, and vast national scope.

- The "big three" partnership: Labor, Industry, and Government.

By carefully harnessing these diverse components into a balanced whole, the Social Security program was successfully created.

The philosophy of the program: Social Insurance

The new Social Security program ideally would promote, not undermine, the work ethic and individual dignity. Therefore, Social Security was established as a *social insurance* program, not a *social welfare* (or public assistance) program.[8]

Social insurance means that the government acts as an insurance company. It insures your paycheck. Much like a private insurance company, Social Security collects premiums from you the worker, and then pays back to you (or your family) a defined amount when certain events occur. In 1935 the insured event was the retirement of the worker, but insured events now include death and disability.

Payments from Social Security are intended to *partially replace lost earnings.*[9] Payments are tied to your contributions to the system (i.e., the payroll taxes you paid). Those payments, then, are owed to you and your family. Your work paid for them; they are an *earned right.* In this way, the system reflects our basic value of *ownership.*

Social Security protects the worker's family as well as the worker. This promotes our basic value of *family.*

Social Security payments are not welfare—not charity, a handout or dole. They're like payments from a private insurance company or pension. And since the payments are earned through work performed, the system encourages productive work, thus promoting another American value: our *work ethic.*

You become eligible for Social Security by passing an *insured test.* Your work record proves you paid into the system, making you insured. A welfare or public assistance program, on the other hand, requires a *means test*—every participant must prove that he is sufficiently *poor* to get payments. Compared to a welfare program, an insurance program is less expensive to run (having no need to prove poverty) and better preserves *individual dignity.*

By the way, the difference between *private insurance companies* and *social insurance* is that social insurance is run for the entire society, and participation is mandatory, enforced by the tax system.

> 🎯 **Reform Target:** Some reform proposals would add a welfare-type means test to Social Security. For example, some propose that retirees with income above, say, $50,000, should have their Social Security reduced or eliminated. This would partially change Social Security from an insurance program to a welfare program.[10]

Examples of social insurance programs include:

- Social Security
- Unemployment insurance (for unemployed workers), and
- Workers' compensation (for those injured at work).

Independent funding

Social Security is *self-funded.* Private insurance companies are funded by premiums from rate-payers. Similarly, Social Security's benefit payments, administrative overhead, and future investment are paid by tax contributions from workers and employers, not government subsidies.[11] (Exceptions are Medicare, which is partially subsidized by the government, and the 2011-2012 "payroll tax holiday," with lost payroll tax revenue replaced by general revenues.)

Self-funding gives the program integrity. Social Security isn't charity and it isn't a drain on government. It is supported *by* workers, *for* workers.

Independent funding also insulates Social Security from the vagaries of government funding. Social Security does not reduce benefits during times of government belt-tightening. It is shielded from the whims of Congress or the President.

The public supports Social Security's independent status. In fact, many question whether Social Security finances should be included in the Federal budget. They have a point—there is little reason to lump Social Security figures into the Federal budget because Social Security is independently financed.

> 🎯 **Reform Target:** Some reformers propose direct government subsidies to Social Security.[12] This would change Social Security from a self-funded system to one dependent on government subsidy.

The scope of the program

We can imagine 1930s critics of Social Security raising a good question: Was a national insurance system even *possible?* The scope of such a system—its sheer size and the blizzard of necessary paperwork—was simply staggering, especially with 1935 technology.

First, a system of *record-keeping* needed to be invented. This would have to be a massive system, dwarfing any other program at that time. Just think: for each industrial worker in the nation, a record would have to be kept every calendar quarter. The record would have to reflect every dollar earned from each employer, even if the worker had multiple employers every month (not so unusual, especially in the Depression), and even if the worker changed names.

The system finally adopted required employers to file the reports necessary for record-keeping. These reports would be broken down worker by worker and quarter by quarter (quarterly reports were replaced by annual reports in 1978). The reports would cover each worker throughout every year of his or her working life. And every employer would prepare and file these reports with no compensation—instead they would be stung with a payroll tax.

The millions of employer reports would be sorted into individual workers' records by the new "Social Security Board" (predecessor to today's Social Security Administration). To do so, the Board had to assign a unique *number* to each worker—otherwise it would have been impossible to properly sort the reports into individual records, given the number of identical names, birthdates and birth cities, even within a single large company. Imagine the controversy: were people being reduced to serial numbers? (See page 216 for more information on Social Security numbers.)

Collecting, sorting, and storing these tens of millions of records was just the beginning. The Social Security Board still needed to create a *payment* system to process claims, recall earnings records, compute benefit payments, and maintain monthly payments for the lifetime of each beneficiary.

Remember, this was 1930s technology. There were no computers, magnetic tapes, or electronic data transfers. We're talking actual paper reports, prepared on manual typewriters, then mailed in and sorted by hand into filing cabinets. Social Security cards were typed by hand and payment computations were performed with adding machines and scratch paper.[13]

Critics of the new system predicted the program would collapse under its own weight. Few could imagine the system working, especially since it required the cooperation of three natural antagonists: Labor, Industry, and Government.

Members of the partnership

The Social Security program created a partnership of the three major sectors of the American economy: Labor, Industry, and Government. Each sector was to play a significant role:

- The *individual worker* would make regular contributions to the program through payroll deductions, and cooperate by accepting the assigned Social Security number.

- *Industry* would match the worker's contribution to the system. Employers would also keep individual records of each worker's earnings and report them quarterly to the government.

- *Government* would hire the staffers, issue the Social Security numbers, maintain the national records necessary to compute payments, process claims from retirees, and issue benefit payments.

The system ca. 1937-1940

Guided by this ambitious blueprint, the first Social Security taxes were collected in 1937: 1% of earnings up to $3,000, for a maximum annual tax of $30.00. Only industrial workers were covered—not farmers, the self-employed, professionals, or the military. The first monthly Social Security benefit payments were issued in January 1940. Benefit categories included:[14]

- The retired worker
- The *wife* of a male worker,
- The child under 18 of a retired or deceased worker,
- The *mother* of a deceased worker's child, and
- The dependent parent, 65 or older, of a deceased worker.

These original benefit categories reflect the values of their time. The worker could be either sex, but only wives and widows were considered dependents of a worker; men got no benefits on their wives' work records. Children were automatically covered, with assumed dependency on the worker. However, parents of the worker needed to prove their dependency. In 1940, then, a simple Retirement and Survivor Insurance program, reflecting the work and family values of the era, was put in place.

The system evolves

Incredibly, the overall framework established in the 1935 Act stands today with relatively minor modifications. Still in place after 83 years is the *philosophy* of insurance rather than welfare, *self-funding*, and the immense *scope* of the system. Even the partnership among government, industry, and the individual remains intact.

Nevertheless, times have changed and Social Security has changed as well. Changes include:

- **New covered workers.** Over the years, farmers, domestic workers, the self-employed, the military, professionals, and many government workers have been brought into the system.

 THE INSIDE STORY

Internal names for SSA programs

The initials of its various programs serve as a kind of "shorthand" inside SSA. As the programs evolved, the shorthand has had to follow suit:

1935-1956	**OASI**	"Old-Age & Survivor Insurance"
1957-1964	**OASDI**	"Old-Age, Survivor, and Disability Insurance"
1965 on	**OASDHI**	"Old-Age, Survivor, Disability, and Health Insurance"
TODAY	**RSDHI**	"Retirement, Survivor, Disability, and Health Insurance"

Employees create partial acronyms to refer to groups of programs. For example, when speaking of the retirement/survivor program but not disability and Medicare, you will hear "RSI;" or in comparing the payment programs with the health program you will hear "RSDI" vs. "HI."

- **New types of benefits.** *Disability benefits* were added to the program in 1956, and further expanded in 1960 (after being proposed since the 1930s). *Medicare* was added in 1965, adding health insurance to the program. (See the "Inside Story" box above for how the Administration's internal jargon has evolved to reflect the added benefit types.)

- **New types of beneficiaries.** *Husbands and widowers* of workers became eligible starting in 1950, joining the wives and widows already eligible.

- **New retirement ages.** *Age 62 early retirement* became an option for women in 1956 and for men in 1961. And currently the "Full Retirement Age" (FRA) is rising from age 65 to age 67.

- **Higher benefit payments and taxes.** Over the years benefit payments increased, first through Congressional action and now automatically with inflation. At the same time the eligible population expanded and new benefit categories were added. These increased costs made higher taxes necessary.

- **New information technology.** With their huge record-keeping and payment tasks, Social Security has always needed efficient data-processing systems. The paper files, typewriters, and adding machines have gone the way of the dinosaur, replaced by computers.

Overall, the changes in Social Security in its first 83 years balance flexibility and stability. Each decade has brought changes to the program, based on what each generation wanted Social Security to do. Yet the basic structure of the system remains.

This balance between flexibility and stability suggests what we can expect in Social Security's future: reforms for each generation's needs within a stable framework of social insurance.

TODAY'S SOCIAL SECURITY

Many people believe that Social Security is merely a retirement program. But Social Security has always been much more than that. Today it is a comprehensive program of worker benefits, covering not only the worker but also family members. In fact, only about 68% of Social Security beneficiaries are retired workers (see Figure 1.1). Categories of protection include:

- *Retirement benefits*—For workers over 62 who retire. Similar to private pensions and annuities.

- *Family benefits*—For dependent family members of a worker who retires or becomes disabled.

- *Survivor benefits*—For surviving family members of a worker who dies at any age. Similar to private life insurance and joint annuities.

- *Disability benefits*—For workers, widow(er)s, or children under Full Retirement Age who become totally disabled. Similar to private disability insurance.

- *Medicare*—Health insurance for retirees over 65, certain disabled persons, and their dependents. Similar to private health insurance.

Thus, the program provides, in the language of insurance, *protection against loss of earned income due to retirement, disability, or death*. This three-fold protection is the mission of the Social Security Administration. In the coming chapters we'll see how SSA carries out its mission, extending insurance coverage to you and other Americans.

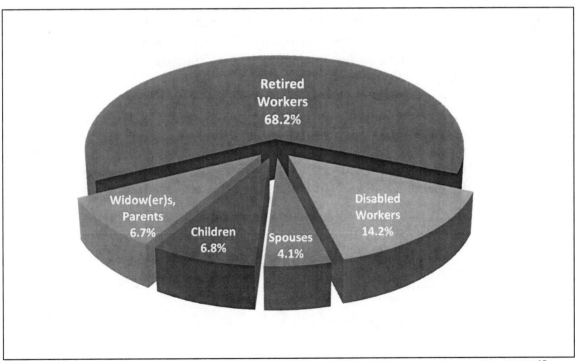

Figure 1.1: Types of beneficiaries in the Social Security program, as of June 30, 2017.[15]

SURPRISING STRENGTHS OF SOCIAL SECURITY

There's good news about Social Security. Here are a few of its strengths:

Inflation-proof

Payments from Social Security are inflation-proof. Every Social Security payment gets an annual increase in January, equal to the inflation rate, as measured by the Consumer Price Index (CPI). This is called a *COLA,* for Cost Of Living Adjustment, and has been required by law since 1975.

Without COLAs, the buying power of your Social Security would steadily erode. That's the situation for most pensions, which are "locked in" at a fixed dollar amount for life. Inflationary erosion can be substantial when compounded over a 30-year retirement.

There were no COLAs in 2010, 2011, and 2016. Quite simply, there was no measurable inflation for those years.

 Reform Target: Many reformers propose to reduce the COLA to less than the inflation rate (e.g. the inflation rate minus 0.5%), or to measure inflation with an index lower than the CPI, such as the "Chained CPI." Over time this would reduce buying power substantially.[16]

Supplemental payments for family

Additional benefits are payable to certain dependent family members. Chapter 3, "Family Benefits," gives details on this provision. Most pension plans don't pay family benefits.

 Reform Target: This provision is also under scrutiny. Many proposals would reduce family benefits.[17]

Insurance, not public assistance

Social Security is an insurance program, not a welfare program. It's a big difference. A welfare program is *needs-based*, and must document all income and assets of the individual or family. That's costly—in time, money, and the dignity of the claimant.

Social Security, on the other hand, is a *social insurance* program. Payments are based on your work history and age. Those are concrete facts, far easier to establish than need. Thus, Social Security is much more efficient than welfare programs, saving taxpayer money. It also preserves individual dignity—you know you paid for your benefits and own them.

> **_Reform Target:_** Some reformers call for eliminating this core principle of Social Security. This usually takes the form of reducing or eliminating benefits for higher-income retirees.[18]

Portability and universal coverage

Ever lose pension coverage when you changed jobs? Thousands of dollars in contributions and a good number of "vesting years" can be lost forever, due to a job change.

Social Security, on the other hand, is totally portable, meaning you carry your coverage with you when you change jobs. And it's nearly universal, covering 94% of all paid jobs in the U.S.[19] Your Social Security coverage continues to grow as your career progresses, wherever your career takes you.

> **_Reform Target:_** Most reform plans call for extending Social Security coverage to more workers, making coverage even more universal.[20]

This is a plus for taxpayers as well. Having one large national system provides economies of scale—it is simpler and more efficient to operate than hundreds of individual pension plans.

Financial soundness

The last few decades brought a series of financial nightmares. We saw the Savings and Loan Crisis, bank failures, huge insurance companies in bankruptcy, stock market volatility, pension plans going broke, housing crashes, and the "Great Recession."

Social Security faced its own financial crisis in the late 1970s and early '80s. Headlines stated the exact month the system would run out of money. Congress tried several fixes between 1977 and 1983. Yet the program continued to slide closer to insolvency.

The 1983 fix finally worked. The 1983 Amendments to the Social Security Act raised taxes and cut benefits, opening the door for a half-century of solvency. Since then the system has run a surplus every year, and Social Security is still "on track" with 1983's projections.

Turns out, Social Security is one of our most sound financial institutions.

That doesn't mean that today's surpluses are permanent. Social Security faces another financial shortfall in about 2034, similar to 1983. Solutions are already being sought. For details about Social Security's long-term solvency, see Chapter 11.

 Reform Target: The shortfalls predicted for the 2030s are the driving force behind most reform plans.

Political soundness

Where does an 800-pound gorilla sit? Wherever it wants. And where does the most popular government program sit politically? You got it.

Politicians know it is very risky to weaken Social Security. The program is just too popular—everyone has a stake. 61 million people[21] (about one in every six Americans[22]) receive Social Security payments every month, and most of them are voters. Right behind them are 171 million other Americans paying into the system and *expecting* a payment someday.[23] Social Security has been called the "third rail" of politics—touch it and you die.

An example of the political power supporting Social Security: there have been proposals since the late 1980s to reduce or eliminate annual cost-of-living raises. Popular opinion won't have it. The raises continue to be tied to the CPI.

Another example: Congress enacted the Medicare Catastrophic Coverage Act of 1989. It was rescinded within a year—it was just too unpopular.

Social Security has proved it can weather political storms. That lends stability to the system, and confidence it will endure.

WEAKNESSES OF THE SYSTEM

The above section makes it sound like Social Security is perfect, as if all problems are solved and everyone is happy.

Obviously, that's not so. Here are the main weaknesses of the program, and how you can counter them.

Payment amount

Social Security payments are low. The maximum amount payable to a 66-year-old in 2018 is $2,788 per month.[24] The average retiree draws $1,404 per month.[25] While the average is above the poverty level, no one gets rich from Social Security.

Of course, Social Security payments were never meant to be your sole retirement income. Rather, Social Security should be considered a *foundation* of retirement income, a base to build other assets and income on.

Other forms of retirement income—pensions, investment income, rental income, and so on—do not reduce your Social Security payment. (Remember, this is an *insurance* program, not needs-based welfare.) The *only* type of income which affects your Social Security retirement payment is work income from wages or self-employment before your Full Retirement Age. (See page 205 for more information on work after retirement.)

The implication is clear: since Social Security alone doesn't ensure a comfortable retirement, and doesn't penalize you for outside income, you should amass as much as you can in the way of pensions, retirement savings, and any other assets to augment your Social Security.

See Chapter 2 for more on your Social Security payments, and Chapter 7 on your Social Security Statement.

> *Reform Target:* Nearly every reform plan envisions lower Social Security payments in the future. Younger workers should expect to provide even more of their own retirement funding.

Complexity

Social Security is a complex program with rules, exceptions to the rules, exceptions to the exceptions, and so on. In fact, Social Security is not "a" program at all. It is a set of linked programs—a retirement/survivor program with disability and health insurance programs grafted on. It can take years of study to understand the system. Claims Representatives at SSA are "trainees" for the first three years on the job. Probably no single individual can master the entire system.

So, is it impossible to understand the program? Not at all. As already noted, the overall structure of the program and its underlying philosophy have been largely unchanged for over 83 years. That framework can be understood, along with the major exceptions to the general frame.

As you read this book you will learn about Social Security's rules and practices. You'll better understand your options and your rights, letting you to make better, more informed decisions about *your* Social Security.

Bureaucracy

With over 1,200 offices, some 65,000 employees,[26] and employee manuals that would stack twenty feet high (if printed), we're looking at dense bureaucracy. Complaints about the bureaucracy range from telephone busy signals, to inability to reach the proper person, to poorly trained personnel. Some callers get different answers from different employees to the same question.

Keep in mind that the agency, though large and complex, is still a human enterprise. SSA is just a group of people working together with a common mission. There are experienced people, harried people, outstanding people, and newcomers. Being human, they make mistakes. This is especially understandable when you consider the program's complexity. To their credit, payment accuracy is over 99.5%.[27]

There are ways to work with this bureaucracy. See Chapter 8, Filing Your Claim, for some ideas. You have a head start on others because you have a strong ally: this book.

FOR MORE INFORMATION...

"Understanding the Benefits"
www.ssa.gov/pubs/10024.html

"A 'Snapshot'"
www.ssa.gov/pubs/10006.html

Chapter Endnotes
1. See p. 34 and https://www.ssa.gov/pubs/EN-05-10024.pdf, p. 6
2. See p. 103 and https://www.ssa.gov/disabilityssi/
3. See p. 60 and https://www.ssa.gov/planners/retire/applying6.html
4. See p. 95 and https://www.ssa.gov/pubs/EN-05-10085.pdf
5. See p. 63 and https://www.ssa.gov/planners/retire/divspouse.html
6. https://www.socialsecurity.gov/policy/docs/ssb/v70n3/v70n3p1.html
7. http://www.cwa-union.org/news/entry/social_security_communist_plot_medicare_called_government_takeover and https://en.wikipedia.org/wiki/History_of_Social_Security_in_the_United_States#Initial_opposition
8. https://www.ssa.gov/history/briefhistory3.html under "The Social Insurance Movement"
9. https://www.socialsecurity.gov/history/reports/gspan7.html under "Social Security.....In The Beginning"
10. See for example http://www.phillymag.com/news/2015/04/14/chris-christie-cut-social-security-for-the-rich/
11. https://ssa.gov/news/press/factsheets/HowAreSocialSecurity.htm
12. For a variation in which FICA taxes are reduced and government makes direct contributions to private accounts, see https://www.ssa.gov/oact/solvency/Warshawsky_20080917.pdf
13. https://ssa.gov/history/cronin.html
14. https://ssa.gov/history/briefhistory3.html under "Monthly Benefits"
15. See www.socialsecurity.gov/OACT/ProgData/icp.html for current percentages
16. http://money.usnews.com/money/retirement/articles/2013/04/29/how-the-chained-cpi-affects-social-security-payments
17. https://www.socialsecurity.gov/OACT/solvency/NASI_20091030.pdf, p. 5, D

18. See for example https://www.socialsecurity.gov/OACT/solvency/JChaffetz_20111109.pdf, Provision 7
19. https://www.ssa.gov/OACT/FACTS/, D.1
20. See for example https://www.socialsecurity.gov/OACT/solvency/BipartisanTaskForce_20101117.pdf, Provision 3
21. https://www.ssa.gov/policy/docs/chartbooks/fast_facts/2017/fast_facts17.html#contributions , OASDI tab, "Beneficiaries in Current-Payment Status"
22. https://www.census.gov/popclock/ for current US population
23. https://www.ssa.gov/policy/docs/chartbooks/fast_facts/2017/fast_facts17.html#contributions, OASDI tab, "Earnings in Covered Employment"
24. https://www.ssa.gov/news/press/factsheets/colafacts2018.pdf
25. Ibid.
26. https://www.ssa.gov/policy/docs/statcomps/supplement/2016/2f1-2f3.html
27. https://paymentaccuracy.gov/programs/retirement-survivors-and-disability-insurance

☆ NOTES ☆

CHAPTER TWO

YOUR RETIREMENT BENEFITS

Retirement Benefits in a Nutshell

- To be eligible, you need 10 years of work where you paid Social Security taxes.

- Your Full Retirement Age (FRA) is between 65 and 67, based on your birth year.

- Starting Social Security at your FRA yields a "100%" payment. It's computed from your highest 35 years of earnings.

- Reduced payments are available as early as age 62. Delaying payments results in higher benefits, up to age 70.

Sam Smith is approaching retirement and wants to know how much he will receive from Social Security. When he calls Social Security, he is told he can receive $2,077 per month if his payments start at age 65.

But Sam is curious. What does his age have to do with his payment amount? Where does the $2,077 figure come from—how is it computed? Is there anything he can do to increase the amount?

Retirement benefits are the heart and soul of Social Security's package of protection. In fact, many Americans think Social Security pays *only* retirement benefits, because many are not aware of the family, survivor, and disability portions of the program. The retirement program was the key achievement of the original Social Security Act and continues to be the centerpiece of the program.

In this chapter you will examine the retirement program. You will see how you as a worker become eligible for a payment, how your payments are computed, and a few of the special provisions in the program. And, most importantly, you will learn what you can do to *affect* the amount of your payment.

ARE YOU ELIGIBLE FOR RETIREMENT BENEFITS?

General information about eligibility

Sally Smith, Sam's wife, wants to know whether she is eligible for a retirement payment of her own. When she and Sam married, Sally quit her 3-year job. Then she did not work again until the children were grown, and worked only part-time the last seven years. Can she get a retirement payment?

Sally Smith and others with a limited work history need to know whether they can get a retirement payment at all. They need to know the *eligibility rules* for SSA retirement benefits.

The short answer: to get a retirement payment you must be 62 and have at least 10 years of part-time work. The rest of this section gives the details.

Remember, Social Security is a "social insurance" program, and that's a good way to think of it—like an insurance company. Before your auto insurance or health insurance will pay a claim, you must be enrolled and paid up. Social Security works the same way.

Note that this section deals only with *eligibility* for a payment, not how much will be paid. For information on payment computations see below under "How your payment is computed."

There are two requirements for eligibility:

- You must meet minimum *age requirements*, and

- You must meet minimum *work requirements*.

Age requirement for eligibility

To collect a retirement payment, you must "attain" at least 62 years of age. The earliest month you can be eligible for a retirement payment is your first full month of being age 62.

Normally this means you are eligible for payments the month after your 62nd birthday—that's the first month you are 62 for the entire month. So, if you turn 62 on June 21, you are eligible for Social Security in July.

But there is an exception: If your birthday is the first of the month, you are eligible the month of your 62nd birthday.[1] The reason is that you "attain" age 62 the day before your 62nd birthday (see "The Inside Story" box below). That exception can result in one extra payment if you are born on the first or second of the month.

But attaining age 62 is not enough in itself for you to gain Social Security eligibility. In addition, you must meet the work requirements.

Sally Smith will be over age 62 when she retires, so she knows she will meet the age requirement. What about the work requirement?

 THE INSIDE STORY

"Attaining" retirement age

We normally think that we reach a certain age on our birthdays. Why does Social Security say we "attain" an age on the day before our birthday?

The story in Social Security training classes: back in the 1800's a man was applying for federal benefits. The law said he had to "attain" a certain age to be eligible. He was born on the first of the month and wanted payments for the month before his birth month. He took the case to federal court and argued that he had lived 365 days on the *day before* his birthday—he had already lived a year on that day. His birthday, he argued, was actually the start of his *second* year. The judge agreed.

A simpler explanation is that the U.S. follows English common law.

Either way, all federal agencies recognize that you *attain* an age the day before your birthday.[2]

Work requirement for eligibility: Work Credits

In short, you need 10 years of work where you paid Social Security taxes to be eligible to receive a payment. The details are a bit more complicated, so let's look at the rules.

You "pay your insurance premium" to Social Security by working—or more accurately, working and paying your Social Security (F.I.C.A. or Self-Employment) taxes. The agency keeps a record of your earnings throughout your working life so it can later determine your eligibility and payment amount.

Your eligibility is determined by how many **work credits** you earn. You can earn up to 4 credits per year, so the credits are sometimes called "quarter credits" or "quarters of work." In 2018, for example, you earn one credit for each $1,320 you earn during the year, up to the maximum of 4 credits. Thus, with as little as $5,280 total earnings in 2018, you would earn all four credits for the year. The cost of credits goes up a bit with inflation each year.

For example, you could earn $5,300 in January and not work the rest of the year. You would receive all four credits for the year based on your $5,300 earnings even though you worked only one month. (Before 1978 you had to earn at least $50 in a *calendar* quarter to receive work credit for that quarter, which is why work credits were called "quarters.")

You need 40 work credits (10 years of work under Social Security) to be eligible, if you were born in 1929 or later. (For earlier births, you generally need one less credit for each year before 1929—see Figure 2.1. For example, for a birthdate in 1926, only 37 credits are required.) Under current law, no one needs more than 40 credits.

Bottom line: you need at least ten years of part-time work to qualify.

Sally has a bit over 10 years of work so she almost certainly has the required 40 work credits. Even though much of her work has been part-time, her earnings were high enough to earn all four credits each year because the credits are so "inexpensive."

Date of Birth	Work Credits Needed
1929 or later	40
1928	39
1927	38
1926	37
etc.	etc.

Figure 2.1. Work credits required for retirement eligibility.[3]

Non-covered work. Notice the words "work under the Social Security system" used throughout this section. In some jobs, you do *not* pay Social Security taxes, and that work does *not* count toward retirement eligibility. Examples include:

- Most foreign work
- Federal work, hired before 1984, under the CSRS system
- Certain state or municipal employees, especially police officers and fire fighters, whose retirement systems never merged with Social Security. (Local governments were given the option but some chose not to participate in the system.)

Foreign employment and totalization. Some people lack 40 work credits, because much of their career was outside the U.S.:

William split his career between work in the U.S. and in the United Kingdom. Because of this split, he is not quite eligible for benefits under either system. If only he could combine his work records into one system, and get credit for his work in both countries.

Fortunately for William and others in his situation, Social Security has international agreements which provide for just such "totalization" of work records. Currently the U.S. has totalization treaties with many European countries, plus Australia, Canada (plus Quebec), Chile, Japan, and South Korea. More are added periodically. If totalization affects you because of a foreign career, see "How International Agreements Can Help You" at www.ssa.gov/pubs/10180.html. You might also check with your foreign consulate or with Social Security.

U.S. military personnel serving overseas are not affected. For details on military service and Social Security, see page 219.

These *eligibility rules* determine whether you can receive a retirement payment, but don't determine the *amount* of payment. If you have ten years of work under the system, you can be sure of two things: you are eligible for payments, and you will eventually receive them if you simply live to retirement age and apply. Computing the *amount* of your payment is a separate operation, addressed next.

HOW YOUR PAYMENT IS COMPUTED

General information about your computation

Sam Smith is positive he meets the age and work requirements—he has had substantial earnings his entire life—but he still wonders how his payment amount is computed, in dollars and cents.

The preceding section explains the rules for becoming *eligible* for a retirement payment. This section explains the method for *computing the amount* of your payment.

Although the computation is fairly lengthy, all you need is grade school arithmetic, and you can learn from computing your own Social Security benefit. Both the text below and Appendix A give sample computations for Sam Smith.

In brief, your payment is roughly proportional to your lifetime earnings, and thus to your payments *into* the system. The rest of this section gives you the details.

Your Social Security payment amount is based on only two factors:

- Your *lifetime average earnings* (earnings factors), and

- Your *age when your payments begin* (age factors).

 Tips For Results: Obtaining Needed Work Credits

If you lack 40 credits, and have no foreign work to add to your earnings record, you still have two ways to get a payment from Social Security:

- You might have a current or former marriage to someone who is eligible (see Chapters 3 and 4 for details).

- Or you could work the additional years necessary to gain coverage. (See Chapter 7 to learn exactly how many credits you have vs. how many you need.) After all, you can earn all four credits available for the year with relatively low earnings—$5,280 earned anytime in 2018 will give you all four credits for the year.

The work credits are posted one at a time on the first day of each calendar quarter. *Example:* Suppose you turn 62 in January of 2018, and have 36 work credits counting your work in 2017. You need 40 credits to receive Social Security. You must earn at least $5,280 in 2018, and you will receive your qualifying 40th work credit on October 1, 2018—the first day of the fourth quarter. You would be eligible for Social Security as of October 2018.

Earnings factors in your computation

Your lifetime average earnings

Like other pensions, your Social Security is based on your earnings history. The higher your earnings during your working career, the higher your payment. The amount of your payment is a percentage of your *lifetime average earnings.*

Therefore, Social Security tracks your earnings—for you and most other U.S. workers. Your employer reports your earnings to SSA every year, and the Administration keeps a record throughout your lifetime. (If you are self-employed, your tax return includes the necessary report of self-employment earnings.) Your *earnings record* will be used to compute your retirement benefit.

The steps of the computation, moving from your earnings record to your Social Security payment amount, are summarized here and detailed in Appendix A (page 271).

Maximum annual amount posted

There is a cap or ceiling on the amount of earnings subject to the 6.2% Social Security tax. In 2018, for example, the maximum taxable earnings for *Social Security* is $128,400.[4] (There is no ceiling on the 1.45% *Medicare* tax). The ceiling increases every year with inflation. The ceiling is called the *taxable earnings base.*

Looking at his earnings record (Appendix A, Figure A-1) Sam Smith sees that Column 2 gives the maximum earnings for each year from 1954 ($3,600) to 2018 ($128,400).

If your earnings are under the annual ceiling, you pay the 7.65% FICA tax on all earnings. In that case, all earnings are posted to your earnings record.

Nationwide, though, about 6% of us earn over the ceiling.[5] If you are one of these high earners, only the first $128,400 of your 2018 earnings would be taxed for Social Security, and only the first $128,400 would appear on Social Security's records. Higher earnings would not increase your eventual Social Security benefit.

Sam's earnings for 1998 were $69,000. His payment computation will use only $68,400 because that was the maximum amount that could be used that year.

Since there is a maximum of posted earnings, there is also a maximum Social Security payment. If a worker had maximum earnings every year and retired in 2018 at age 66, her 2016 Social Security payment would be $2,788 per month.[6]

The three computation steps

Once your earnings are posted to your record, the Social Security computation proceeds through three steps:

1:    An inflation adjustment,

2:    Determining your lifetime average earnings, and

3:    Applying a formula to that average to determine your full payment amount.

PIA: Your full retirement benefit

The end product of these steps is your *full retirement benefit* or *100% benefit*. This is the amount payable at your *Full Retirement Age (FRA)*, defined below under "Age Factors."

Your full retirement benefit is fundamental. It determines how much you will receive from Social Security, and how much family members applying on your record will receive. Think of it as the core number, the basis for every payment made on your record. Inside SSA your full retirement benefit is called your *Primary Insurance Amount* or PIA.

Let's look at how Social Security proceeds through the three steps of computing your PIA.

PIA step 1: Indexing your earnings for inflation

First, Social Security applies an inflation adjustment to every year of your earnings. This makes past earnings comparable to recent earnings.

What figure does Social Security use to adjust for inflation? The figure used tracks *average earnings* over the years.

Sam's computation (Appendix A, Figure A-1) shows the average earnings measured by SSA for each year after 1953 (Column 3). In Sam's case, each year's inflation index factor (Column 4) equals 2013 average earnings divided by each year's average earnings (Column 3).

Why is Sam's inflation adjustment based on 2013's average earnings—why not 2012 or 2014? Because the inflation factor in your Social Security computation is always the one for the year you *attain age 60*. This is called your *Base Year*. Even if the payment computation is not performed until a later year, the adjustment is "locked in" in your Base Year. Using age 60 makes sense, because then all the computation factors will be known at age 62, when you are first eligible. (Stay tuned for how inflation affects later years.)

Sam turned 60 in 2013, so that is his Base Year, and all his earnings are adjusted using 2013's inflation figures. If you turn 60 in a later year, for example 2014, then all your inflation adjustments would be based on 2014's higher average earnings.

Note that the inflation adjustment does not fully cancel out the effects of inflation for high earners:

*Bill Johnson turned 60 in 2013, just like Sam. Bill had **maximum** wages of $14,100 posted in 1975. The inflation factor for 1975 earnings with a Base Year of 2013 is 5.2008546 (Figure A-1, Column 4). That means average earnings increased by a* *factor of 5.2008546 from 1975 to 2013. Applying the inflation factor to Bill's 1975 earnings yields the following calculation:*

$$\$14,100 \times 5.2008546 = \$73,332.05$$

Bill is surprised. He expected that his 1975 wages—the maximum allowed that year—would be inflated to somewhere near \$113,700—the maximum in effect for 2013. Instead, only about two-thirds that amount will be used in Bill's payment computation.

Clearly, SSA's earnings index used does not fully inflate higher earnings. Only if your earnings are exactly *average* would the inflation factor be perfectly fair. *Even after* the inflation index is applied, *recent* earnings are frequently the highest earnings.

Step 1 is essential for fairness. When earnings from 30 or more years ago are used for your payment computation, some inflation adjustment is needed. Basing the adjustment on the increase in average earnings is reasonable for most workers. And the factor is derived from SSA's own records, streamlining the process.

PIA step 2: Your lifetime average earnings

The second step in computing your Social Security payment is to determine your lifetime average earnings.

To determine your lifetime average, Social Security uses your *best 35 years* of work.[7]

Most private pensions, on the other hand, are based on the best three to five years of earnings—frequently the last years on the job, the peak of most careers. The Tips for Results section on page 43 explains the advantages and disadvantages of the 35-year computation.

The years used are the 35 years with the highest inflation-adjusted earnings—in other words, the 35 highest amounts from Step 1 of the computation.

The 35 years chosen do not have to be consecutive nor recent. Wherever the best (highest) inflated years are, they will count—as long as they are after 1950. If you were a child actor, for example, your best years might be very early indeed.

Sam Smith's best 35 years appear in Figure A-1, Columns 7 and 8. Note that his "high 35" years are not a continuous run of years.

Sam is fortunate to have over 35 years of earnings. What if you have fewer work years?

35 years must still be used in the computation, even if some of them are "zero years" (years with no earnings posted to your record).[8]

Sally Smith has only ten years with posted earnings. Yet her Social Security computation must be based on 35 years. Her ten work years will be included because they are her best years. The other 25 years used in the computation will be zero years that will not contribute toward a higher Social Security payment.

Once the 35 years with the highest inflation-adjusted earnings are selected, the adjusted earnings are totaled and averaged.

Sam's earnings in Figure A-1, Column 8 are totaled and averaged. The total is shown as the "Dividend" in Figure A-2. Sam's Dividend is $2,380,480.84.

Social Security uses average *monthly* earnings, so the Dividend—the total adjusted earnings from the best 35 years—is divided by 420, the number of months in 35 years. The result is called your *AIME*, pronounced like the name "Amy." AIME stands for Average Indexed Monthly Earnings. (The "Indexed" part of the name indicates that inflation was counted.)

Sam's AIME, shown in Figure A-2, is $5,667, representing his average monthly earnings throughout his career, adjusted for inflation.

Your AIME is your lifetime average earnings, and is used in Step 3 to compute your Social Security payment.

PIA step 3: Assigning a percentage

Once your average earnings are computed, a formula determines your full Social Security payment amount. The formula basically pays you a percentage of your AIME, but there's a twist: not everyone receives the same percentage. It's a sliding scale.

The higher your lifetime average earnings, the higher your Social Security payments, as you might expect. The average worker can expect a Social Security payment at 66 of about 43% of her AIME. That percentage is called the *replacement rate* because it shows how much of your paycheck is *replaced* by your Social Security payment.

Interestingly, though, higher earners receive a *lower replacement rate*, with very high earners receiving about 26% of their average earnings. Conversely, a retiree with low earnings can expect a higher replacement rate—up to 90% of the AIME for very low earners. The computation is *progressive*, favoring lower earners. This is illustrated in Figure 2.2.

Tips For Results: Your 35-Year Computation

Basing your payments on your best 35 years carries advantages and disadvantages. The **disadvantages** include:

- Your work record may be "spotty," meaning some years have little or no work posted. That could be from taking time off work to raise children, having frequent layoffs, education years outside the workforce, immigrating to the U.S. mid-career, taking lower pay while in military service or volunteer work, etc. Such gaps reduce your lifetime average earnings, so your Social Security will be less, even if the gaps occurred twenty years ago.

- You may have ended your career at the top of the pay scale, but it may have taken you a long career at lower earnings to climb to that level. If so, your *lifetime average* will be lower than a person who had top wages for more years in his or her career.

The biggest **advantage** is that retiring early—say, at age 56 or 58—after a long steady work history, will not reduce your lifetime average earnings much. With 35 years averaged together, some zeros in the last four to six years will have little impact. Your track record is already established, especially if you already have 35 years of work on your record.

Consider Janet Johnson, born in February 1955. She earned maximum wages every year of her work career.

- If Janet retired in February of 2017 at age 62, she would have $2,153 per month payable from Social Security.
- On the other hand, if Janet retired five years earlier at age 57 and had *no further earnings*, her Social Security payment at age 62 would be $2,117—a loss of only $36 per month.[9] (See Chapter 7 and Appendix E to get your own online "what-if" computations.)

Janet loses very little Social Security even with 5 non-work years. Changing 5 years has little impact on the 35-year average.

Why 35 years? Because your *lifetime average earnings* determines your retirement payments. The 35 years are said to represent the 40 career years from age 22 to age 62, with the lowest 5 years dropped out for equity.

Using lifetime earnings makes sense. Payments are then roughly proportional to lifetime FICA contributions. Suppose Sam Smith landed a job with a big paycheck, stayed on the job for three years, and then quit, never to work again. Should Sam get maximum Social Security payments for life, just because he was highly paid for three years? Most of us would say that wouldn't be fair—to get the maximum, Sam should have a longer track record. That's why Social Security uses the "lifetime average earnings" concept.

2017 Earnings	Social Security Payment at 66	Replacement Ratio
$127,200/year (maximum earnings)	$2,788/month	26%
$77,000/year	$2,292/month	36%
$48,000/year (average earnings)	$1,732/month	43%
$22,000/year	$1,050/month	57%

Figure 2.2. Earnings level vs. Social Security payments, illustrating the "progressive" nature of replacement rates. Assumptions: Earnings were steady at the level shown for life, after adjusting for inflation, rounded to nearest thousand (except for maximum). Payment amounts are for filing in 2018 at age 66.[10]

The practice is like IRS's progressive income tax rates, but in reverse. With IRS, when you have higher earnings you not only pay more total tax dollars, you also pay taxes at a higher percentage rate. With Social Security, when you have higher earnings you get a higher payment, but it's a lower percentage of your earnings.

Why does Social Security use the sliding scale? Because lower earners generally have less opportunity to save for retirement. Those with greater means, on the other hand, require less from the system in their retirement years.

Does this mean that Social Security is not insurance? No, it means that Social Security is *social insurance*, striking a balance between a purely private enterprise and a social program. In this case, Congress has decided that the country is better served by using the progressive sliding scale.

Sam's payment computation in Appendix A shows how the formula used in step 3 results in a lower reward for higher earnings. Sam's actual figures are as follows:

AIME	SSA Payment at 66	Replacement Ratio
$5,667	$2,225	39%

Note that the higher your earnings, the higher your Social Security payment will be, even though your replacement ratio may drop. Higher earnings cannot decrease your payment.

This sliding scale has prompted some to observe that *Social Security taxes are regressive, but Social Security benefits are progressive:*

- FICA taxes are *regressive* because they are a fixed percentage for all wage levels and are zero above the taxable earnings ceiling. Therefore, lower earners pay a larger percentage tax than higher earners.

- But benefits are *progressive* because lower earners receive a higher percentage of their taxes back, and there is a ceiling on benefits ($2,788 for a person age 66 in 2018).

To summarize:
- The payment computation is totally separate from the 10-year work requirement to become eligible for payments.

- Social Security computes your retirement payment from your 35 best years of work (even if some are zeros), after adjusting for inflation.

- That computation determines your full retirement benefit at your Full Retirement Age—also called your Primary Insurance Amount or PIA.

The only other factor influencing your payment is your age when payments begin.

 Tips For Results:
Using the Sliding Scale to Your Advantage

The sliding payment scale works to your advantage if you retire before age 62. How? Because retiring early lowers your total lifetime earnings, compared to working longer.

- The *bad news* is that this will reduce your Social Security payment.

- The *good news* is that lower earnings provide a higher replacement percentage.

The result is that your Social Security may not decline as much as you thought. A 10% reduction in your lifetime earnings might mean only a 7% reduction in your Social Security payments. (See the Janet Johnson example in the above "Tips for Results" for an instance of this.)

Age factors in your computation

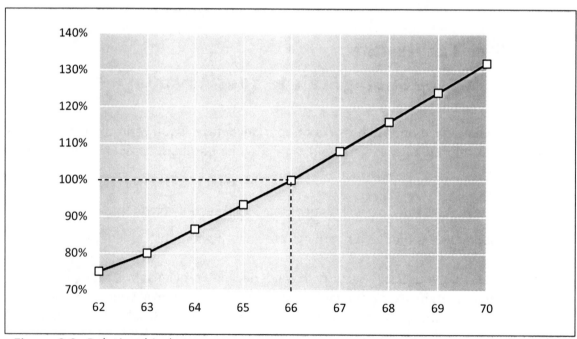

Sam (page 33) wonders why the Social Security representative specified his payment "at age 65." Once he turns 62, does it make any difference how old he is?

The short answer: the earlier you start your Social Security payment, the less you get per month.

The amount paid is based on your birth date and your age when the payments start, so *when you file* will determine how much you'll be paid. While you worked you had little control over your Social Security payments; you simply paid your taxes. But at retirement, you gain control over your Social Security for the first time, by *choosing your payment month.*

Figure 2.3 shows the relationship between age (horizontal axis) and amount paid (vertical axis) for a person born from 1943 through 1954.

To understand the details, let's start by defining the "Full Retirement Age."

Figure 2.3: Relationship between payment amount and age when payments begin, for those with Full Retirement Age of 66.

Payments starting at Full Retirement Age: Full retirement benefit

The full retirement benefit is payable if your payments start at your Full Retirement Age. You would receive 100% of your Primary Insurance Amount (PIA).

Sam's birth year is 1953. Therefore, his FRA is 66 (Figure 2.4). If his Social Security payments start at that age, he will be paid his Primary Insurance Amount: $2,225 each month. (The $2,225 is in 2018 dollars. Sam could receive more due to cost-of-living-adjustments from 2018 to 2019, when he attains his FRA.)

Year of Birth	Full Retirement Age
1937 or earlier	65
1938	65 and 2 months
1939	65 and 4 months
1940	65 and 6 months
1941	65 and 8 months
1942	65 and 10 months
1943 - 1954	66
1955	66 and 2 months
1956	66 and 4 months
1957	66 and 6 months
1958	66 and 8 months
1959	66 and 10 months
1960 and later	67

Figure 2.4: "Full Retirement Age"—the age to receive full Social Security benefits. If your birthdate is January 1, use the preceding year. This chart applies to both workers and spouses;[11] see Figure 4.4 (page 91) for widow(er)s.

Payments starting before Full Retirement Age: Reduced payments from Reduction Months (RMs)

You can claim early retirement payments as young as age 62. The catch: your payment amount is *permanently* reduced. The earlier you file, the lower your monthly payment for the rest of your life.

The reason is simple. By filing early, you will receive more payments, so the amount must be reduced to equalize your lifetime payments with those of older retirees.

The reduction is computed by counting *Reduction Months (RMs)*—the months before your FRA. A two-stage reduction applies:

- Stage 1: For the first 36 Reduction Months, payment is reduced 5/9 of 1% for each month.

- Stage 2: For any additional RMs, payment is reduced 5/12 of 1% for each month.[12]

Example 1: Sally files for Social Security to begin at age 63. Her FRA is 66. Since she files 36 months early, her payment will be reduced 20% (5/9% x 36 RMs = 20%). She will receive an 80% payment.

Example 2: Jeb, like Sally, files for Social Security to begin at age 63. However, his FRA is 67, so he is filing 48 months early. His payment will be reduced as follows:

20% for the first 36 RMs
(5/9% x 36 months = 20%).

5% for the next 12 RMs
(5/12% x 12 months = 5%).

Total reduction: 25% (20% + 5%).

He will receive a 75% payment.

Example 3: Ron files for Social Security to begin at age 64 and 6 months. His FRA is 67. Since he files 30 months early, his payment will be reduced 16.67% (5/9% x 30 RMs). He will receive an 83.33% payment.

We can now understand Sam Smith's payment amount at age 65 (example at top of chapter and Appendix A):

Sam's birth year is 1953. Therefore, his FRA is 66 (from Figure 2.4).

If Sam begins payments at age 65, he will be 12 months early (age 66 minus age 65 is 1 year or 12 Reduction Months).

His payment will be reduced 6.67% (5/9% x 12 RMs = 6.67%). Therefore, his age 65 payment will be 93.33% of his full payment.

His full payment amount (PIA) is $2,225 (from his lifetime average earnings).

Therefore, his age 65 payment will be $2,077 ($2,225 x 93.33%).

Payments starting after Full Retirement Age: Higher payments from Delayed Retirement Credits (DRCs)

If you delay your payments until after your FRA, you will receive a permanent raise. *Delayed Retirement Credits (DRCs)* provide an 8% raise in your payments for each year of late filing, up to age 70. (The amount of the DRC "bonus" could be less for early birth years, as illustrated in Figure 2.5.)

Delayed Retirement Credits are computed on a month-by-month basis, like Reduction Months. For each month of delayed retirement, you receive an increase of 2/3% (1/12 of 8%).

Year of Birth	Yearly Percentage Increase
1916 or earlier	1%
1917 - 1924	3%
1925 - 1926	3.5%
1927 - 1928	4%
1929 - 1930	4.5%
1931 - 1932	5%
1933 - 1934	5.5%
1935 - 1936	6%
1937 - 1938	6.5%
1939 - 1940	7%
1941 - 1942	7.5%
1943 or later	8%

Figure 2.5: Delayed Retirement Credits (DRCs). The annual rate of increase is shown; in practice DRCs are computed monthly.[13]

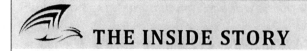

Our Changing Retirement Age

Age 65 was originally set as the retirement age in 1935, when the Social Security Act was first written. But why 65—why not 67 or 63? Social Security lore cites three possible explanations:

- Perhaps Uncle Sam wasn't very generous. Life expectancy in 1935 was only about 61. Therefore, the odds were against living long enough to receive full benefits.

- Or perhaps Uncle Sam wasn't very original. Age 65 had already been set as the retirement age in the world's first Social Security system, Germany's, created under Chancellor Otto von Bismarck in 1889.

- SSA's Historian's Office says 65 was already prevalent in other US systems like state and railroad pensions, and was a practical actuarial choice.[14]

Whatever the explanation, age 65 continued to be the Full Retirement Age from 1935 to 1983, when the age limit was raised as part of the 1983 amendments to the Social Security Act. Two explanations were offered for the change:

- First, people are living longer and healthier lives now than in 1935, so an increased retirement age simply reflects the greater life expectancy. In fact, with the current at-birth life expectancy around 79, the Full Retirement Age would have to be about 83 to mirror the situation in 1935.

- Second, raising the retirement age saves SSA money, strengthening the program's finances—the key goal of the 1983 amendments.

Age 62 was introduced as the "early retirement" age for women in 1956, and extended to men in 1961.[15] It is retained under present law. However, age 62 payments decrease as the Full Retirement Age increases (Figure 2.6). Thus, increasing the retirement age reduces payments for nearly everyone, saving money for the system.

Sam was born in 1953. He could get an 8% increase for every year he delays his Social Security (Figure 2.5).

If he waits until age 70 to file, he would receive an increase for 4 years (age 70 minus his FRA of 66):

4 years x 8% = 32%

Sam would receive a 132% payment. Instead of his PIA of $2,225 per month he would receive $2,937 per month.

Another way to get DRCs and increase your Social Security payment is to *voluntarily suspend* your payments for some or all months from FRA to age 70. For details see Chapter 10, page 241.

You can file any month

You need not file for benefits in your birth month, nor on the first of the year, nor in December, as some people believe. You may start your payments in *any* month, provided you are retired and over 62—or over FRA whether or not you are retired.

Year of birth	Full Retirement Age	Age 62 payment	Age 70 payment
1937	65	80%	132.5%
1938	65 & 2 months	79.17%	131.42%
1939	65 & 4 months	78.33%	132.67%
1940	65 & 6 months	77.5%	131.5%
1941	65 & 8 months	76.67%	132.5%
1942	65 & 10 months	75.83%	131.25%
1943-1954	66	75%	132%
1955	66 & 2 months	74.17%	130.67%
1956	66 & 4 months	73.33%	129.33%
1957	66 & 6 months	72.5%	128%
1958	66 & 8 months	71.67%	126.67%
1959	66 & 10 months	70.83%	125.33%
1960 and later	67	70%	124%

Figure 2.6: FRAs and payment percentages at 62 and 70 for birth years after 1936.[16] If your birthdate is January 1, use the preceding year.

You should file your claim three months before you want your payments to start. (Chapter 9 defines how much work is allowed in "retirement." Chapter 8 gives details on filing claims.)

Sam was thinking about retiring in June so he could start off with a summer trip. Even though that is not the first of the year nor his birth month, Social Security will compute his exact payment by knowing his exact age.

Once you specify your payment start month, Social Security counts how many months that date is before or after your Full Retirement Age. Then the calculation is automatic: a reduction if you are younger than your Full Retirement Age, or an increase if you are older.

Figure 2.6 shows FRAs and payment percentages at age 62 and age 70 for every birth year. It illustrates how changing the FRA changes payment amounts at all ages.

Retroactive payments

If you file before FRA, your benefits start the month you apply, with no retroactive payments.

If you file when older than FRA, you can receive retroactive payments up to 6 months before filing, or back to your FRA, whichever is later. The general rule is that you can't get retroactive benefits if that would cause a permanent reduction of payments.[17]

If you are eligible and want payments to start, don't delay—file immediately so you don't lose a month of payments.

How to get the most.

How can you receive the most money overall—by starting your Social Security at age 62, at Full Retirement Age, or at age 70? Where is the break-even point? See Chapter 10 for answers (page 231).

To summarize: The month your payments begin determines what *percentage* of your full retirement payment (PIA) you will receive. Your payment is reduced for early filing, or increased for late filing.

WEP: Lower payments for some

The preceding sections explain the normal retirement payment computation. However, you might be subject to a different, lower computation called the Windfall Elimination Provision, or WEP.

You're affected if you get a pension from a job where *you didn't pay Social Security FICA taxes.*

Generally, those affected are:

- Certain public-sector workers, including some Federal, State, and local employees whose retirement systems were not part of the Social Security system. This often includes police officers and fire fighters.

- Many foreign workers.

One affected group is Federal employees hired before 1984 who stayed under the old Civil Service Retirement System (CSRS). However, Federal employees retired under the Federal Employee Retirement System (FERS) are *not subject to WEP.* They get a normal Social Security computation. Also exempt are many, but not all, state and municipal workers.

The number of people affected is small, and the list of exceptions is long. Check with Social Security or your employee benefits office to see if you are affected.

The reason for the reduction

See Figure 2.2 on page 44. Now imagine how your Social Security earnings record appears if you have non-FICA work.

For all your non-FICA years, your earnings were exempt from Social Security taxes, and not posted to SSA records. Those years are posted as *zero years* (unless you had moonlighting jobs concurrent with your non-FICA work). Then you retire from your non-FICA career and start collecting a pension based on that work.

Let's say you also have enough "outside" work where you paid FICA taxes—10 years—to get Social Security. But all the years of non-FICA work are zeroes, "hidden from view," never posted to Social Security records. To the computer you look like a low-income worker. That would normally trigger a *better* Social Security computation, with a higher replacement rate, based on the progressive sliding percentage scale (see Figure 2.2, page 44).

That high replacement rate is for *true* low-wage workers. But your earnings aren't really low; they only *look* low to the computer because you worked outside the system.

In your case, then, the high replacement rate for low earners would be an unfair *windfall.*

The reduction

WEP addresses the windfall. WEP eliminates part of the higher percentage bonus for people with non-FICA pensions. It basically removes some of the progressivity in the computation, yielding a lower Social Security payment.

If you are affected, your Social Security will be reduced up to $447.50 per month in 2018.[18] (That's the worst case; the reduction could be less if you have lower Social Security earnings, if you have many years of Social Security earnings posted, or if your non-covered pension is low.)

Betsy had a long career as a police officer, where she paid no FICA taxes. She also worked for several years in the private sector while she was in school. When she retired from her police job, she became self-employed to supplement her police pension. By the time she is 65, she will have well over 10 years of work in the private sector where she paid Social Security taxes.

At 65 she can retire and draw both her police pension and her Social Security. Her police pension will be unaffected by her Social Security, but her Social Security payments may be up to $447.50 per month lower because of her police pension.

Betsy knows the payment estimates on the Social Security Statement don't include the WEP reduction. She remembers to subtract about $447.50 from the estimates shown. Alternatively, she can get a more accurate estimate using the WEP calculator (below).

Note that WEP affects *only* your Social Security payments (not your *other* pension). In addition, WEP applies only if you are eligible for both Social Security and a pension from a job not covered under Social Security. If your other pension is from work where you paid Social Security taxes, your Social Security benefits will *not* be affected.

*Sam Smith earned a company pension while he worked, in addition to his Social Security. His company pension will not affect his Social Security. He can draw full payments from both the company pension and Social Security, because he paid Social Security taxes while he worked under the company pension plan. He did **not** work under a plan where **no Social Security taxes were paid**. WEP does not apply to him.*

WEP phase-out

If you have many years of work where you paid Social Security taxes, WEP's impact may be reduced or eliminated. It has less effect if you have 21-29 years of "substantial earnings" that were taxed for Social Security, and does not apply at all if you have 30 years of such work. The "substantial" level was $23,625 for 2017, and less in past years.

WEP affects *your own* Social Security payments. If you apply for *spousal or widow(er)'s* payments, a different provision, called Government Pension Offset (GPO), could reduce your Social Security payments, if you get a government pension based on non-FICA work. GPO is explained on page 69.

For more information on WEP, go to www.ssa.gov/planners/retire/gpo-wep.html or see the SSA Factsheet "Windfall Elimination Provision," at www.ssa.gov/pubs/EN-05-10045.pdf. A WEP calculator is available at www.ssa.gov/planners/benefitcalculators.html.

Other special situations

Certain other people have special coverage rules or computations, including:

- Self-employed persons
- Corporate officers
- Insurance sales people expecting renewal commissions
- Farmers and ranchers
- Domestic workers
- Clergy

SSA produces fact sheets for each of them. If your work appears on the list or if you think another special rule might apply to you, see www.ssa.gov/pubs/index.html, especially under Topics>General Information, or contact SSA for more information.

RETIREMENT COMPUTATION EXAMPLE

Let's look at another example to further clarify the ideas in this chapter. Meet Maria.

Maria is a fairly typical wage-earner. Over the years she has had some prosperous and lean times, but overall life has been good to her. Now that she is nearing retirement age, she wants to know where she stands with Social Security. She calls the Social Security phone number: 1-800-SSA-1213.

While Maria is on the phone, the Social Security representative is on the computer. She calls up Maria's work record and an estimate of her full payment amount. Maria's wages have been somewhere between average and maximum, so her Social Security payments will be between average and maximum, too. Her full payment is estimated at $2,000 per month.

Maria learns that her Full Retirement Age is 66. She understands that she will get the full $2,000 per month if she waits until 66 to start drawing her retirement payments, but she wants to know what happens if she starts earlier.

You already know the answer: Maria learns that she could draw a payment as early as age 62. At 62 she would be eligible for 75% of her full payment amount, or $1,500 a month ($2,000 x 75% = $1,500).

Next, Maria wants to know what her payment would be if she started her payments somewhere between 62 and 66—for example, at 63 or 64. She learns that at 64, her payments are reduced for 24 months at 5/9 of 1% per month:

24 months x 5/9% = 13.33% reduction.

This leaves her with an 86.67% payment, since 100% - 13.33% = 86.67%.

$2,000 x 86.67% = $1,733.40

Similarly, Maria learns that her average-to-high lifetime earnings will yield her the following benefits:

Age 66	100% payment	$2,000 per month
Age 65	93.33% payment	$1,866
Age 64	86.67% payment	$1,733
Age 63	80% payment	$1,600
Age 62	75% payment	$1,500

. . . and she may file in any intervening month, for a proportional adjustment.

In the following chapters, we examine family and survivor benefits.

FOR MORE INFORMATION...

"Retirement Benefits"
www.ssa.gov/pubs/10035.html

"Social Security Retirement Planner"
www.ssa.gov/retire2/

"How International Agreements Can Help You"
www.ssa.gov/pubs/10180.html

"Windfall Elimination Provision"
www.ssa.gov/pubs/10045.html

"Information for Government Employees"
www.ssa.gov/planners/retire/gpo-wep.html

"Your Retirement Benefit: How It Is Figured" go to
www.ssa.gov/pubs/index.html, select "Retirement" in the "Topics" tab, find the
title, click PDF, and select your birth year in the drop-down box

Chapter Endnotes

1. https://ssa.gov/OP_Home/handbook/handbook.03/handbook-0301.html and
    https://www.socialsecurity.gov/OACT/quickcalc/earlyretire.html, paragraph 2, column 3, and
    footnote b
2. https://secure.ssa.gov/apps10/poms.nsf/lnx/0300615015
3. https://www.socialsecurity.gov/planners/credits.html
4. https://www.socialsecurity.gov/planners/retire/topwages.html and
    https://www.ssa.gov/news/press/releases/2017/#11-2017-1
5. https://www.ssa.gov/policy/docs/chartbooks/fast_facts/2017/fast_facts17.html#page10
6. www.ssa.gov/OACT/COLA/examplemax.html
7. https://www.socialsecurity.gov/OACT/ProgData/retirebenefit1.html, text in left-most column
8. https://www.socialsecurity.gov/policy/docs/statcomps/supplement/2016/apnd.html, first bullet
9. Computed by author using SSA's anypia.exe software.
10. Computed by author using SSA's anypia.exe software.
11. https://www.socialsecurity.gov/planners/retire/agereduction.html. If born on January first,
    refer to the previous year.
12. https://www.socialsecurity.gov/OACT/quickcalc/early_late.html
13. https://www.socialsecurity.gov/OACT/quickcalc/early_late.html#drcTable
14. https://ssa.gov/history/age65.html
15. https://www.socialsecurity.gov/history/puzzles/quiz2a.html
16. https://www.socialsecurity.gov/OACT/ProgData/ar_drc.html
17. https://www.socialsecurity.gov/OP_Home/handbook/handbook.15/handbook-1513.html and
    https://secure.ssa.gov/apps10/poms.nsf/lnx/0200204030
18. https://www.ssa.gov/planners/retire/wep-chart.html

CHAPTER THREE

FAMILY BENEFITS

 Family Benefits in a Nutshell

- If a worker gets Social Security retirement or disability benefits, certain family members are also eligible for payments.

- Eligible family members are spouses, certain former spouses, and certain children.

- Payment amount is a percentage of the worker's full payment amount (PIA).

- A family maximum limits total family payouts.

FAMILY BENEFITS BACKGROUND

Sam and Sally Smith (pages 33-34) are concerned that Sally's payment on her own work record may be very low. Is there some way she could draw part of Sam's payment?

Yes. One of the key strengths of Social Security is the provision for *family benefits* for families of retired or disabled workers. Under certain circumstances, you, as a dependent family member, are eligible for Social Security payments—payments *in addition to* whatever payments the worker gets.

These additional payments, called *auxiliary benefits* inside SSA:

- Recognize the greater costs in a larger family.

- Acknowledge the support the worker received from family during the work years—such as homemaking assistance, transportation, help with child rearing, and other personal maintenance—that increase earning power.

- Support our core value of family.

Eligible family members are the worker's:

- Child(ren)

- Spouse, and

- Former spouse(s)

Family benefits are additional payments for family members. They do not reduce the worker's payment.

As mentioned, payments can be made "under certain circumstances." We'll explore the rules in this chapter. The most important rules are these:

- *A family benefit will be paid unless you (the family member) are eligible for a **higher benefit** on another work record, including your own.* If you are *dually eligible*—eligible in two ways, as a family member and a worker in your own right—you are generally paid the higher of the two benefits.

- *For you to get a family payment on a worker's record, the worker must be getting his or her own Social Security retirement or disability payment.* An exception for former spouses appears below. Another exception is when the worker *suspended* his or her payments before April 30, 2016 (page 241).

- *You must be retired.* That means your earnings must meet the same limits as those used for other Social Security recipients. The limits, which apply only before FRA, are described on page 205.

Figure 3.1 summarizes family benefits, with more detail in the text.

Are you currently unmarried? Read on, because you could be paid as a *former spouse*. In addition, your children might be eligible. If you are a widow or widower, see Chapter 4 for details on survivor benefits.

BENEFITS FOR THE WORKER'S SPOUSE

Spousal benefits are a core family benefit. Here we will closely examine the rules governing spouse payments:

- The definition of a spouse,

- Age rules, and

- Payment amounts,

to see if you or someone in your family might get spousal benefits.

In addition to monthly cash payments, spousal benefits can include Medicare at age 65. See Chapter 6 for details.

Definition of Spouse

A spouse can be either sex—a wife or a husband. A spouse may be *currently* married to the worker, or may be a *former* spouse, i.e. divorced from the worker. There are a few special rules for former spouses which we'll look at in a moment.

A spouse must be legally married to the worker for one year (or 10 years before a divorce). Generally, if state law recognizes a legal marriage relationship between individuals, then so does Social Security. There are a few special areas described below.

Same-sex spouses

Spousal benefits are payable for same-sex couples, if you are (or were) legally married. The following rules apply:

- If you were married in the U.S., SSA recognizes your marriage. SSA acknowledges the June 26, 2015, Supreme Court ruling in *Obergefell v. Hodges,* and recognizes same-sex marriages performed in any U.S. state.

- In addition, SSA recognizes many non-marital but legally recognized same-sex relationships (such as civil unions or domestic partnerships).

- Finally, SSA recognizes same-sex marriages and some non-marital legal relationships established outside the U.S.

In every case, SSA strongly recommends that you immediately file for spousal payments (assuming you meet general qualifications, like age) to protect your rights. See SSA's "Same-Sex Couples" page at www.ssa.gov/people/same-sexcouples/.

Common-law marriages

Common-law marriages are recognized if they are legally entered into. Common-law marriages are legal in several states, and once entered into are recognized by most other states and by Social Security.[2]

PERSON	BENEFIT AMOUNT (Percentage of worker's Full Payment Amount)	
SPOUSE		
Full Retirement Age or older	50%	
Age 62 (depending on FRA)	32.5%-35%[1]	
Any age, caring for the worker's child under 16	50%	
Requirements: • Worker must be getting Social Security (or have suspended payments before April 30, 2016) • Claimant must be age 62+, or caring for worker's child who is on Social Security, and under 16 or disabled		
FORMER SPOUSE		
Full Retirement Age or older	50%	
Age 62 (depending on FRA)	32.5%-35%[1]	
Requirements: • Worker must be age 62+; not necessarily on Social Security • Marriage lasted 10 years or more • Claimant age 62+, and currently unmarried		
CHILD		
Any age	50%	

Requirements:
• Worker must be getting Social Security (or have suspended payments before April 30, 2016)
• Child must be unmarried and either:
   o Under 18, or
   o Under 19 and in high school, or
   o Adult but disabled before age 22.		

NOTE: Family maximum may reduce total amount payable to family. Does not apply to former spouse.		

Figure 3.1: Summary of benefits for family of retired or disabled worker.

Legal impediment

John and Marsha apply for Social Security as a married couple and provide a marriage certificate as proof. Only then do they realize that the certificate was not properly recorded with the state.

In cases like this, SSA looks for "good faith" on the part of the married couple and in most cases will determine a "deemed marriage" exists, and award spousal payments.[3]

For any marriage, if there is a question about your legal status you should discuss the question with Social Security now to clear up any possible problems.

Special rules for former (divorced) spouse

If you apply as a former (divorced) spouse, your former marriage must meet the same legal requirements shown above. In addition, you must meet three special requirements:

- You must be at least 62. You cannot qualify at a younger age even if you have the worker's child in your care.

- You must be *currently unmarried*.

- You must have been married to the worker for *at least ten years* before the divorce. The ten years run from the date of marriage to the date your divorce was final.[4]

Sam Smith's former spouse, Janet, may qualify for former spouse benefits on Sam's work record. Janet is over 62, retired, and currently unmarried. She was married to Sam for 12 years. When Janet applies for her own Social Security, SSA will see if she can draw more on Sam's record than on her own record, and pay her the higher of the two.

Note that *you don't need to wait for the worker to start Social Security,* if you have been divorced at least two years.[4] If you are 62 and retired, you can draw payments on the worker's record as soon as the worker reaches age 62, whether or not the worker gets Social Security.

Janet is already 62 and retired. Her former husband Sam is 62 but still working and not getting Social Security. Nevertheless, Janet gets Social Security on Sam's work record, years before Sam retires.

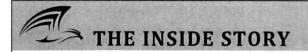

THE INSIDE STORY

Why Special Rules for Former Spouses?

Note that the worker must be 62, but need not be on Social Security for a former spouse to be eligible (page 63), if the divorce is final for at least two years. This is different from the rules for current spouses, where the worker must be getting Social Security.

Before 1985, divorced spouses were subject to the same requirement as a current spouse. That is, the worker had to apply for Social Security. Why did Congress change the rule? Consider the following fictional example:

*When Richard went to claim his retirement payment in 1983, he learned that his former spouse, Eunice, could draw Social Security on his record. Carrying a grudge for many years, Richard responded that, in that case, he would **never apply**.*

Under the old rules, Eunice might have waited and waited for a former spouse payment. Eunice might be destitute, perhaps on public assistance, but would basically be held hostage by Richard's retirement decision, outside her control.

Therefore, an exception was made. Effective in 1985, Eunice could draw on Richard's work record if Richard was over 62, even if Richard never applied for Social Security, provided the divorce was final for at least two years.

The exception recognizes that a *current spouse* has access to the worker's current income; the *former spouse* does not. So the former spouse's payments should not be blocked by the worker's income or retirement.

Age rules for spousal benefits

There are two age rules for spousal benefits. The first rule is that you must be at least 62, just like a retiring worker.

The second rule is an exception to age 62. You may be eligible at *any* age, provided:

- You are currently married to the worker, and

- Have a child of the worker in your care. The child must be:
  - Under age 16 or disabled, and
  - Getting Social Security on the worker's record.[5]

Note that the age 62 exception does not apply to divorced spouses. Former spouse payments are possible only if you are over 62—even if you are caring for the worker's child.[6]

The first rule means that if you have reached the early retirement age of 62, you are potentially eligible for payments on your spouse's or, if currently unmarried, your ex-spouse's work record. You might also be eligible for payments on *your own* work record, making you a "dualie" (see page 68).

The second rule means that if you are caring for your young or disabled child, and your spouse is retired or disabled, *both you and the child* may be eligible for Social Security payments. This is true at any age—say, 35 years old. Keep in mind you must meet the same work limits as most other Social Security recipients; see page 205 for details.

Jack Johnston retires at age 62 and applies for Social Security. He learns that his 14-year-old child, Robert, will also get Social Security. In addition, Jack's wife Jill, 52, will get Social Security because of Jack's and Robert's payments. Her payments will continue until Robert turns 16, if she meets the earnings limits. She will again be eligible at 62 for regular spousal payments.

Payment amount for spouses

If you are eligible for spousal benefits, you will receive a percentage of the worker's *full payment amount* (the PIA, the benefit payable to the worker at FRA).

Your payment is computed on the *full payment*, not on what the retired worker *actually receives*.[7]

Jack's 100% payment is $1000 per month He starts payment at age 62, with a 25% reduction for early retirement. His payment is $750 (75% x $1000 = $750).

However, the spousal benefit for his wife Jill is computed as a percentage of his full $1000 payment, not the $750 he receives. Jill's payment is determined only by Jill's age and Jack's full benefit amount, regardless of Jack's age and payment amount.

Payments for child-in-care—50% payment

If you are eligible for spousal benefits because you are *caring for the worker's child,* you will be paid 50% of the worker's full payment amount, regardless of your age.[8]

Jill's payment is 50% of Jack's full payment amount. 50% of $1000 = $500 per month. Jack will draw a 75% payment at the same time Jill draws a 50% payment.

If you are eligible for spouse benefits *only because of your age* your payment computation is a little more complicated.

Payments started at Full Retirement Age—50% payment

If you are at least age 66 (or other Full Retirement Age—see page 47) when you claim payments, you will be paid the full 50% of the worker's full payment amount. There is no increase for filing after FRA.[7]

> **Reform Target:** Some reform proposals would reduce the maximum spousal payment to 33% of the worker's payment.[9]

Payments starting before Full Retirement Age—reduced payments for early retirement

You can file for early spousal payments as young as age 62. Early payments are reduced as follows:

- Stage 1: For the first 36 months of early filing, payment is reduced 25/36 of 1% for each month.

- Stage 2: For any additional early months, payment is reduced 5/12 of 1% for each month.[10]

This payment reduction is similar to the way retirement payments are reduced (see page 48). The same Full Retirement Age (FRA) is used for workers and spouses. Note that the first stage (25/36 of 1%) is a different reduction rate than retired workers (5/9 of 1%). The second stage is the same rate.

FRAs and payment percentages at age 62 are summarized in Figure 3.2.

John Jones retires at age 66 with a $1000 full payment amount. His wife Marsha files for Social Security on John's record at 62. Marsha's FRA is 66.

Marsha's payment will be reduced as follows:

- *25% reduction for the first 36 months of reduction (25/36% x 36 months)*
- *5% reduction for the next 12 months of reduction (5/12% x 12 months).*
- *Total reduction: 30% from the full 50% spouse payment.*

Marsha's payment amount will be computed as follows:

- *50% payment = $500 ($1000 x 50%).*
- *$500 – 30% = $350.*

Marsha will be paid $350 per month, starting at age 62.

Year of birth	Spousal FRA	Age 62 payment	FRA payment
1937	65	37.5%	50%
1938	65 & 2 months	37.1%	50%
1939	65 & 4 months	36.7%	50%
1940	65 & 6 months	36.3%	50%
1941	65 & 8 months	35.8%	50%
1942	65 & 10 months	35.3%	50%
1943-1954	66	35%	50%
1955	66 & 2 months	34.6%	50%
1956	66 & 4 months	34.2%	50%
1957	66 & 6 months	33.8%	50%
1958	66 & 8 months	33.3%	50%
1959	66 & 10 months	32.9%	50%
1960 and later	67	32.5%	50%

Figure 3.2: Spousal FRAs and payment percentages at 62 and FRA, for birth years after 1936. FRAs are the same as for retirement benefits (p. 47). If your birthdate is January 1, use the preceding year.[1]

Retroactive payments

If you file before FRA, your spousal benefits start the month you apply, assuming you meet all eligibility requirements, with no retroactive payments.

If you file when older than FRA, you can receive retroactive payments up to 6 months before filing, or back to your FRA, whichever is later. The general rule is that you can't get retroactive benefits that would cause a permanent reduction of payments.[11]

If you are eligible and want payments to start, don't delay—file immediately so you don't lose a month of payments.

Dual entitlement: "Dualies"

If you are *dually eligible*—eligible in two ways, as a family member and a worker in your own right—I unofficially call you a "dualie." You will receive the *higher* of the two payments. You cannot receive both added together. Basically, spousal payments are a guarantee that your Social Security payment will be no smaller than ½ of your spouse's payment.

If dually eligible, your own retirement benefit will be paid first. Then, if you can get more as a spouse, your own payment will be supplemented up to the level of the spousal payment.[12] (See exception below.)

Sally Smith can draw $300 on her own work record at age 66. Sam Smith's full payment amount is $2,225, so Sally could draw $1,112 as Sam's spouse (50% of $2,225). She will draw her full $300 on her own record and have an additional $812 added to her payment from Sam's record. Her payments will not affect Sam's payments in any way.

If you are eligible for more on your own record than as a spouse, spousal payments are impossible. No spousal claim will be taken. You will draw only your own retirement payment.[13] (See exception below.)

Deemed filing

If you are dually eligible, you will be *required* to apply for both your own retirement and your spousal payment. This is called *deemed filing,* i.e. you are *deemed* (assumed) to file for both benefits when you file for one. Your own benefits and your spousal benefits are like a "bundled package." Under deemed filing, claiming your retirement benefits = claiming for spousal benefits, and vice versa.[14]

Exception: Deemed filing will *not* apply if:

- You first file at FRA or above, *and*

- You were born before January 2, 1954.

Then you can file a Restricted Application for spousal-only payments without filing on your own work record, holding your own higher payments in reserve. The two benefits are "unbundled." You can use this as a strategy to maximize total lifetime Social Security benefits (see page 248).

However, if you were born on January 2, 1954, or later, deemed filing applies at all ages, both before and after FRA. You cannot file a Restricted

Application. If you file for one benefit you are deemed to file for the other simultaneously.[15]

GPO: Lower payments for some

If you receive a pension from a federal, state, or local government based on *work not covered by Social Security,* your government pension may reduce your Social Security benefits. Your pension may reduce Social Security payments on *your own* work record; that reduction is called the *Windfall Elimination Provision,* and is described on page 52. Your government pension also reduces, or *offsets,* Social Security *spousal* payments you get on your spouse's work record. The provision for reducing your spousal benefits is called *Government Pension Offset (GPO).*

Government Pension Offset affects spousal and widow(er)'s benefits. The amount of the reduction is two-thirds of your government pension.

Grace is a retired county employee. She did not pay Social Security taxes at her county job. Grace receives a county pension of $300 per month.

Grace's husband Gus has a full Social Security payment of $2,200 per month. Grace would normally be eligible for a $1,100 spousal payment from Social Security at FRA (50% of Gus's $2,200). However, due to her government pension the $1,100 will be offset, or reduced, by $200 (two-thirds of her $300 county pension). Her spousal benefit will be $900 instead of $1,100. The same $200 reduction will apply to future widow's payments she might receive.

The GPO offset is often enough to eliminate any Social Security spousal payment.

For more information on the offset, see the SSA Factsheet "Government Pension Offset," available at www.ssa.gov/pubs/EN-05-10007.pdf. A GPO calculator is at www.ssa.gov/planners/retire/gpo-calc.html.

To summarize:

- You can receive spousal payments on the work record of your spouse or former spouse.

- If you are dually eligible as a spouse *and* as a worker in your own right, your payment is the higher amount.

- Then your payment is made up of your own payment first, plus any excess from your spousal payment.

- *Exception:* If filing at FRA and if born before January 2, 1954, you may opt to claim only the spousal payment and delay your own.

- Your spousal payment may be further reduced by GPO if you receive certain government pensions.

For more information about how spousal benefits will work in your case, see the "Examples" section below.

BENEFITS FOR THE WORKER'S CHILD

Will a minor child be part of your retirement? Are you disabled and raising children? Or are you concerned about your disabled adult child in your later years? Keep reading.

Social Security will pay benefits for your child if you are retired or disabled, if you get Social Security and your child meets certain requirements.

This section affects you if *you* are a minor or are disabled and your parent is retired or disabled. If so, you will learn how you can receive payments on your parent's work record. (If the worker is deceased, see Chapter 4, Survivor Benefits, for more information.)

Definition of child

For your child to qualify for child's benefits, *you* must be getting your own Social Security payments as a retired or disabled worker, and your *child* must meet the definitions in this section. The child must be:

- Your child, and
- Unmarried, and be:

  o Under 18, **or**

  o Under age 19 and a full-time elementary or high school student, **or**

  o Age 18 or over and under a total disability. The disability must have begun before age 22. For details see page 117.[16]

The child is your child if she is:

- Your legitimate child, or

- Your natural child (if acknowledged as your child in writing or in legal documents), or

- Your legally adopted child, or

- Your stepchild.[17]

The rule of thumb is that if State law would recognize the child as your heir in its intestacy inheritance laws, then Social Security will recognize your child as well.

There is also limited provision for a grandchild or step-grandchild to receive payments on your work record. The grandchild's parents must be deceased or disabled. In addition, the grandchild must be your dependent and live with you.[18]

Example of child benefits

Chuck has a natural son Dave and a stepdaughter, Erin, both in their teens.

Both can get child's payments on Chuck's record once Chuck gets Social Security retirement or disability.

Erin is a high school senior when she turns 18. Her Social Security payments stop in June, when she graduates.

Dave turns 19 shortly before his own graduation. His payments stop when he turns 19.

Payment amount for child's benefits

If eligible, your child is entitled to 50% of your full payment amount, regardless of what percentage you, the worker, receive.[19] Thus, the child's computation is similar to a spouse computation, described on page 65. However, there is no reduction for a child's age.

Chuck's 100% benefit is $1000. Erin is entitled to $500 per month.

Since Chuck has two eligible children, they might *each* receive $500 per month. However, there is a limit to total family benefits, known as the *family maximum payment*.

FAMILY MAXIMUM PAYMENT

Kathy has a large family. At 66, she applies for a 100% Social Security payment on her own record. Her husband will get a 50% spousal payment on Kathy's record. Each of her 4 minor children is also eligible to receive a 50% payment. Could Kathy's family be paid more from Social Security than they ever got in paychecks?

There is a limit to payments for Kathy's family members. Every Social Security computation includes a *Family Maximum Payment*.[20] The family maximum ranges from 1.5 to 1.8 times the worker's full payment amount, based on a four-stage formula.[21]

Once the maximum is being paid to a household, no higher payments will be issued, even if another individual becomes eligible. If, say, another child is added to a record already paying the maximum, the same dollar amount is simply divided into smaller shares to be distributed to the new, larger household.

In other words, if someone else sits down to dinner, everyone gets a smaller serving.

There are two kinds of benefits *not* affected by the family maximum: Payments to *the worker* and payments to a *former spouse*.[20]

- The worker's payment remains a fixed amount no matter how many other family members are added to the payment record; the worker is *primary*.

- Former spouses are a separate family unit, so their payments do not affect anyone else on the record.

Let's look at our example family to see how the family maximum works.

Kathy is receiving a $1,200 age-66 payment. Her family maximum is then $1,868, an amount computed from her $1,200 full payment (using the 2018 formula).[21]

If Kathy has one eligible child, the child is entitled to $600 (50% of Kathy's full $1,200). Total family payments are then:

Kathy	*$1,200*
+Child 1	*+$600*
Total	*$1,800*

Since this total payment is under the family maximum, the entire $1,800 is paid.

What if Kathy has two eligible children? Without a family maximum, the computation would look like this:

Kathy	*$1,200*
Child 1	*$600*
+Child 2	*+$600*
Total	*$2400*

*But since this exceeds the $1,868 family maximum, the children will **not** receive full payments. Instead, the children's benefits are computed in two steps, while still ensuring that Kathy gets the full amount she is due:*

STEP 1:

Family Maximum:	*$1,868*
—Kathy's share:	*—$1,200*
Amount available for dependents:	*$668*

STEP 2:

Amount available for dependents:	*$668*
Divided by number of dependents:	*÷2*
Amount for each child:	*$334*

Final payment schedule:

Kathy	*$1,200*
Child 1	*$334*
+Child 2	*+$334*
Total	*$1,868*

Similarly, if we were to add more children, or a spouse, to Kathy's family, the $668 available for family members would simply be split among them, in smaller and smaller shares. Kathy would always get her full $1,200, and all other family members would split the $668 evenly.[22]

Former spouses and the family maximum

The family maximum *does not apply to former spouses.* If Kathy has a former husband eligible on her record, for example, he will get up to his full $600 payment (50% of Kathy's $1,200) even if Kathy's immediate household family is already receiving the family maximum.

Why? Because the ex-spouse is a separate family unit. By treating former spouses as separate family units, Social Security stays out of family conflicts.

Combined family maximums

A child may be eligible as the child of *two* working parents. In that case, an additional computation is performed, yielding a *combined family maximum* for the child and any siblings. This combined family maximum can be as much as the sum of the two maximums together, but with a combined maximum limit.[23]

Callie is eligible for up to $600 as Kathy's daughter. But because her brother Carl is also drawing on Kathy's record, Callie can only receive $334.

Later Callie's father, Ken, starts receiving Social Security. Because Callie and Carl are eligible on Ken's higher record as well as Kathy's, their family maximums can be combined. The children each receive $650 instead of $334.[24]

EXAMPLES

John and Marsha

 John and Marsha Jones are married. Both have a Full Retirement Age of 66, and John's full payment amount is $1,000. Let's examine spouse benefits, using a variety of different work histories for Marsha.

Let's take the basic case first. Assume that John and Marsha are both 66. That makes John eligible for his full $1,000 payment. Marsha's payment depends on her own work history. Here we will consider four different possibilities, summarized in Figures 3.3 - 3.6:

Both start at age 66.

(1)   If Marsha is *not eligible* on her own work record: $500.

If Marsha lacks her own 40 work credits (see page 36), she will get a spousal payment of 50% of John's full payment. Marsha's payment is *in addition to* John's, and does not reduce John's payment. Therefore, Marsha will receive $500 per month (50% of John's $1,000). John and Marsha together will receive $1,500 per month (John's $1,000 + Marsha's $500).

(2)   If Marsha is eligible for a *smaller* payment on her own work record: $500.

Let's say Marsha is eligible for her own $400 Social Security payment. That makes her a dualie, dually eligible as a worker and as a spouse. Her payment will be the *higher* of the two. She will receive her own $400 payment, plus a $100 spousal payment, to equal the $500 total payment. John and Marsha together will get $1,500 per month, just as in the previous situation.

Note: If Marsha is subject to "deemed filing" (page 68), she *must file for both payments.* She cannot take first one and delay the other.

(3)   If Marsha has substantial work: She will draw only her own payment.

Suppose Marsha's own Social Security is $800. Since her $800 is higher than the spouse payment ($500), she will receive the $800. John and Marsha together will receive $1,800 per month (John's $1,000 + Marsha's $800).

BOTH START AT FRA			
John's Own Payment	Marsha's Own Payment	**Marsha's Payment**	**Family Total**
Example 1: Marsha not eligible for her own payment.			
$1,000	$0	**$500**	**$1,500**
Example 2: Marsha eligible for $400 on her own.			
$1,000	$400	**$500**	**$1,500**
Example 3: Marsha eligible for $800 on her own.			
$1,000	$800	**$800**	**$1,800**
Example 4: Marsha eligible for $2,200 on her own.			
$1,000	$2,200	**$2,200**	**$3,300**

Figure 3.3: Summary of John and Marsha's benefits if started at age 66 (or other FRA). Note that in Example 4, John will receive a 50% spousal payment of $1,100 (50% of Marsha's $2,200).

(4)   If Marsha out-earns John: She will draw only her own payment.

Let's say Marsha earns more than John, so her own Social Security payment is $2,200. Like the previous example, she will then receive her own payment, since it is higher than the spousal payment.

John and Marsha will receive a total of $3,300 per month together. The total will be $3,300, not $3,200, because John will get a spousal payment of $1,100 (50% of Marsha's $2,200).

Note: Social Security calculations are gender-neutral. If John's and Marsha's work histories were reversed, John would be eligible for the same benefits listed above for Marsha.

Figure 3.3 summarizes the four spouse cases just described.

Both start at age 62

If John and Marsha are both 62, John is eligible for 75% of his full $1,000. John's own payment would be $750.

Marsha's *spousal* benefit at 62 is computed using a special formula for reduced dualie benefits, yielding $370 for her.[25]

BOTH START AT AGE 62			
John's Own Payment	Marsha's Own Payment	**Marsha's Payment**	**Family Total**
Example 1: Marsha not eligible for her own payment.			
$750	$0	$350	$1,100
Example 2: Marsha eligible for a full benefit of $400 on her own.			
$750	$300	$370*	$1,120
Example 3: Marsha eligible for full benefit of $800 on her own.			
$750	$600	$600	$1,350
Example 4: Marsha eligible for full benefit of $2,200 on her own.			
$750	$1,650	$1,650	$2,470*

*Figure 3.4: Summary of John and Marsha's benefits if started at age 62, assuming FRA of 66. *In Example 2, a special computation applies when Marsha is dually eligible for reduced retirement and reduced spousal payments, so she gets $370 (her own $300 + $70 as John's spouse). Using the same computation in Example 4 yields a total benefit of $820 for John (his own $750 + $70 as Marsha's spouse).*[25]

The Marsha in Example 3 would be eligible for more on her own record than she could get on John's. At 62 she can get 75% of her own $800 full payment, or $600.

The Marsha in Example 4 would be eligible for 75% of her own $2,200 full payment, or $1,650. John's payment would be computed using the special formula for reduced dualie benefits, yielding $820 for him.[25]

Figure 3.4 summarizes these four cases.

Mixed ages

What happens if John and Marsha are not the same age? If John is 62 and Marsha is 66, John's work record might pay $750 to him (75% of his full retirement benefit of $1,000) and $500 for her (50% of the same $1,000).

Note that Marsha's spouse benefit is computed on John's *full* age-66 payment, even if he is drawing a reduced payment because of early retirement. Each person's payment is computed based on *that person's age when that person's payment begins*, regardless of the other spouse's age or payment.

Figure 3.5 summarizes this information.

STARTING AT MIXED AGES			
John's Own Payment	Marsha's Own Payment	**Marsha's Payment**	**Family Total**
Example 1: John age 62 and Marsha age 66.			
$750	$0	**$500**	**$1,250**
Example 2: John age 66 and Marsha age 62.			
$1,000	$0	**$350**	**$1,350**

Figure 3.5: Summary of John and Marsha's benefits starting at mixed ages. (Examples assume Marsha is not eligible on her own work record, and both FRAs are 66.)

Madam X

When John and Marsha apply for Social Security, the application asks, "Did you have any previous marriages?" Their prior marital history must be explored, to see if anyone else might get paid on their work records, and if they might be paid more on another work record.

John responds that he had a former wife, Madam X. John and Madam X were married for ten years and Madam X is over 62. This is a *claims lead* that Social Security must resolve by either paying Madam X or determining that no payment is possible. Social Security must attempt to locate Madam X to see if payments are possible.

When Social Security contacts Madam X, she confirms that she was married to John for ten years, that she is currently unmarried, and that she is 66 and retired. Therefore, Madam X could be eligible for former spouse benefits, depending on how high her own payments might be.

Quite logically, her payment amount will be whichever is higher, her own Social Security, or spousal payments on John's record. This means that Madam X is eligible for the same payment schedule as Marsha (Figure 3.6). Since she is over 66, she might even be able to claim "Spousal-Only" payments (see page 248).

In this case:

- Madam X's payments will not affect payments to John and Marsha, and vice versa.

- The Family Maximum will not apply because Madam X is considered a separate family unit.

- John and Marsha will never know if Madam X is on John's record, and Madam X will never know about John and Marsha's payments, because of the Privacy Act.

Note different eligibility rules for Marsha and Madam X:

- Marsha, John's current spouse, can get spousal payments only if John is *getting his own Social Security.*

- Madam X, though, can get former spousal payments *even if John gets no Social Security,* as long John is 62 and the divorce was final for at least two years. This special rule for former spouses is explained on page 63.

FORMER SPOUSE "MADAM X," STARTING AT FRA		
John's Own Payment	Madam X's Own Payment	**Madam X's Payment**
Example 1: Madam X not eligible for her own payment.		
$1,000	$0	**$500**
Example 2: Madam X eligible for a full benefit of $400 on her own.		
$1,000	$400	**$500**
Example 3: Madam X eligible for full benefit of $800 on her own.		
$1,000	$800	**$800**
Example 4: Madam X eligible for full benefit of $2,200 on her own.		
$1,000	$2,200	**$2,200**

Figure 3.6: Madam X's payments if started at FRA.

Tom & Harry

Let's make our example even more complex. When Madam X applies for Social Security, *her* marital history must also be explored, to see if anyone might get paid on her work record, or if she might get more on someone else's record. Therefore, the Social Security representative asks, "Did you have any other marriages?" Madam X responds that she was married to Tom for eleven years and Harry for twelve years.

How will Social Security handle this situation? Will Madam X be eligible under the first marriage? The last? The longest-lasting?

The solution is simple: she will be paid on whichever record *pays highest*. Therefore, Madam X now has *four* work records to choose from: her own, John's, Tom's, and Harry's. Madam X will be paid from whichever record pays the most.

The "best" record might change over time. For example, Madam X might be drawing a $500 benefit on John's record. Then, Harry turns 62. Suppose Harry's age 66 payment is $1,800 compared to John's $1,000. When Harry turns 62, Madam X should switch to *his* payment record to receive $900 per month. Thus, it pays Madam X to note when former spouses turn 62, and check with SSA to see if higher payments are possible. I call it "changing seats on the bus."

Madam Y and Z

Let's add one more detail to our John and Marsha example. Suppose John had several ten-year marriages—not only to Madam X, but to Madam Y and Madam Z as well.

In that case, current spouse Marsha, and former spouses Madam X, Madam Y and Madam Z, could *each* draw $500 payments on John's work record. The family maximum doesn't apply because each spouse is a separate family unit. The former spouse payments would not affect Marsha's payment amount, nor would they affect each other.

Other Examples

Marsha may have ex-husbands, just as John has ex-wives. Mr. A, B, and C, if we call them that, might be eligible for payments on Marsha's record, if Marsha's payments are high enough and assuming they are not eligible for a higher payment on another record. The rules would be the same as those for Madam X, Y, and Z applying on John's record.

Here's a quiz: could John or Marsha become eligible on the records of *their* former spouses? Why or why not?

The answer is that neither John nor Marsha are eligible on other records because they are currently married. You must be *currently unmarried* to draw former spouse benefits.

THE INSIDE STORY

Examples vs. Real Life

The examples used here are not far-fetched. I remember my first day of "real" claims, as part of Claims Representative training. My fellow trainees and I had practiced on textbook cases. We had role-played retirement interviews. We felt our instruction and testing had prepared us for the real world, so we were given some hand-picked "simple" cases to process.

In no time, our naive confidence evaporated, as the "simple" cases revealed former spouse issues, earnings problems, special computations, or any of the thousands of other complications that arise when working with real people.

The lesson: government tries to have a rule for every situation, a category for every individual. But that is impossible. No matter how complex the rules and categories, a real person will have a life much more complicated than the rules. The examples above, with their Madam X, Y, and Z, represent any number of cases Social Security deals with every day.

You might be a John, a Marsha, a Madam X, or a Mr. A, and you need to know how your current and/or former marriages affect your Social Security.

Furthermore, these examples illustrate an important rule: It is SSA's *duty* to pay you the most you can get. If a higher benefit is overlooked, it is an employee error. Every possible way to determine your highest legal payment must be explored.

There are reasonable limits to this policy. If you refuse to apply for benefits, you can't be paid. If you delay filing, back pay could be reduced. But once you telephone or otherwise contact SSA, the Administration must pursue every possible payment for you. By reading this book, you'll know why SSA asks about former marriages, and you can help SSA search for every possible payment without overlooking a higher payment on another record.

The next chapter deals with a sensitive subject: death. Specifically, we will explore what Social Security benefits are payable to those left behind after a death, focusing on *who* is eligible, *when* they are eligible, and *how much* their payments can be.

FOR MORE INFORMATION...

"Retirement Benefits/Family Benefits"
www.ssa.gov/pubs/10035.html, and scroll to "Family benefits "

"Retirement Planner: Benefits for you as a spouse"
www.ssa.gov/planners/retire/applying6.html

"Same-Sex Couples"
www.ssa.gov/same-sexcouples/

"Benefits for Children"
www.ssa.gov/pubs/10085.html

"Government Pension Offset"
www.ssa.gov/pubs/10007.html

"Information for Government Employees"
www.ssa.gov/planners/retire/gpo-wep.html

Chapter Endnotes

1. https://www.socialsecurity.gov/planners/retire/agereduction.html and https://secure.ssa.gov/apps10/poms.nsf/lnx/0300615205
2. https://secure.ssa.gov/apps10/poms.nsf/lnx/0200305060
3. https://secure.ssa.gov/apps10/poms.nsf/lnx/0200305055
4. https://ssa.gov/planners/retire/divspouse.html
5. https://ssa.gov/OP_Home/handbook/handbook.03/handbook-0305.html, D.2.
6. https://ssa.gov/OP_Home/handbook/handbook.03/handbook-0311.html, "Note"
7. https://ssa.gov/planners/retire/applying6.html under "How Much Will I Receive?"
8. https://www.ssa.gov/OP_Home/handbook/handbook.03/handbook-0320.html, 3201.1 C.
9. See https://www.socialsecurity.gov/OACT/solvency/provisions/summary.html, D2,for example
10. https://www.ssa.gov/OACT/quickcalc/spouse.html#calculator
11. https://www.socialsecurity.gov/OP_Home/handbook/handbook.15/handbook-1513.html and https://secure.ssa.gov/apps10/poms.nsf/lnx/0200204030
12. https://ssa.gov/OP_Home/handbook/handbook.03/handbook-0320.html, 320.1 B.
13. https://ssa.gov/OP_Home/handbook/handbook.03/handbook-0305.html, C. Note that the actual comparison is between your own full payment amount (PIA) and ½ of the worker's PIA.

14. https://secure.ssa.gov/apps10/poms.nsf/lnx/0200204035 A. and https://secure.ssa.gov/apps10/poms.nsf/lnx/0200204020, D.1.b; note use of term *reduced* RIB or spouse's benefits, i.e. before FRA.
15. https://secure.ssa.gov/apps10/poms.nsf/lnx/0200204035 B.1.a.
16. https://ssa.gov/OP_Home/handbook/handbook.03/handbook-0323.html
17. https://ssa.gov/OP_Home/handbook/handbook.04/handbook-0411.html
18. https://ssa.gov/OP_Home/handbook/handbook.03/handbook-0325.html and https://secure.ssa.gov/apps10/poms.nsf/lnx/0200306235
19. https://ssa.gov/OP_Home/handbook/handbook.03/handbook-0338.html
20. https://ssa.gov/OP_Home/handbook/handbook.07/handbook-0731.html
21. See https://www.socialsecurity.gov/OACT/COLA/familymax.html for current formula. Past formulas are found at https://www.socialsecurity.gov/OACT/COLA/bendpoints.html.
22. https://ssa.gov/OP_Home/handbook/handbook.07/handbook-0732.html
23. https://ssa.gov/OP_Home/handbook/handbook.07/handbook-0737.html
24. Illustration only, not reflecting an actual computation.
25. https://secure.ssa.gov/apps10/poms.nsf/lnx/0300615250. Basically the spouse benefit at FRA is reduced, and then added to the worker's own reduced benefit, rather than reducing the total benefit at once.

CHAPTER FOUR

SURVIVOR BENEFITS

Survivor Benefits in a Nutshell

- If a worker dies, certain surviving family members are eligible for payments.

- Eligible family members are widow(er)s, certain former spouses, certain children, and dependent parents.

- Survivor payments are possible even if the deceased was young and never got Social Security.

- Payment amount is a percentage of the worker's full payment amount (PIA).

- A family maximum limits total family payouts.

Fran Ferguson is desperate. Her husband Fred died last month from a sudden illness. Her son Frank and her daughter Karen are still in high school. Fran does not work. How will she pay her bills?

Fran learns that she and Frank can get Social Security survivor payments. Karen, as Fred's stepdaughter, will also be eligible.

SURVIVOR BENEFITS BACKGROUND

Did you know that when you pay your Social Security taxes, you are also buying protection for your family in case of your death? *Survivor benefits* work somewhat like life insurance, and can be worth hundreds of thousands of dollars for your family members if they are left without your support.

Survivor benefits are like family benefits, except they are payable after your death. Like family benefits, your eligible family members will get a monthly payment based on your earnings level, and a family maximum caps payments to larger families.

However, compared to family benefits, each survivor gets a higher percentage of your full payment amount. Survivors can also get higher payments because your absence means one less payment counted against the family maximum.

Figure 4.1 lists the types of payments available. Each type is detailed in the sections below.

The Four Types of Survivor Benefits

- Payments to your widow or widower, and/or your former spouse.

- Payments to your surviving unmarried children.

- Payments to your dependent parents.

- A one-time, lump sum payment to your spouse or children.

Figure 4.1. Types of survivor payments.[1]

Here are two key features of survivor payments. Your survivors can get Social Security even if, at the time of your death:

- You were not getting Social Security payments, and

- You were not retirement age.

Even if you die well before retirement, say at age 30, your family will receive monthly Social Security payments until the children are grown, provided you meet the work requirements below.

Harold died at the age of 28, leaving his wife, Hannah, age 27, and two minor children. Hannah and the children will receive Social Security payments until the children are grown (provided that everyone meets the work limits described on page 205).
Hannah will again be eligible for payments at age 60.

WORK REQUIREMENTS FOR SURVIVOR BENEFITS

Before your family members are eligible for survivor payments, you the worker must earn coverage through working and paying Social Security taxes.

Your work is measured in *work credits*. These are the same credits used to establish your eligibility for Social Security *retirement* payments (see page 35).

You need 40 work credits to get retirement benefits. But workers who die at a young age have less chance to earn the full 40 credits required for retirement:

When Harold died at 28, he had only 30 credits on his work record, because of his schooling and a few years of low earnings. Hannah is concerned that she and the children will not be eligible because Harold has fewer than 40 credits.

Since younger workers have fewer work years, fewer credits are required for survivor benefits after an early death.

There are two ways to meet the work requirement: *fully insured status* or *currently insured status.*

Fully insured status—comprehensive protection

"Fully insured status" provides comprehensive coverage for your family. Fully insured status means you have earned enough work credits to provide Social Security payments to your survivors of *all types*—a spouse over 60, a younger spouse caring for your children, your children, and your dependent parents.

The number of credits needed depends on your age when you die. The older you are, the more work credits required, up to the maximum of 40 credits. Figure 4.2 shows the number of work credits needed for fully insured status. Once you have 40 credits, you are *permanently insured* for all your family members.[3]

Since Harold was 28 when he died, he needed only 6 credits for fully insured status for survivor benefits, not the full 40 credits required for retirees. His 30 work credits ensure that Hannah and the children will be eligible for Social Security.

Fred Ferguson died at 62. He needed 40 work credits to make Fran and his children eligible for Social Security.

Currently insured status—fallback protection

Currently insured status is a special rule for those who do not qualify for fully insured status. Think of it as backup that gives partial protection for your family.

If you are only "currently insured," only two types of survivors can be paid:

- your children, and
- your widow who is caring for your children.[4]

No payments will be possible to your parents or your widow not caring for your children.

Work Credits Needed for Survivor Benefits (Fully Insured Status)	
Age at death	**Credits Needed**
28 or younger	6
29	7
30	8
31	9
32	10
33	11
34	12
35	13
36	14
37	15
38	16
39	17
40	18
41	19
42	20
43	21
44	22
45	23
46	24
47	25
48	26
49	27
50	28
51	29
52	30
53	31
54	32
55	33
56	34
57	35
58	36
59	37
60	38
61	39
62 or older	40
See text for exception to these requirements.	

Figure 4.2. Work credits needed for survivor benefits (fully insured status).[2]

You are currently insured if you die with at least 6 work credits in the previous 13 calendar quarters—in other words, at least 1-1/2 years of work in your final 3 years.[4]

Note that this rule applies *only* when surviving children are involved, or for the payment of the Lump Sum Death Benefit (described below). No payments will be available for others.

*Ken died at age 32 with only 8 work credits. He is not **fully** insured because he needed 10 work credits for fully insured status (see Figure 4.2). However, 6 of his work credits were earned in his last 3 years; therefore, he is **currently** insured. His children will get Social Security on Ken's work record until they are grown. His wife Carol will also get Social Security while she is caring for the children, until the youngest is 16.*

*When the children are grown and Carol reaches retirement age, she will not be eligible for widow's benefits on Ken's record because his **currently** insured status does not provide that type of benefit.*

If you meet the work requirement, your survivors may get Social Security. The following sections describe in detail the various types of payments, their special requirements, and the amount paid.

BENEFITS FOR WIDOWS AND WIDOWERS

The most common type of survivor payment is for the widow or widower after a worker's death.[5] If you are a widow(er), this section will tell you if and when you are eligible for a payment and how much to expect. Figure 4.3 summarizes available benefits.

Definitions of widow, widower, and surviving divorced spouse

The definition of a widow(er) is nearly identical to the definition of a spouse for family benefits (see page 61). Basically, if you were married to the worker for at least 9 months at the time of his or her death, you will meet the definition of a widow(er).[6]

Same-sex spouses may get widow(er)'s payments. SSA urges same-sex survivors to file a claim.[7]

If you were divorced from the worker at the time of death, you might still qualify for Social Security payments as a *surviving divorced spouse*. Again, the requirements are similar to those for family benefits: your marriage to the worker must have lasted at least ten years.[8] (The ten-year marriage requirement is waived if you are caring for the worker's eligible child who is under 16 or is disabled.[9])

Rules for a widow (survivor benefits) are different from rules for a spouse (family benefits). Particularly, *remarriage rules* and *age requirements* are different, as discussed in the next two sections.

PERSON	BENEFIT AMOUNT (Percentage of worker's Full Benefit Amount)
WIDOW OR WIDOWER	
Full Retirement Age or older	100%
Age 60	71.5%
Any age, caring for worker's entitled child under 16	75%
Requirements: • Must be currently unmarried **or** • Remarried after age 60	
SURVIVING DIVORCED SPOUSE	
Full Retirement Age or older	100%
Age 60	71.5%
Any age if caring for worker's entitled child (child under 16 or disabled)	75%
Requirements: • 10-year marriage **or** have child in care, **and** • Currently unmarried **or** remarried after age 60. (If eligible because of child in care, remarriage at any age terminates payments.)	
NOTES: Family maximum may reduce total amount payable to family. If the worker was eligible for a reduced retirement payment before death, a survivor payment may not exceed the worker's payment or 82.5% of the full payment amount, whichever is greater. Surviving spouses or surviving divorced spouses who are fully disabled may be eligible at ages 50-59; see Chapter 5, Disability.	

Figure 4.3. Summary of benefits for surviving spouses.

Remarriage rules for surviving spouses

One important rule applies to all widows, widowers, and surviving divorced spouses: you must be currently unmarried *or remarried after age 60*.[10]

Maud, age 62, draws a widow's payment on the record of her deceased husband. She and Greg wish to marry. If they do, Maud can continue to receive her widow's payment because her remarriage is after age 60.

*Kristen, age 58, plans to draw a widow's payment on Dan's record when she turns 60. She also wishes to marry Hank. If she marries Hank before she turns 60, she cannot draw a widow's payment on Dan's record. (But she could draw a **spouse** payment on **Hank's** record when she reaches 62.)*

Age requirements for widow(er)'s benefits

Eligibility age for widow(er)s is 60. There are exceptions below.

The age 60 requirement is unique, not 62 like retirement or spouse payments. The younger age limit recognizes the greater hardship that many widows and widowers face.

 THE INSIDE STORY

Remarriage Rules for Widow(er)s

There is a good reason for the rule permitting remarriage after age 60. In the 1970s a widow(er)'s remarriage was never permitted; Maud would lose her widow's payment if she married Greg. Thus, there was incentive for them to live together without marrying.

The media trumpeted the situation, with headlines claiming "Seniors forced to live in sin."

In response, Congress amended the Social Security Act to allow remarriage after age 60 without stopping widow(er)s' payments.

Note that remarriage at any age continues to end benefits for a surviving divorced spouse who is eligible because of caring for the deceased worker's child.

Maud lost her husband Mark when she was 57. Her children were grown. She had been a homemaker and volunteer for years with little or no paid work. She lived on life insurance proceeds and savings, plus some part-time work, after she was widowed. She was relieved to start getting Social Security on Mark's record at age 60.

There are two exceptions to the age 60 rule:

- You can get *disabled widow(er) benefits* at ages 50-59, if you are disabled and meet other requirements. See page 116 for details.

- You may be *any age,* if you are *caring for the worker's child*[11]:

  o The child must be under age 16 or disabled.

  o The child must be getting Social Security on the worker's record.

  o In addition, a surviving divorced spouse must be unmarried to be paid as the child's parent.[12]

The child-in-care rule provides payments to millions of young widows and widowers.

When Harold died, Hannah was 27 and caring for their two children. Because the children got Social Security, Hannah also qualified for payments. She drew Social Security payments for two years until she returned to work. The children's payments continued through high school.

Note that you can qualify with a child in care whether you were married to or divorced from the worker at the time of death. (If the worker were still alive, a *former* spouse must wait until age 62 to be eligible.)

Cal and Irene were divorced when Cal died. Irene was raising their son, Bill. Irene and Bill can each draw Social Security on Cal's work record.

Payment amount for widow(er)s

Like family benefits (Chapter 3), widow(er)'s benefits are computed as a percentage of the worker's full benefit amount (PIA). There are three differences, though, between family benefits and widow(er)'s benefits:

- First, the worker may not have lived to retirement age (see the next section immediately below). In the event of a younger death, a full benefit is computed *as if the worker were Full Retirement Age (FRA) at the time of death.*

- Second, the percentages paid to survivors are higher—up to 100% of the worker's full payment, as shown in Figure 4.3.

- Third, the Full Retirement Age for widow(er)s is slightly different from the FRA for workers and spouses, with a later phase-in to age 67, as shown in Figure 4.4.[13]

Payments for child-in-care—75% payment

If you are eligible because you are caring for the worker's child, you will receive 75% of the worker's full benefit amount.[14]

Year of Birth	Full Retirement Age
1939 or earlier	65
1940	65 and 2 months
1941	65 and 4 months
1942	65 and 6 months
1943	65 and 8 months
1944	65 and 10 months
1945 - 1956	66
1957	66 and 2 months
1958	66 and 4 months
1959	66 and 6 months
1960	66 and 8 months
1961	66 and 10 months
1962 and later	67

Figure 4.4: "Full Retirement Age" for widow(ers). Note differences from FRAs for workers and spouses (Figure 2.4, page 50, and Figure 3.2, page 67).[13]

Payments starting at Full Retirement Age—100% payment

If you start widow(er)'s payments at your FRA or older:

- In general, you will receive 100% of the payment the worker *was receiving*.[15]

- Filing after FRA will not increase your payment, except for Cost of Living Adjustments (COLAs). There is no advantage to waiting past FRA for widow(er)'s benefits.

- If the deceased worker was receiving reduced payments because of early retirement (page 48), your payment will also be reduced to that level or 82.5% of the full payment amount, whichever is greater.[16]

- If the worker was receiving increased payments because of delayed retirement (page 49), your payment will include that increase.[17]

- If the worker died before FRA, without ever receiving Social Security, you will receive 100% of the full payment amount.[18]

- If the worker died after FRA, without ever receiving Social Security, your payment will be increased by Delayed Retirement Credits up to the age at death.[17]

Frances lost her husband Tom when she was 68. Tom's payment would have been $2,000 at his FRA of 66, but he was receiving only $1,500 (75%) because his payments started at 62. Frances' widow's payment will be $1,650 (82.5% minimum).

Sharon lost her husband Shel when she was 68. Shel's full payment amount was $2,000 at his FRA of 66, but he delayed retirement until he was 70. Therefore, Shel's Social Security was $2,640 (132%). Sharon's widow's payment will be $2,640.

Bella's husband, Don, died at 68 without ever getting Social Security. His full payment amount was $2,000 at his FRA of 66. Bella's widow's payment at her FRA will be $2,320 (116%), including 2 years of Delayed Retirement Credits, because Don had not gotten Social Security.

Note that when you opt for a reduced early retirement payment, you are also reducing payments for your surviving spouse.

When Tom opted for a reduced age-62 retirement payment, he also chose a reduced widow's payment for Frances, whether he knew it or not.

Conversely, delaying your own Social Security past FRA could mean increased payments for your widow(er). Choosing early or delayed payment has long-term financial consequences, affecting your own lifetime payments and your spouse's.

Payments starting before Full Retirement Age—reduced payments for early filing

If you first draw a widow(er)'s payment before your FRA, and don't have the worker's eligible child in care, payments can start as early as age 60 (or 50 if you are disabled):

- You will be paid a smaller percentage of the worker's full payment amount.

- The amount will be proportional to your age when your payments begin.

- The monthly reduction varies, depending on your FRA, but always results in a 71.5% payment at age 60.[19]

- Disabled widow(er)s ages 50-59 are paid 71.5%, the same as age-60 widow(er)s (see page 115).[20]

- If you have work earnings before FRA, your Social Security payments may be reduced by the work rules (see page 205).

The monthly reduction from age 60 to FRA is simply 28.5% divided by the number of months from 60 to FRA.

For example, if your FRA is 66, you are eligible up to 72 months before FRA (age 66 – age 60 = 6 years or 72 months). The monthly reduction is 28.5% divided by 72, or 0.396% per month.

Eugene was retired and 59 when his wife Eunice died. Eunice was already 66 and drawing a full 100% Social Security retirement payment of $600. When Eugene turns 60 he can draw a widower's payment of $429 (71.5% of $600), no matter what his FRA is.

Maud started drawing widow's payments on Mark's record when she turned 60. Mark's full payment amount was $800, but he was only receiving $600 because he chose a reduced age-62 payment. Maud's widow's payment is $572 (71.5% of the full $800). If Maud postponed her payments until FRA, she could be paid $660 (the minimum of 82.5% of Mark's full payment amount.)

Retroactive payments

If you file before FRA, your widow(er)'s benefits can start the month you apply, assuming you meet all eligibility requirements, with no retroactive payments. *Exception:* If you file in the month immediately after the worker's death, your payments can start the month of death.

If you file when older than FRA, you can receive retroactive payments up to 6 months before filing, or back to your FRA, whichever is later. The general rule is that you can't get retroactive benefits if that would cause a permanent reduction of payments.[21]

If you are eligible and want payments, don't delay—file immediately so you don't lose a month of payments.

What if the worker never received Social Security payments?

You may be eligible for survivor payments even if the deceased worker never received Social Security, and even if the worker never reached retirement age.[22]

This provision is particularly important if your working spouse dies at an early age, leaving you with young children to raise. In this case:

* The payment amount is based on your spouse's full benefit amount, which would be computed *as if he or she were Full Retirement Age at the time of death,* based on his or her average earnings up until death.[23]

* The children would receive payments until they are grown (see details below).

* You could receive payments as the children's parent until the youngest child is 16.

* The payment amount would be subject to the Family Maximum Payment (page 71).

These payments could easily amount to tens or hundreds of thousands of dollars while your children mature, helping offset the loss of your spouse's wages.

Be sure to consider these Social Security payments when you make your life insurance decisions. Social Security provides a foundation for survivors' income, with pensions, life insurance and savings providing the rest.

Hannah drew payments for herself and the children years ago, following Harold's death. When the children were grown, the Social Security payments stopped. Now that Hannah is 60 and retired she re-applies for widow's payments. Harold's full payment amount is now $1,000—it has been automatically adjusted for inflation over the years. Hannah will receive $715 (71.5% of Harold's full payment amount).

GPO: Lower payments for some

If you receive a *pension from work not covered by Social Security,* your widow's benefit may be reduced by the *Government Pension Offset,*[24] described on page 69.

BENEFITS FOR SURVIVING CHILD(REN)

Definition of surviving child

The definition of a surviving child is the same as the definition of a child used for family benefits: he or she must be unmarried and the worker's legitimate child, natural child, legally adopted child, or stepchild. He or she must also be:

- Under 18, **or**

- Under age 19 and a full-time elementary or high school student, **or**

- Age 18 or over and under a total disability that began before age 22.[25]

Fred died when his children were both minors—Frank was 17 and Karen, his stepdaughter, was 15.
Karen is still in high school when she turns 18. Her Social Security payments do not stop until June, when she graduates.
Frank turns 19 shortly before his own graduation. His payments stop when he turns 19.

Henry is disabled. His mother died while he was still in high school. Henry drew survivor payments on his mother's work record.
*Henry's payments continue after high school because of his disability. He is still drawing payments when he turns 30 and gets married. Then his payments must stop because he is no longer **unmarried**.*

UNMARRIED SURVIVING CHILD	BENEFIT AMOUNT (Percentage of worker's full payment amount)
Under 18 (or 19 if in high school)	75%
Any age, disabled before age 22	75%

NOTE: Family maximum may reduce total amount payable to family.

Figure 4.5. Summary of benefits for surviving children.[26]

There is also limited provision for a grandchild or step-grandchild to receive payments on the deceased's work record.

- The grandchild's parents must be deceased or disabled, or
- The grandchild must be adopted by a surviving spouse of the deceased grandparent.
- In addition, the grandchild must have been dependent on the deceased.[27]

Payment amount for surviving child

A surviving child is paid 75% of the worker's full benefit amount.[26] (As noted above, if the worker never received Social Security payments, her full benefit amount is computed as if she died at Full Retirement Age.)

*Fred's full 100% benefit was $800. Frank and Karen will **each** be paid 75% of that, or $600, per month.*

Henry's mother had a $1,000 full payment amount. Henry was paid 75%, or $750, per month until his marriage made him ineligible.

The **family maximum payment**, described on page 71, may limit payments if multiple persons are paid on one work record.[28]

BENEFITS FOR SURVIVING DEPENDENT PARENTS

Definition of surviving dependent parent

Figure 4.6 summarizes the benefits payable to the dependent parents of a deceased worker. To qualify for these parent payments, you must meet certain requirements:

- You must be the *parent* of the deceased worker. You will qualify if you are the natural parent, or if you became the worker's stepparent or adopting parent before the worker reached age 16.[29]

- You must be *dependent* upon the deceased worker. This means you received one-half of your support from the worker before he or she died (or before he or she became disabled, if applicable).[30]

- You must be at least age 62.[31]

Payment amount for parent

Your payment amount is based on the worker's full payment amount (PIA), like other survivor payments. If one parent is enrolled, the payment is 82.5% of the worker's PIA. If two parents are enrolled on the same earnings record, the payment is 75% of the PIA for each parent.[32] Payments may be limited by the **family maximum** (see page 71).[32]

DEPENDENT PARENTS	BENEFIT AMOUNT (Percentage of worker's full payment amount)	
One parent over age 62	82.5%	
Two parents over age 62	75% each	
NOTE: Family maximum may reduce total amount payable to family.		

Figure 4.6. Summary of benefits for surviving parents of a deceased worker.[32]

Before Don died he was supporting his father, Tom. Tom had a very small Social Security payment; Don's support was over 50% of Tom's total income.

When Don died, Tom qualified as his dependent parent. Tom's small Social Security payment was raised to 82.5% of Don's full payment amount. Since Don's full payment was $1,500, Tom was paid $1,237.

Lynn was supporting her two parents before she died. Her full payment amount was $1,600.

Each parent will receive 75%, or $1,200, from Lynn's work record, for total Social Security payments of $2,400 per month.

DUAL ENTITLEMENT FOR SURVIVORS: "DUALIES"

You can be a "dualie"—dually eligible for both survivor benefits and your own retirement benefits. If so, your payment will equal the *higher* of the two amounts—unless you request otherwise to strategically time your payments.

Tom (above) had received $500 Social Security on his own record until his son Don died. Don had provided most of Tom's support. Tom's payment was raised to $1,237 because Tom's payment on Don's record was higher than the payment on Tom's own record.

But some special rules apply, different from the rules for worker/spouse dualies (page 68):

- You can choose to file for only one of the two benefits, with no requirement that you file for the other. *Deemed filing* does not apply to survivor benefits like it does to spousal benefits (page 68).[33]

- There is no carry-over from one benefit to the other of any reduction for early filing.[34]

- Therefore, you could take the lower benefit first and hold the higher benefit in reserve. You could delay the higher benefit until it maximizes (your FRA for survivor benefits, or age 70 for retirement benefits).

Louise was widowed at age 56 when her husband Tim passed away. Tim's full payment amount is $1,000 per month, computed from his earnings up to death. Louise's FRA is 66 and her own full payment amount is $2,000 per month.

Louise retires at age 60 and claims only her widow's benefit. Her payment is $715 (71.5% of Tim's $1,000 payment).

At 70, Louise claims her own retirement benefit. Her payment is $2,640 (132% of her own $2,000 payment) for the rest of her life. The fact that her widow's payment was reduced for early filing has no effect on her own payment.

George was widowed at 65 when his wife Grace passed away. Grace's full payment amount is $2,000 per month. George's FRA is 66 and his full payment amount is $1,600 per month.

At 66 George files only for his widower's benefit. His payment amount is $2,000 (100% of Grace's $2,000 payment).

At 70 George files for his own retirement benefit. His payment is $2,112 (132% of his own $1,600 payment) for the rest of his life.

Same example as "George" above, except George retires at 62 and files for his own Social Security. His payment amount is $1,200 (75% of his own $1600 payment).

Grace passes away when George is 65. George decides to stay on his own Social Security and delay his widower's payment until it maximizes at 66.

At 66 George files for his widower's benefit. His payment amount is $2,000 (100% of Grace's $2,000 payment) for the rest of his life. The fact that his own payment was reduced for early filing has no effect on the widower's payment.

You could even be eligible three or more ways.

Pam's first marriage ended in her husband's death. She remarried, then divorced 13 years later.

At 66, Pam applies for Social Security. She learns that she is eligible three ways: as a worker, a widow, and a divorced spouse.

SSA examines all three payment amounts and suggests that Pam take widow's payments at 66 (they were larger than the spousal payments), and her own retirement payments at 70 (which by then would be larger than the widow's payments.)

SPECIAL ONE-TIME DEATH BENEFIT

The various kinds of *monthly* payments available for survivors are not the only payments possible. You may also be eligible for a special one-time payment called the *lump sum death payment*, or LSDP.

The LSDP is a one-time payment of $255, made in addition to any monthly benefits that may be due.[35] The payment amount is small—it has been the same since the 1940s—but it can help with funeral expenses or other final expenses after a death.

The LSDP can be paid to you under three circumstances:

1. You are the worker's surviving spouse, and you were *living with the worker* at the time of death. You are "living with" your spouse even if there was a temporary absence because of work or medical treatment.[36]

2. You were married to but not living with the worker at the time of death. You must be *eligible for survivor benefits* on the worker's record in the month of death.[37] (You are *eligible* for benefits if you could have filed for and received payments. You don't need to actually get payments.)

3. You are the child of the deceased worker, eligible for benefits on the worker's record in the month of death, and there is no qualifying spouse. If there are other such children, you will split the payment with them.[38]

Note that the LSDP cannot be paid to a former spouse. Nor can it be paid to a funeral home, although that was the general practice some years ago.

You must claim the LSDP within two years of the worker's death, or show good cause for late filing.[39] The application is filed like any other Social Security application—see Chapter 8 for a full description. *Exception:* no application is needed if you were already receiving spousal benefits from the deceased at the time of death; payment will be automatic.

When Harold died, and Hannah applied for survivor benefits for herself and the two children, she also filed for the Lump Sum Death Payment. It was included with her first payment.

To summarize:

• Social Security survivor payments provide valuable benefits for family members after a worker's death.

• Surviving spouses, children, surviving divorced spouses, and dependent parents can receive payments.

• Survivor benefits provide valuable protection for the worker's family members—protection similar to life insurance, paid for by Social Security taxes.

Note the previous three chapters, on retirement, family, and survivor payments, describe the original Social Security system, created as "Old-Age and

Survivor Insurance" (OASI). In the next two chapters you will explore newer, more recent additions to the system: disability and Medicare protection.

FOR MORE INFORMATION...

"Survivors Benefits"
www.ssa.gov/pubs/10084.html

"Survivors Planner"
www.ssa.gov/planners/survivors/

"Survivors Planner: If You Are The Survivor"
www.ssa.gov/planners/survivors/ifyou.html

"Important Information for Same-Sex Couples"
www.ssa.gov/same-sexcouples/

Chapter Endnotes

1. https://www.ssa.gov/pubs/EN-05-10084.pdf, pp. 2-3
2. https://ssa.gov/OP_Home/handbook/handbook.02/handbook-0203.html, 203.1 B.2 and 203.4
3. https://www.socialsecurity.gov/OACT/ProgData/insured.html
4. https://www.ssa.gov/OP_Home/handbook/handbook.02/handbook-0206.html
5. https://www.ssa.gov/policy/docs/statcomps/supplement/2016/5f.html#table5.f7
6. https://ssa.gov/OP_Home/handbook/handbook.04/handbook-0401.html, F.1.
7. https://www.socialsecurity.gov/people/same-sexcouples/
8. https://ssa.gov/OP_Home/handbook/handbook.04/handbook-0403.html
9. https://www.ssa.gov/planners/survivors/ifyou3.html
10. https://ssa.gov/OP_Home/handbook/handbook.04/handbook-0401.html, E., and https://ssa.gov/OP_Home/handbook/handbook.04/handbook-0406.html, 406.1.
11. https://ssa.gov/OP_Home/handbook/handbook.04/handbook-0415.html and https://ssa.gov/OP_Home/handbook/handbook.04/handbook-0416.html
12. https://ssa.gov/OP_Home/handbook/handbook.04/handbook-0416.html, C.
13. https://ssa.gov/OP_Home/handbook/handbook.07/handbook-0723.html, 723.6
14. https://ssa.gov/OP_Home/handbook/handbook.04/handbook-0418.html
15. https://ssa.gov/OP_Home/handbook/handbook.04/handbook-0407.html
16. https://secure.ssa.gov/apps10/poms.nsf/lnx/0300615320, A.2.
17. https://secure.ssa.gov/apps10/poms.nsf/lnx/0300615702, B.1. and https://ssa.gov/OP_Home/handbook/handbook.07/handbook-0720.html, 720.3.D.
18. https://secure.ssa.gov/apps10/poms.nsf/lnx/0300207002, A.1.
19. https://secure.ssa.gov/apps10/poms.nsf/lnx/0300615301, B.1.b.
20. https://ssa.gov/OP_Home/handbook/handbook.07/handbook-0724.html, 724.1.C.
21. https://www.socialsecurity.gov/OP_Home/handbook/handbook.15/handbook-1513.html and https://secure.ssa.gov/apps10/poms.nsf/lnx/0200204030
22. https://secure.ssa.gov/apps10/poms.nsf/lnx/0300207001. Note that the worker had to meet insured requirements but there is no age or payment requirement.

23. https://secure.ssa.gov/apps10/poms.nsf/lnx/0300605016, A.3. and https://secure.ssa.gov/apps10/poms.nsf/lnx/0300605017, 1.b.
24. https://www.ssa.gov/pubs/EN-05-10007.pdf
25. https://ssa.gov/OP_Home/handbook/handbook.04/handbook-0410.html
26. https://ssa.gov/OP_Home/handbook/handbook.04/handbook-0412.html
27. https://www.ssa.gov/OP_Home/handbook/handbook.04/handbook-0411.html, F.
28. https://ssa.gov/OP_Home/handbook/handbook.04/handbook-0412.html
29. https://www.ssa.gov/OP_Home/handbook/handbook.04/handbook-0421.html, H.
30. https://www.ssa.gov/OP_Home/handbook/handbook.04/handbook-0421.html, E.
31. https://www.ssa.gov/OP_Home/handbook/handbook.04/handbook-0421.html, C.
32. https://ssa.gov/OP_Home/handbook/handbook.04/handbook-0425.html
33. https://secure.ssa.gov/apps10/poms.nsf/lnx/0200204035, A, and https://secure.ssa.gov/apps10/poms.nsf/lnx/0200204020, D.1.b., deemed filing applies for RIB (retirement) and spouse benefits only.
34. https://secure.ssa.gov/apps10/poms.nsf/lnx/0300615150, A, https://secure.ssa.gov/apps10/poms.nsf/lnx/0300615160, A.1., and https://secure.ssa.gov/apps10/poms.nsf/lnx/0300615020, where A = RIB = retirement benefit, and D = WIB = widow(er's) benefit. Note that all combinations of A then D or D then A use calculation Method B, where both benefits are reduced independently.
35. https://ssa.gov/OP_Home/handbook/handbook.04/handbook-0428.html
36. https://ssa.gov/OP_Home/handbook/handbook.04/handbook-0430.html
37. https://ssa.gov/OP_Home/handbook/handbook.04/handbook-0431.html
38. https://ssa.gov/OP_Home/handbook/handbook.04/handbook-0432.html
39. https://ssa.gov/OP_Home/handbook/handbook.04/handbook-0433.html

CHAPTER FIVE

DISABILITY BENEFITS

 Disability Benefits in a Nutshell

- There are three ways to get Social Security disability benefits: as a worker, widow, or adult child.

- Disabled workers get a 100% payment, like retirement payments at FRA.

- Disabled widows and adult children get a percentage of their related worker's full payment.

- Special rules apply to working while getting disability payments.

- Disability payments qualify you for early Medicare.

DISABILITY BENEFITS BACKGROUND

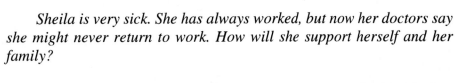

Sheila is very sick. She has always worked, but now her doctors say she might never return to work. How will she support herself and her family?

A young worker has a 30% chance of becoming disabled before retirement age, according to the Social Security Administration. Can Social Security help if you become disabled during your working years?

The answer is yes. If you become disabled before retirement age, SSA provides a protection package to partially replace your lost wages, including:

- Monthly disability payments for you,

- Monthly payments for your spouse and children, and

- Medicare health insurance, after 2 years of disability benefits.

Over 8.7 million American workers receive monthly Social Security disability payments, with another 1.7 million family members eligible because of the worker's disability.[1]

Age at disability	Lifetime Work Credits Required	Recent Work Credits Required
24 or less	6	All earned within last 3 years
25	8	All earned after age 21
26	10	
27	12	
28	14	
29	16	
30	18	
31-42	20	20 earned within last 10 years
43	21	
44	22	
45	23	
46	24	
47	25	
48	26	
49	27	
50	28	
51	29	
52	30	
53	31	
54	32	
55	33	
56	34	
57	35	
58	36	
59	37	
60	38	
61	39	
62 or over	40	

Figure 5.1. Work credits required for disability eligibility at various ages.[2]

If you are disabled and do not qualify for disabled worker benefits, you might still qualify as a disabled widow(er) of a deceased worker, or as a disabled adult child of a worker who is retired, disabled, or deceased. These types of benefits are outlined later in this chapter.

Social Security disability is yet another kind of "insurance" you are buying with your Social Security FICA taxes, much like the retirement insurance, survivor insurance, and health insurance provided by the program.

ELIGIBILITY FOR DISABILITY BENEFITS

To receive disabled worker payments, you must first meet the eligibility rules. The eligibility criteria are more restrictive for disability, partly because disability is more difficult to prove than retirement or death. You must meet both the *work requirements* and the *medical requirements* detailed below.

Work requirements for disability eligibility

The work requirements for disability payments consist of two standards: you must have both *substantial lifetime work* and *recent work* to be eligible for disability. If you become disabled before age 31, both these standards are combined into a *special age 31* requirement. Figure 5.1 summarizes the work requirement for those who become disabled at various ages.

Substantial lifetime work standard

To meet this standard, you must have between 1-1/2 and 10 years of work where you paid Social Security taxes, depending on your age when your disability begins. Your work is measured in Work Credits, just as it is for retired workers (see page 35 for details).

The idea here is that a younger worker has less time to earn work credit, so fewer credits are required.

The lifetime work required is shown in the second column of Figure 5.1.

Sheila is 35. She had 12 years of part-time and full-time work before she became disabled. Since she needs only 20 credits (5 years of work) she meets the substantial lifetime work standard.

Recent work standard

In addition to the total number of lifetime credits required, some of your work credit must be recent. In the 40 calendar quarters (10 years) immediately preceding your disability onset, you must have earned 20 work credits (5 years' credit). To meet this requirement, you must have worked sometime in the last 5 years before your disability, or at least have worked steadily up until 5 years before. The recent work requirement is shown in the third column of Figure 5.1.

The reason: Social Security insures you against *loss of earned income due to disability*. If you were not depending on current or recent earnings, then your disability did not cause an insured loss. The "20-40 rule"—requiring 20 work credits in the last 40 quarters—determines if disability caused you any actual loss of earnings.

Sheila became disabled in 2018. She had nearly steady work from 2006 to 2016—she had some time between jobs, and a maternity leave, but she earned 4 credits in each year. Therefore, she meets the recent work standard. Since she meets the substantial lifetime work and recent work requirements, she meets all work requirements for Social Security disability payments.

Charles became disabled this year. He has over 40 work credits. However, he retired 6 years ago, and hasn't worked since. He does not meet the recent work standard (5 out of the last 10 years must be work years). Therefore, he does not qualify for Social Security disability, no matter his medical condition. He can receive retirement payments when he reaches early retirement age at 62.

Special age 31 rules

The two work requirements above are combined into a unified rule if you are under age 31 when your disability starts. In that case, you need credit for having worked half the time between your 21st birthday and the time you become disabled. The *minimum* requirement for those under 24 is 6 work credits in the last 3 years. For example, if you are age 25, you need credit for two years of work (out of the 4 years since age 21). If you are 19, you need to meet only the minimum requirement of 6 credits in the past 3 years.

This opens the door to very young workers receiving disability payments. The youngest I know of was this example, a true story:

*"Ken," a 14-year-old boy, suffered an accident resulting in permanent disability. However, he had run a paper route for two years, and had earned Social Security work credits by paying his taxes. He applied for and received monthly Social Security disability payments **on his own work record**.*

Medical requirements for disability eligibility

In addition to meeting the work requirements above, you must meet strict medical requirements. Among the many definitions of disability used in government, insurance, and industry, Social Security's is perhaps the strictest. SSA defines disability as:

> *The inability to engage in any Substantial Gainful Activity by reason of any medically determinable physical or mental impairment which can be expected to result in death, or which has lasted or can be expected to last for a continuous period of not less than 12 months.*[3]
>
> *"Substantial Gainful Activity" is defined as earnings of $1,180 per month (or $1,970 for blind individuals) in 2018.*[4]

In short, you must have a verifiable medical condition that prevents virtually all work (severity) *and* it must be expected to last at least a year or be terminal (duration). Examples demonstrate how strict this definition is.

> *Patty lost her ability to practice her skilled trade because of a serious illness. She can never again perform her accustomed work. She finds that all she can do is a part-time job in a fast-food restaurant, making $1,300 per month.*
>
> *When Patty applies for Social Security disability. However, her claim is denied. Why?*
>
> *She does not meet the **severity** rule. The definition of "substantial gainful activity" is earnings of $1,180 per month ($1,970 for blind) in any work, whether or not it is her accustomed work. Since Patty is performing substantial gainful activity, she does not meet the definition of disability.*

> *Greg was in a severe automobile accident. He will be hospitalized for 7 months and have another 4 months of daily therapy after that. He will be restricted to part-time work for another two years after his course of therapy.*
>
> *However, Greg will not qualify for Social Security disability, since he can return to part-time work within a year—he does not meet the 12-month **duration** rule.*

The point is this: you must be *totally and permanently disabled,* or nearly so, to qualify for Social Security disability. There is little or no provision for partial or temporary disability, as there is under Veterans Administration benefits, certain state-run plans, and many private insurance policies. Many people do not understand this, and they apply even though their impairments are partial or temporary. In fiscal year 2015, only 32% of disability claims were approved, largely because of this misunderstanding.[5]

That same year, over 775,000 disability claims were approved for payment.[5]
Here are some examples of impairments which do or do not meet the standards:[6]

Cancer

Few cancer claims are approved. Many patients claim disability payments shortly after detection or during medical treatment. However, at that point the chances for recovery are high enough that many claims are denied.

If a malignancy has *recurred* after medical treatment or is *untreatable*, and limits daily activities, the claim may be allowed. Also allowed are cases where the medical treatment itself, or the treatment combined with the disease, causes inability to work for at least a year.

 THE INSIDE STORY

How Your Disability Is Evaluated

Social Security employees don't directly determine whether your condition is disabling. Rather, SSA contracts with state governments across the nation to make these determinations, with SSA providing the rules, training, and quality reviews to ensure compliance with federal regulations. This "Disability Determination Service," usually part of your state's department of health, might also be charged with making disability determinations for state programs such as vocational rehabilitation and workers' compensation.

The state disability evaluator obtains and weighs extensive evidence in your case, including:

• Your first-hand reports on your medical condition,

• Your medical records from your doctor, hospital, or other care provider, and

• Your vocational and educational background.

Whether your doctor does or does not subjectively deem you disabled is not material. Rather, your medical records must show objectively that your condition meets certain standards, or *listings*, which specify precisely how severe an impairment must be to be disabling.

For example, the listing for emphysema may include requirements for X-ray evidence, lung capacity tests within certain parameters, and tests for blood gases with certain values.

The disability evaluator must order any tests that are either missing or not current, then determine whether the severity of your impairment meets the disability listings. Your vocational history and education are generally considered, to determine your suitability for retraining for other types of work.

In many cases, keen judgment is necessary. For example, you may have a combination of impairments; perhaps no one of them alone is disabling, but in combination they are.

Approximately 65% of claims are denied at the initial claims level.[5] Many of these denials result from public misunderstandings about SSA's requirement for near-total, near-permanent disability. (For example, many people file claims for a broken leg or for a temporary severe illness.)

If your claim is denied—or *any* time you receive an "adverse determination" from SSA—you may file an *appeal* to have a new decision made by a different person or team. Among disability claims pursued to the *hearing level (*a higher and more elaborate level of appeal; see page 199) more than half are approved for payment.[7]

The process takes a long time. In 2015, the average disability claim took nearly 4 months to be decided.[8] Appealing to the hearings level is taking 596 days on average.[9]

Coronary disease

This is another area where many claims are denied, usually because the disease still allows some low-stress work activity, or because the acute phase of the illness is not expected to last a year. Extremely serious coronary disease which truly and permanently prevents all work will, of course, be allowed. Severity must generally be documented with specific imaging, ECG, or blood chemistry evidence.

Back injury

Back pain can be severe and immobilizing. But SSA requires a disability to be *medically determinable,* and this is sometimes difficult. Claims with imaging evidence of arthritis or osteoporosis, or with persistent motor, sensory, and reflex loss, are allowed for disability. Some of these claims are initially denied but awarded at a higher level of appeal where an individual's level of pain or suffering is assessed in person by a judge.

AIDS

Infection by HIV (the AIDS virus) is not by itself considered disabling. However, many conditions associated with HIV can qualify if persistent, including but not limited to:

- Sepsis
- Meningitis
- Pneumonia
- Septic arthritis
- Endocarditis

Loss of limb

Loss of a limb—or loss of use of a limb, e.g. after a stroke or spinal cord injury—is generally not by itself sufficient for a disability allowance. Exceptions are made for loss of a leg with other complications. Loss of function in *two* limbs, e.g. paraplegia or double amputation, is considered disabling.

Loss of vision

Blindness is defined as either visual acuity no sharper than 20-200 *corrected* vision, or a visual field no wider than 20° (tunnel vision), in your better eye.

Psychiatric disorders

Impairments such as depression, schizophrenia, or autism are considered disabling if they result in persistent marked restriction of daily activities, constriction of interests, and a seriously impaired ability to relate to other people. In these cases, Social Security takes a close look at your daily living patterns, in addition to your medical records, to determine the severity of the impairment.

These examples illuminate what is or is not considered disabling. As you can see, the decision process is a detailed and objective process of assessing whether the impairment will prevent substantial work for at least a year.

To summarize: The twin hurdles of a stiff work requirement and a strict medical definition of disability act as substantial barriers to many claims. Nonetheless, you may, like millions of other claimants, meet these standards and receive disability benefits. The payments and other benefits you could receive are detailed in the next section.

DISABILITY BENEFITS: PAYMENTS AND MEDICARE

Once approved, Social Security disability offers three kinds of benefits: cash payments, Medicare eligibility, and a chance to return to work without immediately losing your disability payments.

Cash payments

Your cash payments are computed much like 100% retirement payments as if you were Full Retirement Age.[10] The average disability payment in 2018 is $1,197 per month, about the same as the average retirement payment.[11] The maximum is about $2,700—again, like retirement payments.

In addition to your own payment, family members like your spouse and child(ren) may also be eligible. Family benefits for a disabled worker are paid just like family benefits for a retired worker (see Chapter 3).[12]

Five-Month Waiting Period

There is a "catch." Your cash benefits begin only after a *five-month waiting period.* During the first five full months of your disability, no payments can be made to you or your family members. But since the five months must be *full* months, it is more accurate to say the waiting period is six months; see "The Inside Story" on page 112.[13]

Sheila became disabled on January 10. Her waiting period runs from January 10 to June 10—five full months later. Her first month of eligibility is July, the first month after the waiting period.

Retroactive payments

Although no payments are possible during the 5-month waiting period, you may qualify for *back payments,* also called retroactive payments:

- You can qualify for up to 12 months of payments *before you file* your Social Security claim, if you became disabled at least 18 months before filing your claim (to allow for the waiting period).[14]

- When your first payment comes, it can include the back payments for up to 12 months before you filed your claim, plus payment for any months you have waited for your claim to be processed after filing.

THE INSIDE STORY

The Five-Month Waiting Period

The five-month waiting period might more accurately be called a *six*-month waiting period, since only "full" months count.

To illustrate, suppose your disability onset is April 4. (Your onset is generally the date your impairment first made you unable to work, or when you stopped working.) You will have waited five full months on September 4, so you would first be entitled to Social Security disability payments in October. The October payment is paid in November, meaning you waited six months for eligibility and nearly seven months for payment.

Note that disability *entitlement* begins at the end of the waiting period. Therefore, if you recover or die within the five months, no disability payments are due, even as "back pay," either to you or your survivors. (But your survivors might get Social Security survivor benefits.)

The waiting period saves Social Security money. Some private insurance policies, whether for health coverage, disability, or nursing care, specify a waiting period of days, months, or years. A longer waiting period makes the insurance policy less expensive, since fewer benefits will be paid.

- Note that no more than 12 months of back payments are possible, so if you have been disabled for over 18 months you should file your claim *as soon as possible* to avoid loss of payments.

Sheila became disabled January 10. She filed her Social Security claim in September, and it took until November to approve and pay her claim.

On November 15, she received her first payment and a letter to explain the payment. The payment included back payments for 4 months (July, August, September, and October). Sheila cannot be paid for her 5-month waiting period (January 10 to June 10), but she can be paid back payments for July and the following months. All these payments can be made because Sheila applied within 18 months of her disability onset.

Sheila's next payment will be in December, when she is paid for the month of November.

Bob became disabled January 15, 2012. He waited two years to file for Social Security, finally filing on January 5, 2014.

Bob's claim took 3 months to process. His first payment arrived in April 2014 and included payments for January 2013 through March 2014. He can get back payments only to January 2013—12 months before he filed his claim—plus the three months of processing time after he filed his claim. Social Security cannot pay Bob for months before January 2013 because back pay is available only for the 12 months before his claim was filed. Bob will never be paid for the earlier months he was disabled.

Bob's next payment will arrive in May, when he is paid for the month of April.

Other government benefits

Your Social Security disability payments might be affected by other government benefits. The exact effects depend on the type of government benefit you receive:

- *Pension from non-covered work.* Your disability payment may be reduced if you get a pension from work not covered by Social Security, just like Social Security retirement payments. This is called the *Windfall Elimination Provision (WEP)* and is explained on page 52.[15]

  Harold received a state pension before he became disabled. He did not pay Social Security taxes at his state job. He can still receive Social Security disability, but he is subject to a special WEP computation and lower payments.

- *Government pension for disabled widow(er).* Social Security disabled widow(er)'s benefits are reduced by two-thirds of the amount of certain *government pensions.* This is called the *Government Pension Offset (GPO)* and is explained on page 69.[16]

  Grace receives a county pension of $600 per month. She did not pay Social Security taxes at her county job. She is also eligible for disabled widow's benefits of $715 per month from Social Security. Two-thirds of her county pension—$400—will be counted against her widow's benefit, leaving $315 payable on her Social Security ($715–$400).

- *Workers' Compensation.* If you are disabled due to a job-related injury or illness, you may get *workers' compensation* payments. If so, total family payments from workers' compensation and Social Security are capped at 80% of your "average current earnings" before your disability.[17] Either your

SSA or your workers' compensation payments may be reduced, depending on local laws.

> *Bob gets a workers' compensation benefit and his claim for Social Security disability is approved. His combined income from the two programs cannot exceed 80% of his "average current earnings" before he was disabled. Either his workers' compensation or his Social Security will be adjusted to keep his total benefits under the 80% limit.*

- *Other disability payments.* Certain disability payments from Federal, State, Civil Service, or military programs may trigger a similar limit. Total compensation from some such programs, combined with your Social Security benefits for you and your family, is capped at 80% of your "average current earnings" before your disability.[17]

Your Social Security representative will inform you if any of these provisions affects your payments.

Employer or union disability payments

There can be a long wait for Social Security disability, between the Waiting Period and the long SSA processing times, not to mention the high denial rate. Your employer or union might be able to help:

- Sometimes *sick pay* can support you during the claims process and waiting period.

- Some employers offer *temporary disability benefits* in addition to sick pay. These typically last for six months—just enough to get through the Social Security waiting period.

- Large employers sometimes provide *long-term disability benefits*, but beware: many such plans require an SSA disability approval to trigger employer benefits. Your employer may also subtract your Social Security payment from your employer payment. That means (1) you must wait for SSA's decision, (2) you could be denied employer benefits if your Social Security claim is denied, and (3) you might receive little or no employer money beyond your Social Security payments.

Every employer or union plan is unique. Ask your benefits office how your organization's disability coverage works, and how it fits with Social Security. And be sure to apply for any employer or union benefits if you become disabled.

Medicare

In addition to your cash payments, you will also get Medicare health insurance. Medicare coverage starts after you have gotten disability payments for 24 months. *Exception:* If you are disabled by kidney failure or ALS, your Medicare is effective the first month of disability payments. Note that you must be *getting payments*, so the 24-month period starts after the five-month waiting period.[18]

Sheila became disabled January 10, filed her claim in September, and received her first payment on November 15. She received back payments to July 1, the date her payments commenced. Two years later, on July 1, she will be covered by Medicare.

Bob became disabled January 15, 2010. He filed for disability two years later, on January 5, 2012. His back pay is computed from January 1, 2011 (12 months' back pay). His Medicare is effective January 1, 2013—two years after his payments.

Your Medicare coverage is the same as Medicare for age-65 retirees. See Chapter 6, Medicare, for details.

Some large employers or unions will extend your group medical insurance until Medicare starts. This means that if you become disabled, you will not have a period without health insurance. Check with your benefits office for their policy.

Sheila stopped work due to disability on January 10. Her Medicare starts in July two years later.

Sheila's employer provided medical coverage until her Medicare coverage started.

OTHER DISABILITY BENEFITS: WIDOW(ER)S, CHILDREN

Background on Disabled Widow(er)'s and Disabled Adult Child's Benefits

The provisions described above allow you to receive disability payments on *your own* work record. That is, you apply on your own record and payments are proportional to your own work history.

Social Security provides two other disability programs:

- *Disabled widow(er):* If you are a disabled widow or widower, you can apply on your deceased spouse's (or former spouse's) work record.

- *Disabled adult child:* If you are an adult, disabled since before age 22, with a parent who is Social Security-eligible as a retired, disabled, or deceased worker, you can file on your parent's work record.

In these cases, you may have had little or no opportunity to earn disability protection under your own work record, so Social Security makes payments possible through your family relationship to the worker. These additional disability programs provide monthly payments and Medicare to many individuals who would otherwise be ineligible.

Disabled Widow(er)'s Benefits

If you are a disabled widow or widower aged 50-59, you may be eligible for this type of disability payment.

Payments can be made on the earnings record of the worker (your deceased spouse or former spouse). Payments are proportional to the deceased worker's lifetime earnings. You would be paid 71.5% of the worker's full benefit amount.

Mimi worked and supported her disabled husband, Joseph. Mimi died when Joseph was 52. He had no means to support himself.

Joseph learns that he could receive disabled widower's payments. Mimi's work yielded a full payment amount of $800. Joseph is eligible for 71.5% of the $800, or $572 per month. With this Social Security money, plus some life insurance and pension payments, Joseph makes ends meet.

The general requirements are largely the same as for other widow(er)'s benefits, described in Figure 4.3 on page 88. You must have been married to the worker at the time of death or, if divorced, you must have been married for at least 10 years and be currently unmarried. In addition to the general requirements shown in Figure 4.3, you must meet these special requirements for disabled widow(er)s:[19]

- You must be at least *age 50.* Since you are eligible for regular widow's payments at age 60, this effectively limits disabled widow(er)'s benefits to ages 50-59. (See below for an exception regarding your Medicare eligibility.)

- Your disability must have started before the worker's death or *within 7 years after* the worker's death. Alternatively, if you were previously eligible for Social Security payments because you were caring for the worker's child (see page 90), your disability must start before those payments end or within 7 years after they end.

- You must meet the same definition of disability as a disabled worker.

In other words, to qualify for disabled widow(er)'s payments you must be within a certain age range, your disability must start within a specified period, and your disability must be severe.

If you qualify, your payments will begin after a 5-month waiting period (see pages 111-112).

Two years after your payments begin, you will be eligible for *Medicare*, just like a disabled worker. Under a special provision, you can also get Medicare from age 60 - 64 because of your disability. At 65, you will be eligible for Medicare based on age rather than disability.

Disabled Adult Child's Benefits

If you are the disabled adult child of a worker who is retired, disabled, or deceased, you may be eligible for this type of disability payment.[20] For you to be eligible, your parent must be entitled to Social Security retirement or disability payments or, if deceased, your parent must have been "fully" or "currently" insured for Social Security survivor payments (see pages 84-87).[21]

You will be paid a percentage of your parent's full benefit amount (PIA)— 50% of a living parent's or 75% of a deceased parent's full benefit.

The general requirements are the same as for other child benefits (see page 70). These include the requirement that you must generally be unmarried to receive child's benefits.

In addition, you must meet the *disability requirements:*

- You must meet the same definition of disability as a disabled worker, and

- Your disability must start or have started before you reach age 22.[20]

The age requirement raises some issues. If you are already receiving Social Security child's payments at an early age, payments normally stop when you turn 18 or leave high school. If you are disabled, however, your payments can continue past 18 and you will be eligible for Medicare coverage as well.[22] You could file a disability claim shortly before turning 18, to ensure that your payments continue.

Ted received child's benefits on the record of his retired mother, Irene. Normally Ted's benefits would stop when he turned 18 or finished high school.
However, Ted qualified for disabled adult child's benefits. His "child's" benefits continue into his adulthood until he marries, recovers, or proves an ability to perform substantial work.
If Irene dies at some date in the future, Ted's payments continue but are raised from a 50% payment to a 75% payment.

THE INSIDE STORY

RIB, DIB, DAC

SSA staffers have a shorthand language to refer to the various types of claims and benefits. It's an interesting vocabulary that sounds a bit like Pig Latin:

RIB   Retirement Insurance Benefit. "She wants RIB at 62."

WIB   Widow(er)'s Insurance Benefit. "He didn't take WIB because his own RIB was higher."

DIB   Disability Insurance Benefit. "He filed for his DIB right after his accident."

DWB   Disabled Widow(er)'s Benefit. (Pronounced "dwib.") "Her DWB was denied because of the 7-year time limit, but she'll get DIB."

DAC   Disabled Adult Child. "His mom gets RIB, so he filed as a DAC." (Officially this should be "CDB" for Childhood Disability Benefit, but no one can pronounce that acronym.)

Overlapping eligibility rules make for interesting interesting language at SSA. Examples: "He was 62 and disabled so we filed a RIB-DIB. Then I found out he had a disabled child, so we turned it into a RIB-DIB-DAC." "She could get RIB or WIB but we took a DWB to get early Medicare."

Another possibility: You may be disabled at an early age, but your Social Security payments cannot begin until your parent retires and files for Social Security—that might be the first time you are eligible on any work record. At that point, you can start receiving *child's* benefits, even though you may be in your 30s, 40s, or more.

An issue then is how to prove that you have been disabled since before age 22. Sometimes medical records from 20 or more years ago can be difficult to find. However, SSA will work to help process the claim.

Heather is 35 and has been disabled since birth. When her father, Greg, retires at age 62, his SSA claims representative asks if he has any disabled children (this question appears on every application).

Heather applies for disabled adult child's benefits, and her medical records prove she has been disabled since before age 22. Her claim is approved, and she is paid 50% of Greg's full payment.

Jay became disabled in an auto accident when he was 21. He is 40 when his mother dies. As a surviving child Jay can receive 75% of his mother's full payment amount because he has been disabled since before age 22.

If you qualify, your payments will begin *without* a 5-month waiting period—unlike worker's or widow(er)'s disability payments.[23] Just like those programs, however, you will be eligible for Medicare two years after your payments begin.[22]

WORKING WHILE DISABLED

One of the valuable features of the Social Security disability program is that it encourages you to work whenever you are able. Many determined individuals return to work despite disability.

While getting disability, always report any work you do, no matter how small.[24]

SSA's policy is to help you return to work *before* stopping disability payments and Medicare benefits, in order see if the work attempt is successful.

The programs that help you return to work are called *work incentives.* They include:

- Continued cash benefits,

- Continued Medicare coverage,

- Help with disability-related work expenses, and

- Access to work training or other rehabilitation services.[25]

The general idea is that if you want to return to work, you should have some time to try it without immediately losing all Social Security support. In other words, your Social Security and Medicare eligibility can be *extended* when you return to work.

Here are some conditions to qualify for work incentives:

- Your *medical* disability must continue for you to qualify for the eligibility extensions described below.[26]
- SSA will periodically review your medical condition to ensure that you still meet the medical definition of disability.[27] SSA might initiate such a review when you start working.

- *If your impairment is no longer disabling,* SSA must stop your payment two months later.[28]

- An exception is made if you are engaged in a *vocational rehabilitation program,* including the SSA "Ticket To Work" program, when your medical condition improves. If so, your payments can be continued until the rehabilitation services are completed or until you discontinue receiving services. The rehabilitation program must be expected to enable you to return to work permanently, and you must be making timely progress.[28]

The following extensions of eligibility serve as work incentives. (Also see the summary in Figure 5.2.)

9-month Trial Work Period.

When you return to work, SSA will continue your payments with no reduction or other penalty for a minimum of nine work months, called a *Trial Work Period (TWP).* The rules are as follows:

- To count as a Trial Work month, you must earn $850 or more (2018 figure)[29], and/or have 80 hours of self-employed work. Lower earnings do not count in any way—you could have unlimited months of earnings below the Trial Work limits without affecting your disability payments.[30]

- The nine Trial Work months need not be consecutive. They may be scattered over many years of brief work attempts.[31]

- All nine Trial Work months must occur within a 60-month (5-year) time span to complete your Trial Work Period. This is termed a *rolling 60-month* Trial Work Period. In short, if you never complete nine Trial Work months within a 60-month period, the Trial Work Period will continue indefinitely.[32]

When all nine months have been exhausted within one 60-month span, your work activity will be evaluated to see if it indicates an ability to perform "Substantial Gainful Activity" (SGA). Generally, this means work averaging over $1,180 per month, or $1,970 for blind individuals, in 2018.[29] If you demonstrate such ability (e.g. you earn substantial earnings), your payments will be stopped after a one-time grace period of three consecutive months.

This means that you could make many work attempts, each lasting several months, before SSA would evaluate your work activity. It also means that even after you started a steady, well-paying job, you could receive up to another year of Social Security payments—nine trial work months plus the three-month grace period.

Sheila makes several work attempts, each lasting only a few months. After three such attempts in three years, she still has used only 8 of her 9 Trial Work months. Her disability payments continued without interruption or reduction.

Bob makes several work attempts and uses 7 Trial Work months in the space of two years. After these short-term attempts, he succeeds at a steady, well-paying job. The first 2 months at his new job use up his last 2 Trial Work months. His third, fourth, and fifth months of work use up his 3-month grace period. His Social Security payments stop after his fifth month on the new job.

36-month Extended Period of Eligibility

What if your disability payments do stop after your Trial Work Period, and then your earnings decline or end? Do you need to re-apply for your disability payments?

Probably not. Once you complete your nine Trial Work Period months, SSA keeps your claim open for an additional three years. During this 36-month *Extended Period of Eligibility (EPE),* your disability benefits can be paid for any month your earnings are below the Substantial Gainful Activity level, but cannot be paid for any month your earnings exceed that level. Basically, your Social Security payments start and stop depending on your work income.[33]

The 36 months of extended eligibility are consecutive calendar months, starting with the month after the ninth Trial Work Period month (see Figure 5.2). The EPE acts as a safety net in case your work attempt does not lead to permanent, substantial employment.

After a year at his new job, Bob's condition worsens, and he must stop work due to his impairment. Since he is still in his Extended Period of Eligibility, Bob does not have to repeat the extensive disability application process. He notifies SSA that he stopped work and his Social Security starts the next month.

Six months later, Bob returns to work with substantial earnings. His Social Security payment must stop for every month his earnings are substantial.

After another year of work Bob must again leave his job due to his impairment. Bob is still in his Extended Period of Eligibility, so his Social Security again resumes when his work stops.

Expedited reinstatement

If your benefits are stopped because of substantial earnings, you have access to Expedited Reinstatement (EXR) during the next five years. If you stop performing SGA and your disability continues, you can request EXR, rather than

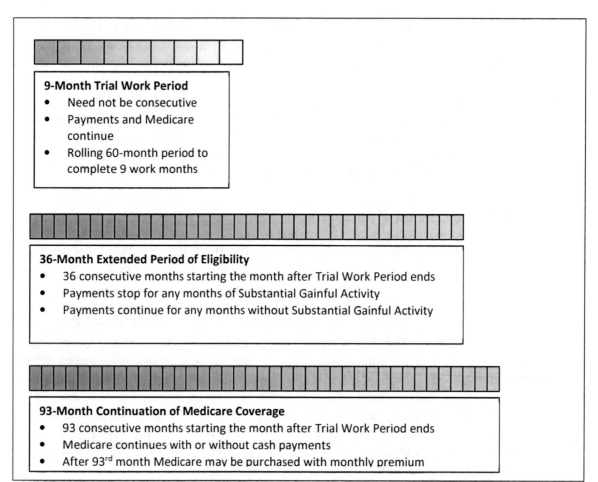

9-Month Trial Work Period
- Need not be consecutive
- Payments and Medicare continue
- Rolling 60-month period to complete 9 work months

36-Month Extended Period of Eligibility
- 36 consecutive months starting the month after Trial Work Period ends
- Payments stop for any months of Substantial Gainful Activity
- Payments continue for any months without Substantial Gainful Activity

93-Month Continuation of Medicare Coverage
- 93 consecutive months starting the month after Trial Work Period ends
- Medicare continues with or without cash payments
- After 93rd month Medicare may be purchased with monthly premium

Figure 5.2. Summary of the Trial Work Period, Extended Period of Eligibility, and Continuation of Medicare Coverage.

re-filing for Social Security disability. Your payments would begin immediately while your medical condition is reviewed, assuming you meet other requirements.

If approved, your EXR would give you payments during a 24-month reinstatement period. The months do not have to be consecutive.

At the end of the 24 months you would receive a new Trial Work Period, Extended Period of Eligibility, and extended Medicare coverage.[34]

Bob returns to substantial work two years later, after his Extended Period of Eligibility has ended. His Social Security payments must be stopped. However, his work again ends three years later due to his impairment. He contacts Social Security. Since he is within five years of his benefit termination due to work, his payments begin immediately under Expedited Reinstatement, without re-applying for disability.

93-month Continuation of Medicare Coverage

Your Medicare will also continue in force during your Extended Period of Eligibility, at least 93 consecutive months after your Trial Work Period ends (36 months corresponding with the Extended Period of Eligibility, plus a 57-month additional period).[35]

After the 93 months, your Medicare will stop unless you opt to purchase the coverage with a monthly premium. See Chapter 6 for more on Medicare, including Part A and Part B premiums.

Remember:

- All these extensions are possible *only if* your medical impairment continues. If you recover from your disability, your payments must stop within three months.
- You must report *all* work activity so your SSA representative may properly tally the months of your extended benefits.

EXAMPLES OF DISABILITY PAYMENTS

The examples below will illustrate the age, work, and disability requirements described in this chapter.

Example 1: Disabled Worker

Abe is a 42-year-old machinist who works full-time for a large aircraft manufacturer. He is married to Jane, 41, and has two children living at home. Derek, 14, is Jane's son by a prior marriage, and Amy, 10, is Abe and Jane's daughter. Jane works part-time as an accounts clerk for a bank.

On March 5, Abe is driving to work when he is hit by a truck that lost its brakes. Abe suffers a spinal injury and paraplegia. His company benefits office puts Abe on sick pay and his company medical plan covers most of the doctor bills.

In May, Abe enters rehabilitation and calls the company benefits office. He learns that his company will continue his sick pay and medical insurance for some months, but he must apply for Social Security disability for extended coverage.

On May 20, Abe calls Social Security's toll-free number to start the application process. His application is completed by telephone and mail on June 7. By August 3, SSA obtains the necessary medical documentation and certifies that Abe meets all work and medical requirements for disability payments. His disability onset is set at March 5, the day of the accident. His first Social Security payment arrives on October 3, based on this calendar:

March 5 - August 5	5-Month Waiting Period (No payments possible).
September	First month of eligibility.
October 3	Payment issued for month of September.

Abe's monthly payments are $1,600. His payment amount is based on his wages over his work years—wages which were higher-than-average because of his work as a skilled machinist, but with gaps due to periodic layoffs.

Derek and Amy will also be eligible for payments from SSA, Derek as Abe's stepchild and Amy as Abe's natural child. They are each eligible for *up to 50%* of Abe's payment amount.

However, Abe's family maximum is 150% of his payment, or $2,400. Since Abe will draw $1,600, that leaves $800 for Derek and Amy to split. Each will receive $400 per month on Abe's record.

Since the children are minors, their payments will be made payable to either Abe or Jane as the parent.

Each child's payment will continue until age 18 (or 19 if still in high school). Note that once Derek's payment stops, Amy's will no longer be limited by the family maximum payment, so her payment will rise to the full 50%, or $800. Thus, the family will continue to receive the same $2,400 total payment.

Jane is also potentially eligible. However, she decides not to apply when she learns that her own part-time earnings would reduce her Social Security payment, and that the total amount payable to the family would be the same $2,400 whether she applies or not, because of the family maximum.

Medicare. Two years after his first Social Security eligibility, in September, Abe will also be eligible for Medicare. Fortunately, Abe's company medical coverage will continue until the Medicare begins. Furthermore, the company can provide a small disability pension to supplement the Social Security payments. (Many employers' health and disability benefits are designed to dovetail with Social Security in this manner.)

Outside income. Abe also receives a large settlement from the trucking company which caused his injuries. That settlement does not affect Abe's SSA payments because Social Security is insurance, not welfare. The interest he receives by investing part of the settlement is also not counted against his payments. Similarly, Jane's paycheck is not counted against any of the three Social Security payments.

Example 2: Disabled Widow

Jean was 52 when her husband Paul died. Since the children were grown no Social Security was payable to the children, nor to Jean, since she was not yet age 60. Jean managed to live on Paul's life insurance proceeds and a part-time job she started once the children were on their own.

Now, a second disaster has struck. At age 54, Jean has a serious bout with cancer which causes her to quit work in February. Surgery, chemotherapy, and a long recuperation are expected to keep Jean out of work for at least a year, and perhaps permanently. The social worker at Jean's hospital recommends that Jean apply for Social Security disability payments.

Jean contacts SSA. She is initially concerned because they tell her she probably can't get disability payments on her own work record because she does not have sufficient work. However, she might qualify under the record of her deceased husband, Paul, as his disabled widow aged 50-59.

Jean's widow's claim is approved. Her first payment arrives in September, after her 5-month waiting period. She will receive $1,287 per month, which is 71.5% of Paul's $1,800 full payment amount. She will also be eligible for Medicare two years later.

Jean has a chance for medical recovery, to the point that she might be able to return to work next year after her long recuperation. Because of this, SSA flags her case for a medical review in 18 months. At that point, and again in future years, SSA will re-contact Jean and her doctors to see if her disability continues. If she recovers, her payments will be stopped three months later. If that happens, she would have to wait until age 60 to receive regular widow's payments based on her age.

Example 3: Disabled Adult Child

Hal is 35 and has always had a developmental disability. His IQ is in the 50s and he has some difficulty caring for himself on a day-to-day basis. He lives in an Adult Home not far from his parents' house, and he is enrolled in a training program to develop his daily living skills. Most of Hal's income comes from SSI (a federal public assistance program described at page 227), but he also works in a recycling center designed to employ disabled workers. His earnings from his job are low enough that they do not interfere with his disability status.

Hal's mother Carol retires at age 62 and claims her Social Security. She is asked if she has any minor or disabled children. Because Hal is Carol's child and has been disabled since before age 22, he is entitled to child's benefits on Carol's work record. Hal's payment starts the same month as Carol's retirement payment, without a 5-month waiting period. He is paid $600, 50% of Carol's $1,200 full FRA payment amount. (Carol receives $900, or 75% of her full payment amount, at age 62.)

Hal's $600 Social Security payment is not quite high enough to replace his SSI. Because the Social Security counts as income against SSI aid, Hal's SSI is reduced by the amount of the Social Security. In a way, Hal hasn't come out ahead yet—he still must deal with all the paperwork required by SSI, since SSI is a public assistance or welfare program.

Next year, though, Hal's father Kenneth retires at age 65. Hal then qualifies for payments as Kenneth's disabled child. He switches from Carol's record to Kenneth's and receives 50% of Kenneth's full payment amount. Kenneth's full payment is $2,000, based on his higher lifetime earnings, so Hal receives $1,000. This will stop the SSI permanently and leave Hal with higher income. He will also have far less bureaucracy to deal with, since Social Security is an insurance program, not public assistance like SSI.

To summarize:

- Disability payments are available to disabled individuals who are workers, widows or widowers of a worker, and adult children of a worker.

- A disabled worker is paid as if he or she were a Full Retirement Age retiree (100% of the full payment amount). The full payment amount is based on average earnings up to the date of disability onset.

- A disabled widow(er) age 50 to 59 is paid like a 60-year-old widow(er) (71.5% of the worker's full payment amount).

- A disabled adult child is paid like a minor child (50% of the worker's full payment amount if the worker is living, or 75% if the worker is deceased).

- In addition to monthly cash payments, disabled individuals are given Medicare medical coverage two years after their entitlement begins.

- If a disabled individual returns to work, special rules delay the termination of the Social Security payments to ease the transition toward being self-supporting.

In the next chapter, we will examine Medicare—who is eligible, what benefits are provided, and how to deal with medical bills not covered by Medicare.

For More Information...

"Disability Benefits"
www.ssa.gov/pubs/10029.html

"Disability Evaluation Under Social Security" (The Blue Book)
www.ssa.gov/disability/professionals/bluebook/

"Working While Disabled—How We Can Help"
www.ssa.gov/pubs/10095.html

"Incentives To Help You Return To Work"
www.ssa.gov/pubs/10060.html

"Red Book (Summary Guide to Employment Supports for Persons With Disabilities)"
www.ssa.gov/redbook/eng/main.htm

"Choose Work" (SSA videos on work incentives)
www.youtube.com/user/choosework

Choose to Work webinars
www.choosework.net/wise

Chapter Endnotes

1. https://www.ssa.gov/policy/docs/quickfacts/stat_snapshot/index.html, Table 2.
2. https://secure.ssa.gov/apps10/poms.nsf/lnx/0300301120,
    https://secure.ssa.gov/apps10/poms.nsf/lnx/0300301105, and
    https://secure.ssa.gov/apps10/poms.nsf/lnx/0300301140
3. https://www.socialsecurity.gov/OP_Home/cfr20/416/416-0905.htm
4. https://www.socialsecurity.gov/OACT/COLA/sga.html
5. https://www.socialsecurity.gov/policy/docs/statcomps/supplement/2016/6c.html, Table 6.C7.
6. In each case, author's summary from "The Blue Book,"
    https://www.socialsecurity.gov/disability/professionals/bluebook/AdultListings.htm.
7. In 2015 the allowance rate for all Social Security disability claims at the hearing level or above was 56.2%, per
    https://www.socialsecurity.gov/policy/docs/statcomps/di_asr/2016/sect04.html, Table 63.
8. https://www.socialsecurity.gov/open/data/Combined-Disability-Processing-Time.xlsx, Fiscal Year 2015 showing 114 days
9. https://www.ssa.gov/appeals/, under "National Hearings Average Processing Time," FY 2017
10. For detailed breakdown, see
    https://www.socialsecurity.gov/policy/docs/statcomps/di_asr/2016/background.html, "Benefit Calculations"
11. https://www.ssa.gov/news/press/factsheets/colafacts2018.pdf
12. https://www.socialsecurity.gov/pubs/EN-05-10029.pdf, p. 10

13. https://www.socialsecurity.gov/pubs/EN-05-10029.pdf, pp. 9-10, and https://ssa.gov/OP_Home/handbook/handbook.05/handbook-0502.html
14. https://ssa.gov/OP_Home/handbook/handbook.15/handbook-1513.html, 1513.1.
15. http://www.socialsecurity.gov/pubs/EN-05-10045.pdf
16. https://www.socialsecurity.gov/pubs/EN-05-10007.pdf
17. https://ssa.gov/OP_Home/handbook/handbook.05/handbook-0504.html, 504.2.
18. https://www.socialsecurity.gov/pubs/EN-05-10043.pdf, p. 4
19. See https://ssa.gov/OP_Home/handbook/handbook.05/handbook-0513.html for this entire section.
20. https://ssa.gov/OP_Home/handbook/handbook.05/handbook-0516.html
21. https://secure.ssa.gov/apps10/poms.nsf/lnx/0300203001, A.1.a.
22. https://secure.ssa.gov/apps10/poms.nsf/lnx/0600801146, B, showing that DIB, DWB, and CDB benefits all qualify after 24 months (Disability Insurance Benefits, Disabled Widow(er) Benefits, and Childhood Disability Benefits)
23. https://ssa.gov/OP_Home/handbook/handbook.05/handbook-0502.html, 502.2 B
24. https://www.ssa.gov/pubs/EN-05-10153.pdf, p. 9
25. https://www.ssa.gov/pubs/EN-05-10095.pdf, p. 1
26. https://ssa.gov/OP_Home/handbook/handbook.05/handbook-0520.html, 520.4.
27. https://www.ssa.gov/pubs/EN-05-10153.pdf, p. 18
28. https://ssa.gov/OP_Home/handbook/handbook.05/handbook-0506.html, 506.1 A.
29. https://www.ssa.gov/news/press/factsheets/colafacts2018.pdf
30. https://ssa.gov/OP_Home/handbook/handbook.05/handbook-0520.html, 520.6
31. https://ssa.gov/OP_Home/handbook/handbook.05/handbook-0522.html
32. https://www.socialsecurity.gov/redbook/eng/ssdi-only-employment-supports.htm, under "Trial Work Period"
33. https://www.socialsecurity.gov/redbook/eng/ssdi-only-employment-supports.htm, under "Extended Period of Eligiblity"
34. https://www.socialsecurity.gov/redbook/eng/ssdi-and-ssi-employments-supports.htm, under "Expedited Reinstatement"
35. https://www.socialsecurity.gov/redbook/eng/ssdi-only-employment-supports.htm, under "Continuation of Medicare Coverage"

C H A P T E R   S I X

MEDICARE

Medicare in a Nutshell

- You are eligible for Medicare health insurance at 65 (or earlier if getting Social Security disability).

- "Original" Medicare—Parts A and B—will pay a portion of your hospital and medical bills.

- Part A is usually premium-free. Part B premiums are based on your income.

- Enrollment dates are strict. Late filing can lead to life-long penalties.

- This book's "three pathways" approach clarifies your options for supplementing your Medicare coverage.

- Powerful resources can help you find the right supplemental coverage.

MEDICARE BACKGROUND

Medicare provides basic health insurance coverage when you are over 65, disabled, or a patient with chronic kidney disease. Its function is virtually identical to private health insurance, but it is specially tailored and financed for its unique beneficiary pool.

Enacted in July of 1965, Medicare has a huge job:

- As one of the largest health insurance programs in the United States, it supplies hospital and medical insurance for about 58 million people.[1]

- It onboards 3.6 million new enrollees per year.[2]

- It must process 1 Billion healthcare claims per year.[3]

- It must minimize overhead by making the claims process faster and cheaper, while making the claims process simpler for the consumer.

- It needs to crack down on insurance fraud by carefully reviewing Medicare claims.

- Finally, it must lead the way in controlling the runaway rise of health care costs.

Despite Medicare's many tasks, it is successful. Medicare satisfies most users, paying health claims accurately and timely. For health providers such as hospitals and doctors, working with Medicare is like working with other insurance programs.

Features

Medicare's benefits are divided into four separate programs, or "parts":

- Part A is called "Hospital Insurance" and covers hospital room and board, plus other services.

- Part B is called "Supplemental Medical Insurance," or simply "medical insurance," and covers medical bills inside or outside the hospital, such as visits to your physician's office or inpatient doctor care.

- Part C consists of "Medicare Advantage" plans. These are private insurance plans that replace Parts A and B's services and may offer additional benefits.

- Part D is Medicare drug coverage, available from private companies. It partially covers costs of prescription medicines.

Reform Target: The Affordable Care Act of 2010—ACA, or "Obamacare" increased Medicare coverage, added new taxes to fund Medicare, and extended Medicare's solvency.

At time of publication, Congress was debating repealing ACA. Repeal would alter many of the provisions described here.

Parts A and B are the core of Medicare. Together, they're called *Original Medicare* and provide basic hospital and medical coverage. They're both run by the federal government. Virtually all retired people over 65 are on Parts A and B. (There are a few exceptions such as older workers with health insurance from current or previous work.) By contrast, Parts C and D are private alternatives or supplements to Original Medicare, and assume you already have Parts A and B.

Other features of Medicare include:

- *Paperwork.* Doctors and other healthcare providers bill Medicare directly. This saves you paperwork and increases the efficiency of the system.

- *Fee cap.* Doctors' charges for Medicare services are capped at 115% of the Part B approved charge, for any doctor accepting Medicare.[4] Most providers do not charge more than the approved charge (see pages 146 and 151).

- *Options to supplement Medicare.* You can purchase a Medigap policy to fill gaps in Medicare's coverage (page 154),[5] and/or a Part D plan to cover prescription drugs (page 164). [6]

- *Option to replace Medicare coverage.* You can purchase a Medicare Advantage plan so a private insurance company will provide all services (page 160).[7]

Medicare is an important benefit for retired and disabled Americans. Medicare covers people with the highest healthcare costs—older and disabled citizens. Without it, coverage would be costly or unavailable for many, and more people would turn to *Medicaid*, the public assistance healthcare program for the needy. Medicaid is more complex, more expensive, accepted by fewer health-care providers, and preserves personal dignity less than Medicare.

In this chapter, you will learn who is eligible for Medicare, what Medicare costs, and what it covers. Most importantly, you will learn what Medicare does *not* cover and how to fill those gaps.

ELIGIBILITY FOR MEDICARE

Medicare's four components, Parts A, B, C, and D, will be explained in the next section. First, let's find out who is eligible for Original Medicare—the core programs, Parts A and B—and how to apply.

General requirements for Medicare eligibility

First, you must be a US citizen or permanent resident. Then there are three ways to become eligible for Medicare:[8]

- *Age.* You gain Medicare eligibility when you turn 65.

- *Disability before age 65.* You are eligible if you are disabled and entitled to Social Security or Railroad disability benefits for at least two years.

- *Chronic kidney disease.* If you have End Stage Renal Disease (ESRD) and require treatment by transplant or regular dialysis, you qualify for Medicare if you are *currently insured* (meaning you have 6 work credits in the past 3 years).

Tony retired at age 63. When he turns 65, he is eligible for Medicare.

Sheila became disabled at age 35. She is eligible for Medicare two years after eligibility for disability payments.

Edward is 30 and requires kidney dialysis. He is currently insured. His Medicare pays for the treatments.

Most people gain Medicare eligibility because of age. Then you gain coverage on the first of the month in which you *attain* age 65.[9] Remember, you attain age 65 the day *before* your birthday, so if you were born on the first of the month you are eligible one month early (see page 35).

Tony turns 65 on March 14. His Medicare coverage begins March 1.

Henny turns 65 on August 1. That means she attains age 65 on July 31. Her Medicare coverage begins July 1.

Additional requirements for Medicare eligibility

In addition to the age, disability, or ESRD requirements, you must either meet certain work requirements or pay a premium to gain Medicare eligibility.

Free Part A work requirement

You qualify for *premium-free* Medicare Part A (explained below) if your work record meets these requirements:

- You are eligible for Social Security retirement, disability, family, or survivor payments, or

- You are eligible for a pension from the Railroad Retirement Board, or

- You or your spouse worked long enough in government work, and paid Medicare taxes.

In these cases, your work automatically makes you, your qualifying spouse, and your qualifying former spouse eligible for Medicare, including free Part A.[8]

Henny has over 40 work credits on her Social Security work record. Therefore, she is eligible for Social Security retirement payments at age 62, and for Medicare at age 65. Her husband is also eligible through Henny's work.

Chip's career was with the railroad under the Railroad Retirement Board. Since he qualifies for RRB retirement benefits, he also qualifies for Medicare at age 65. His wife will also qualify when she is 65.

Jane is a retired firefighter, not covered by Social Security. She is eligible for Medicare because she paid Medicare taxes at her government job.

What about an older spouse married to a younger worker? A special provision allows a non-insured spouse over 65 to get Medicare once the working spouse attains age 62. Neither spouse needs to apply for Social Security payments. This allows a "bridge" to Medicare eligibility 3 years early for the non-insured older spouse.[10]

Note that to qualify for premium-free Part A, you must be *eligible* for Social Security payments. However, you do not need to apply for Social Security to get your Medicare.

Miguel is turning 65 and still working. He has not applied for Social Security, but he does have enough work to qualify. He could enroll in Medicare at age 65, if he chooses to do so.

For *Medicare based on ESRD,* the work requirements are not as stringent as those for Medicare based on age or disability. To qualify, you must meet *one* of these standards:

- Meet *fully insured status* on your own work record (defined the same as Figure 4.2, page 86), or

- Meet *currently insured status* on your own work record (defined as 6 work credits earned in the past 13 quarters), or

- Be the spouse, former spouse, widow(er), or dependent child of a worker who is or was fully or currently insured.[11]

If you are filing on another's record, he or she does not have to be receiving benefits for you to become eligible.

Because of the many ways to become eligible for ESRD Medicare, it is highly likely that you will meet the work requirement. Anyone with chronic kidney disease should contact Social Security promptly to enroll.

Premium Part A

Part A is premium-free if you or your spouse meet the work requirement above. Otherwise, you can purchase Medicare Part A coverage for a premium.

To purchase "premium Part A," you need to meet these conditions:

- If 65 or over, you must be enrolled in Medicare Part B, and either be a citizen, or be a legal resident for at least 5 years.[12]

- If disabled and under 65, your free Part A must have ended because you returned to work (see page 123).[13]

The premium varies with the number of Work Credits (see page 35) on your or your spouse's work record. Here are the premium requirements for 2018:

Work Credits	Monthly Part A Premium (2018)
40+	$0 (free)
30-39	$232
Under 30	$422[14]

Kevin does not qualify for free Medicare Part A but he wants the health coverage. When he turns 65, he enrolls in premium Part A and pays for his Medicare coverage.

Premium Part B

Part B has a monthly premium. In 2018 the standard premium is $134 per month per person, but it can be higher or lower depending on several factors.[15]

Lower premium. Your 2018 Part B premium is "protected" at a lower level averaging $130 if all the following are true:

- You were enrolled in Part B in 2017

- Your premiums were deducted from your Social Security

- You were not subject to higher premiums due to high income

The rule that protects the lower premium is "hold harmless." Under hold harmless, Medicare premiums can't increase more than the Social Security increase. Since the 2018 Social Security COLA was only 2.0%, Medicare premium increases were limited.[15]

Your 2018 premium will be $134 or more if any of the following are true:

- You enroll in Part B for the first time in 2018

- You don't get Social Security, so you are directly billed for the premium

- You have both Medicare and Medicaid, and Medicaid pays your premium

- Your income in 2016 was above the amounts in Figure 6.1.

None of these groups are protected against premium increases by hold harmless rules.

Higher premium. If you have high income, you will pay a higher premium (Figure 6.1). The increased premiums are called Income-Related Monthly Adjustment Amount (IRMAA).

The income used to determine the increased Part B premium is your Modified Adjusted Gross Income (MAGI) from two years prior. Your MAGI is your Adjusted Gross Income plus tax-fee interest income. IRS supplies the figure to SSA automatically. If your income has declined—for example, through retirement or divorce—contact SSA to use a different tax year.

There is no work requirement for Part B. Anyone who is eligible for Part A may enroll in Part B. Normally, you must purchase Part B by paying the premium (unlike Part A, which is usually free).

Because it costs money, Part B is optional. However, it is also an outstanding insurance value, since the standard premium is only about 1/4 of the cost of the program. The federal government pays the remaining 3/4 from general revenues (not Social Security or Medicare taxes).

Henny enrolls in Part A and B at the same time. Since she is eligible for free Part A, she gets full Original Medicare coverage by paying only the Part B premium, $134 per month.

While enrolling in Premium Part A, Kevin also enrolls in Part B. He receives full Original Medicare coverage even though he does not meet the work requirement. His Part A and Part B premiums total $566 per month ($422 for Part A and $134 for Part B).

2016 Yearly Income (MAGI)			2018 Part B Monthly Premium
Single Individual	Married, Filing Joint Tax Return	Married, Filing Individual Tax Return	
$85,000 or less	$170,000 or less	$85,000 or less	$134.00[A, B]
$85,001 - $107,000	$170,001 - $214,000	Not Applicable	$187.50[A]
$107,001 - $160,000	$214,001 - $320,000	Not Applicable	$267.90[A]
$160,001 - $214,000	$320,001 - $428,000	$85,001 - $129,000	$348.30[A]
Above $214,000	Above $428,000	Above $129,000	$428.60[A]

[A]Does not include late filing penalties, if applicable. See text, page 141.
[B]Limited to average of $130 if not subject to IRMAA and premiums were deducted from Social Security in 2017.

Figure 6.1. Your 2018 Medicare Part B monthly premium depends on your 2016 income level.[16]

Certain low-income individuals and families may qualify for state programs that pay the premium, resulting in free Parts A and/or B coverage. These are called "Medicare Savings Programs." In addition to paying premiums, some of these programs also pay Medicare deductibles and coinsurance. Your local public assistance office can give you more information about the savings programs. Also see page 146 and www.medicare.gov/Pubs/pdf/10126-Getting-Help-With-Your-Medicare-Costs.pdf.

Kevin investigates the Medicare Savings Programs to see if his state will pay his Medicare premiums. His public assistance office tells him that he does not meet the income and asset guidelines because of his savings, but that he might qualify next year since his savings are declining.

Most American citizens and legal residents, then, are eligible for Original Medicare—Parts A and B—if they are age 65 or disabled, and eligible for Social Security, Civil Service, or Railroad benefits.

APPLYING FOR MEDICARE

In addition to the requirements mentioned above, you must *enroll* to gain your Medicare coverage. Some enrollments are automatic, and some require filing an application. The following guidelines explain when and how to enroll in Medicare.

Automatic enrollment

The following people are automatically enrolled at the times indicated:[17]

- If you are getting payments from Social Security or the Railroad Retirement Board (RRB), you will be auto-enrolled effective the first of the month when you attain age 65.

- If you're under 65 and getting Social Security disability payments or certain RRB disability payments, you'll be auto-enrolled after 24 months of payments.

- If you have ALS (Amyotrophic Lateral Sclerosis, also called Lou Gehrig's disease), you'll be auto-enrolled the month your Social Security disability benefits begin.

In these cases, you do not need to file an application. You will receive your Medicare card about 3 months before eligibility. Your automatic enrollment will include both Part A and Part B, with an option to drop Part B if you wish. (Parts A and B are explained below.)

*Tony started drawing Social Security at age 63. Therefore, his Medicare enrollment is automatic. He automatically receives his Medicare card, good for Parts A and B, three months before his 65th birthday, along with an option to refuse Part B enrollment. Medicare also sends him a **Medicare and You** handbook describing the program.*

When to enroll

If you are *not* drawing Social Security or railroad pension at 65, you must apply. You have three opportunities to enroll in Medicare:

- The *Initial Enrollment Period*
  - If you retire at or before age 65
  - Enroll on or close to your 65th birthday
  - Enrollment is automatic if you already get Social Security or railroad benefits

- The *Special Enrollment Period*
  - o If you or your spouse work past age 65 and have employee health coverage
  - o Enroll on or close to your retirement date, or when your health coverage stops
- The *General Enrollment Period*
  - o For late enrollment
  - o Late fee will be added to Part B premium
  - o Coverage is delayed

In short, you can either apply for Medicare at 65 or have two opportunities later. Each is detailed below, but a simple rule of thumb appears in Figure 6.2.

Applying for Medicare

- If you receive Social Security or Railroad Retirement payments at age 65, Medicare enrollment is automatic.

- Otherwise, contact Social Security 3 months before age 65 to discuss your options.

Figure 6.2. Summary of Medicare enrollment rules.

Initial Enrollment Period: For Medicare at 65

If not getting Social Security, most people should apply for Medicare at 65. To do so, you must file within 7 specific months: the month you attain 65, the 3 months before, and the 3 months after (see Figure 6.3).[18]

If you enroll during the first 3 months, your Medicare coverage starts with the month you attain 65. If you enroll during the last 4 months, your Part B coverage will start 1 to 3 months after you sign up. In other words, for coverage to begin promptly when you turn 65, you *must* apply 1 to 3 months early.

Note that like other Social Security benefits, you attain age 65 the *day before* your birthday (page 35). Therefore, if your birthday is on the first of the month, you are Medicare-eligible the *preceding* month.

Georgette turns 65 on June 15. She applies for Medicare in May. Her coverage begins June 1.

Rosemary turns 65 on January 10. She applies for Medicare in March. Her coverage begins June 1.

Initial Enrollment Period						
7 Months: Birth Month, 3 Months Before, and 3 Months After						
Month 1	Month 2	Month 3	Birth Month	Month 5	Month 6	Month 7
Coverage starts 1st day of Birth Month			Coverage starts 1st month after enrollment	Coverage starts 2nd month after enrollment	Coverage starts 3rd month after enrollment	

*Figure 6.3. Summary of Medicare Initial Enrollment Period. "Birth Month" is the month you **attain** age 65; for birthdates on the first of the month use the previous month.*[18]

Special Enrollment Period: For Medicare at retirement after 65

The Special Enrollment Period applies if you are over 65 and covered by an employer's health plan. Your health insurance must stem from *current active employment* by you or your spouse (i.e. insurance for active employees). COBRA or retiree insurance do not qualify you for a Special Enrollment Period; they're based on *past* work.

If you are already covered by your employer or your spouse's, you may choose to *delay* enrolling in Medicare until the coverage from work ends.

Why would you delay enrollment? For three good reasons:

- *Little coverage.* If you are dually covered by an employment health plan and Medicare, Medicare is the *secondary payer*. Since Medicare is only *basic* health insurance, it may pay little or nothing after your employment plan pays.

- *Premium cost.* If you enroll in Part B, even accidentally, while still working, you will have to pay the Part B premium of $134 per month (in 2018) even though you get no real benefit from the coverage—again, because Medicare will be the secondary payer.

- *Lost guarantee.* Finally, if you enroll in Part B prematurely, you may lose your Medigap enrollment guarantee (see page 159 for more information). Then you might find you can't get a Medigap policy.

In short, if you have health coverage at work, enrolling in Medicare could cost you money, give you no extra coverage, and could deny you an important right.

If you have employment coverage, there's a middle course: apply for "Part A only" coverage at 65. Later, when you retire, the Special Enrollment Period would allow you to file for Part B with no late fees.

To help you decide whether to delay enrollment, contact your employer's benefits office and Social Security (1-800-SSA-1213) to explore your options.

Here are the rules for the Special Enrollment Period, summarized in Figure 6.4:[19]

- You may enroll at any time while covered by the employer's health plan as an active employee, or

- You may enroll during the 8-month period beginning with the first full month either employment ends or work health insurance ends, *whichever comes first.*

- If you enroll after the month of termination, Medicare coverage is delayed until the month after you enroll.

- You will need to prove that you were covered by the employer plan. A letter from your benefits office will serve.

Special Enrollment Period							
8 Months: Work or Insurance Termination Month, and 7 Months Following							
Termi-nation Month	Month 2	Month 3	Month 4	Month 5	Month 6	Month 7	Month 8
Coverage starts 1st day of enroll-ment month	Coverage starts first day of the month after enrollment						

Figure 6.4. Summary of Medicare Special Enrollment Period. "Termination Month" is the first full month your work health insurance stops due to end of coverage or employment, whichever comes first.[19]

Miguel was still working when he turned 65, and was covered under his health plan at work. Rather than enroll in Medicare at 65, he chose to postpone enrolling until his retirement.

He retired at age 67 and signed up for Medicare A and B **then,** *with no penalties or delays in coverage. He still had the 6-month Medigap enrollment guarantee period (page 159), because he did not enroll in Part B earlier. He used the 6-month period to shop for a private Medigap policy with good coverage and a good price.*

William worked past age 65 and was covered by the health plan at work. He signed up for free "Part A only" coverage when he turned 65. He retired at age 66 and enrolled in Part B **then**, *without penalty or delay in coverage. That started* *his 6-month Medigap enrollment guarantee period, so he had plenty of time to shop for a Medigap policy.*

General Enrollment Period: Medicare for late enrollees

The General Enrollment Period is for late enrollees who missed the Initial and Special Enrollment Periods. This is an "open enrollment" period each year in January, February, and March. Penalties apply for late enrollment in Part B. Here are the facts, summarized in Figure 6.5:[20]

- Enrollment is limited to Jan. 1 - Mar. 31 each year.

- Coverage begins July 1 of the year you enroll.

- Premiums are permanently increased 10% for each year of delay.

James retired at 64, but waited until he was 67 to apply for Medicare. He learns in April that he could enroll only during the next General Enrollment Period (January to March the following year). His coverage would not begin until the following July. He did not want to be uninsured for 15 months, but there was no recourse.

Since he applied 2 years late, his Part B premium was permanently raised 20% over the usual premium.

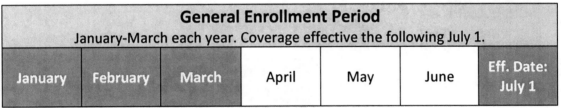

Figure 6.5. Summary of Medicare General Enrollment Period.[20]

Notice the *three penalties* for delaying your enrollment: limited enrollment dates, delayed coverage, and increased premiums.

Note also that you can find yourself trapped between a rock and a hard place, with penalties for enrolling too *late* or too *early*. Because of the complexity of the decision, *Social Security strongly urges everyone approaching 65 to contact Social Security to discuss Medicare.* This is a wise course—it is extremely important to enroll at the proper time, and an SSA representative can give you expert, personalized advice.

To summarize:

- You are eligible for Medicare if you are 65 or disabled, and have the required coverage from work performed by you, your spouse, your former spouse, or in certain cases, your parent.
- If you are getting Social Security, you will be enrolled in Medicare automatically.
- Otherwise you must apply through SSA.
- Always contact SSA before your 65th birthday to explore your best application date.

Once enrolled, you'll get a Medicare card (Figure 6.6). The new design, not displaying a Social Security Number, will be issued to new enrollees starting in April 2018; existing enrollees will receive new cards by April 2019.

Show the card to most doctors and hospitals, and Medicare will pay part of the bill, based on Medicare's benefits, described in the next section.

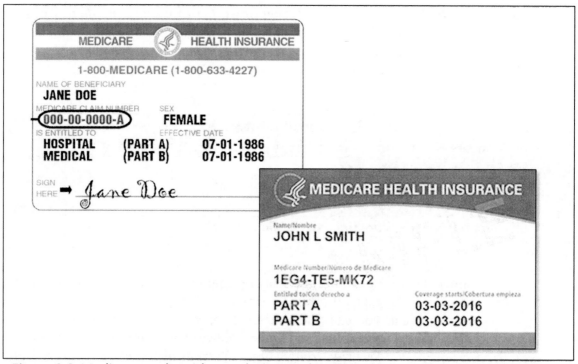

Figure 6.6. Medicare cards, with new design on the right. These are typical "A-B" Medicare cards showing the claim number and eligibility for both Parts A and B.

MEDICARE COVERAGE

Medicare provides *basic* health coverage. It is not a Cadillac, but gives good coverage for most people's needs. Government subsidies keep the price low.

Medicare's benefits are divided into four separate programs, or "parts." Parts A and B comprise *Original Medicare*. Parts C and D are optional approaches to fill the gaps in traditional Medicare. We'll focus first on Original Medicare.

Part A is called "Hospital Insurance," and covers you when you are in a hospital or other care situation (see Figure 6.7). Part B is called "Supplemental Medical Insurance," or simply "medical insurance," and covers medical bills inside and outside the hospital, such as visits to your physician's office.

In the following sections, we will *summarize* what Medicare covers, its costs, and the coverage gaps that can cost you money. For more detail, download the free *Medicare and You* handbook at www.medicare.gov/Publications/Pubs/pdf/10050.pdf, or request it from Social Security by calling 1-800-SSA-1213. See also the list of additional resources at the end of this chapter.

Part A Hospital Insurance

Medicare Part A helps pay for inpatient hospital care, inpatient care in a "skilled nursing facility" (described below, and not to be confused with "nursing home" care), home health care, and hospice care (see Figure 6.7). There are limits to the number of days of care under each category.

Medicare Part A Summary

Coverage:

- Inpatient hospital care

- Skilled nursing care after hospitalization

- Home health care

- Hospice care

Costs:

- Coverage is normally premium-free
- Deductibles and co-insurance costs apply

Figure 6.7. Summary of major Part A benefits and costs.[21]

Part A Hospital Benefits

Medicare Part A covers 100% of inpatient hospital room and board, plus medications, for the first 60 days, after you pay a deductible. In 2018 the deductible is $1,340 per *benefit period*.[21] A benefit period starts when you enter a hospital or skilled nursing facility, and ends when you haven't received inpatient care for 60 days in a row. If you are re-admitted after the benefit period ends, you will pay a new deductible.

Figure 6.8 shows the escalating charges you pay for hospitalizations over 60 days.

Both the deductible amount and the daily care charges increase annually with inflation.

Days 1-60	Days 61-90	Days 91-150	Days 151 & Up
$1,340 deductible (Once per 60-day benefit period)	$335 per day	$670 per day (Using 60 one-time "Lifetime Reserve" days)	You pay all charges

Figure 6.8. Hospital charges you must pay under Medicare (2018 amounts shown).[22]

For more on hospital care, see "Medicare and Your Hospital Benefits" at www.medicare.gov/Pubs/pdf/11408-Medicare-Hospital-Benefits-Getting-Start.pdf, and "Are You a Hospital Inpatient or Outpatient? If You Have Medicare—Ask!" at www.medicare.gov/Pubs/pdf/11435.pdf.

Part A Skilled Nursing Facility Benefits

Medicare Part A will help pay for the costs of care in a Skilled Nursing Facility (SNF), if both the facility and your treatment plan meet Medicare's strict definition.

SNF care is a higher level of care than the "custodial" care provided by a nursing home. Skilled nursing care means daily, continuous therapy such as physical therapy or intravenous injections requiring a doctor or registered nurse. This level of care is very close to full hospitalization. In fact, Medicare will not pay for SNF care unless it follows a hospital stay of at least three days.

If your doctor orders such care, Medicare will pay all recognized charges for the first 20 days. After that you will pay some or all charges.[23]

For details, see "Medicare Coverage of Skilled Nursing Facility Care" at www.medicare.gov/Pubs/pdf/10153.pdf.

Part A Home Health Services Benefits

While you are confined at home, Part A partially covers nursing care, therapy, and medical supplies and equipment ordered by a doctor and provided by a Medicare-certified home health agency.[24]

Details can be found in "Medicare and Home Health Care" at www.medicare.gov/Pubs/pdf/10969-Medicare-and-Home-Health-Care.pdf.

Part A Hospice Care

Terminally ill individuals may choose to receive pain relief, symptom management, and supportive services from an approved hospice organization at home or in a facility. Medicare Part A will cover all care, as long as your doctor continues to certify your eligibility. Virtually all services are covered, including nursing services, doctors' services, home health care, grief counseling, medications, and more.[25]

For details, see "Medicare Hospice Benefits" at www.medicare.gov/Pubs/pdf/02154-Medicare-Hospice-Benefits.PDF.

Other Part A Coverage

- Part A also covers inpatient mental health care in a hospital or specialty psychiatric hospital. See "Medicare and Your Mental Health Benefits" at www.medicare.gov/Pubs/pdf/10184-Medicare-Mental-Health-Bene.pdf.

- Medicare will help pay for inpatient hospital and skilled nursing services in a certified Religious Non-Medical Health Care Institution, such as a Christian Science sanatorium.[26]

- Medicare normally does not cover *foreign care*, except in a few restricted circumstances.[27]

For more information on the special kinds of coverage, consult "Your Medicare Benefits" at www.medicare.gov/Publications/Pubs/pdf/10116.pdf.

Part B Medical Insurance

Medicare Part B medical insurance, the other half of Original Medicare, helps pay for health costs not covered by Part A, including:[28]

- Doctor's bills, whether outpatient or inpatient

- Outpatient hospital care like day surgery

- Diagnostic tests like lab work

- Durable medical equipment like oxygen or wheel chair

- Ambulance services

- Limited preventive care like flu shots and an annual checkup

- Limited services from chiropractors, podiatrists, dentists, and optometrists.

Medicare does not cover routine dental and vision care. With few exceptions, prescriptions are not covered by Part B, but by optional Medicare Part D drug policies.

The Part B *payment schedule* is similar to private medical insurance.

You must pay a *deductible* of $183 per year (2018)[21] before Medicare begins its coverage.

After the deductible is met, Medicare pays 80% of all Medicare *approved charges*. You are responsible for:

- The other 20% of approved charges ("coinsurance"), *and*

- Any portion of medical charges that exceed the Medicare allowable amount ("excess charges").

Medicare Part B Summary

Coverage:

- Physician's and outpatient services

- Certain other medical equipment and services

Cost:

- Basic monthly premium: $134 per person (see pages 134-136 for variations)

- After annual deductible of $183 per person, Medicare pays 80% of approved charges

---

Figure 6.9. Summary of Part B coverage and costs. (2018 amounts shown.)[15]

If you are low income

Several programs can help with your medical bills if you are low-income:

- *Medicaid.* If you are very needy, *Medicaid* can cover virtually all your medical bills. Your Medicare premiums and deductibles will also be paid.

You are automatically eligible for Medicaid if you get SSI (see page 227), or you can apply on your own if you meet the stringent income and resource limits.

- *QMB (Qualified Medicare Beneficiary).* The QMB program (pronounced "quimbee") will pay your monthly Medicare Parts A and B premiums, deductibles, coinsurance, and copayments.

- *SLMB (Specified Low Income Medicare Beneficiary).* The SLMB Program (pronounced "slimbee") will pay your monthly Medicare Part B premium.

- *QI-1 and QI-2 (Qualifying Individual 1 and 2).* These programs can pay part of your Medicare Part B premium if you have slightly higher income levels.

- *QDWI (Qualified Disabled and Working Individuals).* Pays Part A premiums only, for working disabled individuals.

Each of these programs has different income limits and resource limits. Not all income is counted. Resources include money in bank accounts or other investments, but do not include your home, household items, and one car.[29]

These programs are provided by your state. For more information or to apply, contact your local public assistance office. For their number, call 1-800-MEDICARE (1-800-633-4227) and say "Medicaid." See also "Get Help with your Medicare Costs" at www.medicare.gov/Pubs/pdf/10126-Getting-Help-With-Your-Medicare-Costs.pdf, and "Get Help Paying Costs" at www.medicare.gov/your-medicare-costs/help-paying-costs/get-help-paying-costs.html.

To summarize:
- Original Medicare—Part A hospital insurance and Part B medical insurance—offers basic health coverage.

- Medicare includes major coverage for most hospitalizations and medical care, without providing 100% coverage.

- You must apply for Medicare on time when you turn 65, or when your health insurance from current work ends, whichever is later.

- Always contact SSA 3 months before your 65th birthday to be sure you apply properly and timely.

In the next section, you will learn more about the gaps in Medicare coverage and your various options for plugging these gaps.

SUPPLEMENTING MEDICARE

These are perhaps the most important questions you can ask as you approach Medicare eligibility:

- Where does Medicare leave me at-risk?

- How can I supplement Medicare in those areas?

In other words, what are Medicare's gaps and how can I fill them?

Medicare is *basic* coverage, just as Social Security is a basic pension program. Medicare doesn't cover 100% of health bills, just as Social Security doesn't cover 100% of your retirement costs. Just paying the bills that Medicare doesn't cover could potentially wipe out your retirement savings.

Fortunately, there are many options to supplement Medicare coverage.

First, let's look at the gap itself. Instead of looking at what Medicare covers, let's see what it doesn't cover.

Identifying Medicare's gaps

Pre-Medicare gap

The first Medicare gap is obvious: Medicare starts at 65, and you need health insurance before then, especially if you're not working.

There are three pathways to help you get to age 65 or other Medicare eligibility, summarized in Figure 6.10 and explained here:

- *Retiree medical.* You might be eligible for retiree coverage from an employer or union. This is sometimes offered by public employers, large companies, or unions, after some years of service. Remember to explore this option not just from your latest employer, but past ones as well. For example, you might have Tricare or VA coverage from military service years ago. To explore retiree health plans, contact benefits offices from your previous employer(s) or union(s).

- *Employer group plan.* You might be able to get insurance from an employer group plan in one of three ways:
  - *COBRA.* Any time you leave an employer with 20 or more employees, they must offer you COBRA coverage. Under COBRA, you can stay on your work health plan for 18 months after you leave employment. Contact your benefits office to learn more. Note that you could retire at age 63-1/2, have COBRA for 18 months, and then switch directly to Medicare with no gap in coverage.

- o *A job with benefits.* You could get health benefits at a job with benefits.

- o *Spouse's work.* If you have a working spouse, you might get benefits from that job.

- • *Individual plan ("Obamacare").* You could obtain individual coverage through insurance companies or your insurance exchange. For more information, contact insurance companies, www.HealthCare.gov (or 1-800-318-2596), or your state's insurance commissioner. Find your state's commissioner at www.shiptacenter.org.

One of the three pathways, or some combination of them, will get you to age 65 or other Medicare eligibility:

Bill was laid off at age 62. He received COBRA coverage for 18 months, then COBRA ended. He then obtained individual coverage through his state's insurance exchange. Three months before his 65th birthday, he applied for Medicare. His Medicare coverage was effective the first day of his birthday month, and he cancelled his individual plan.

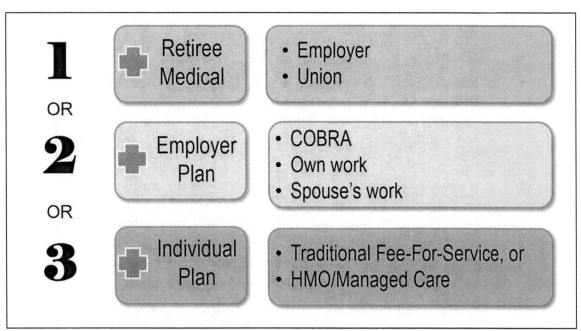

*Figure 6.10. Three pathways for health insurance **before** Medicare eligibility.*

Gaps in Part A hospital insurance

Once you are on Medicare, there are still gaps to cover. Here are the largest Medicare gaps (2018 figures):

- *The Part A deductible.* You must pay the $1,340 deductible per benefit period. The way benefit periods are defined, you could pay up to five deductibles per year, for total deductibles of $6,700 per year.

- *The phase-out period for long hospital stays.* If you are hospitalized for over 60 days you must pay $335 per day for days 61-90, and $658 per day for days 91-150 (Figure 6.8, p. 144). After that, you must pay all costs. For example, if you were hospitalized for 150 days (highly unlikely, but possible), you would pay the deductible of $1,340 plus daily fees of $50,250, for a total of $51,590.

- *Foreign care.* Medicare will not cover healthcare while you travel or live outside the U.S.

- *Long-term care (LTC).* Medicare pays a tiny fraction of the nation's long-term care bill. The only types of LTC that qualify are Skilled Nursing Care and home health care, and both are limited. That leaves you or your family exposed to huge long-term care bills. For example, nursing home median cost in 2017 was over $85,000 per year, according to Genworth.[30]

Gaps in Part B medical insurance

- *The deductible.* You must pay the $183 deductible per year (2018).

- *Medical bills: 20% "coinsurance."* Even if your health-care provider charges only the Medicare allowable fee, you will still be responsible for the 20% remainder after Medicare pays its 80% share. The 20% you must pay is called the "coinsurance," represented by the middle block in Figure 6.11.

- *Medical bills: 15% "excess charges."* Your health provider can charge up to 115% of the Medicare allowable fee. You would then be responsible for the 15% "excess" charges, represented by the top-most block in Figure 6.11.

- *Prescriptions.* Medicare covers almost no prescription drugs unless you're hospitalized. Prescriptions can be a sizeable expense. Many people spend $1,000 to $10,000 per month on prescription medications.

- *Dental, vision, and hearing care.* Medicare does not cover routine dental, vision, or hearing services.

- *Foreign care.* Neither Part A nor Part B covers you while travelling or living outside the U.S.

Unlimited liability

Note that ***Medicare has no out-of-pocket maximum, either annual or lifetime.*** Your risk exposure is unlimited.

Take another look at Figure 6.11 and imagine that the doctor bill is $230,000 for heart surgery, a year of chemotherapy, or other expensive procedure. Medicare's approved charge would be $200,000, of which Medicare would pay $160,000. Your responsibility would be $70,000.

You might need such procedures repeatedly in one year or for following years, and would have to pay your share over and over.

How to fill Medicare's gaps

There are three mainstream pathways to fill Medicare's gaps, plus some options to reduce your health costs. Let's start with some background on self-pay and assignment pay, and then explore the three pathways.

If you are low-income see pages 146 and 167 for help options.

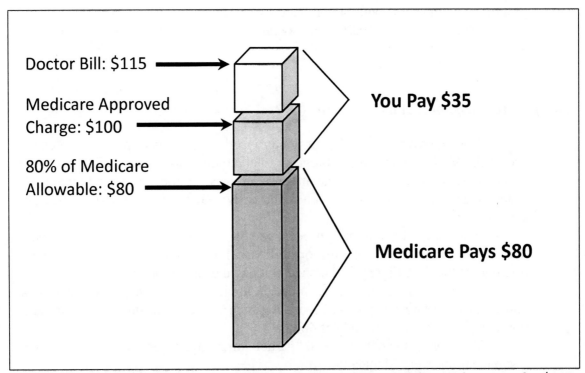

Figure 6.11. Example of Part B coverage and patient responsibility in the case of a $115 medical charge (The 2018 yearly deductible of $183 is already paid).

Self-pay

One option is to pay your medical bills yourself, from income or savings.

Under any insurance plan, you will share some costs with the insurance company. However, if Medicare is your sole insurance, can you afford to pay all the health costs that Medicare doesn't cover? Remember that Medicare has *no maximum out-of-pocket payment,* either annual or lifetime—costs are potentially unlimited.

Self-payment is an option, but is not recommended for retirement security or peace of mind. Remember: you exercise this option whether you *decide* that Medicare will be your sole insurance, or you never pursue *another* option.

With self-pay, you increase the chance of financial hardship, particularly if you develop a chronic disease or require nursing home care. You could have hundreds of thousands of dollars per year in medical bills not covered by Medicare, for the rest of your life.

There are two variations on this option. One is that your *family* can help pay your bills. This is quite common, especially with nursing home stays.

Another variation is that you pay as much and for as long as you are able, until your funds are exhausted. Then you can get *Medicaid,* the public-assistance program that pays medical costs for low-income Americans. Medicaid is an aid program not connected with Social Security or Medicare.

Medicaid is a vital part of our social safety net, but most of us hope to avoid depending on it if possible.

Using doctors who accept assignment

You can save money if your doctor or other health-care provider agrees to accept the Medicare-approved charge as total payment for services. This is called "accepting assignment" on your health-care services.[31] For example, in Figure 6.11, a doctor accepting assignment would charge no more than the $100 Medicare-approved amount.

You save with this option because you avoid the 15% "excess charges" doctors can charge. Your total responsibility will be only your 20% "coinsurance" (the middle block in Figure 6.11), once you pay the annual deductible.

Many doctors accept assignment on a case-by-case basis. Ask about it if you are facing a single expensive procedure, such as outpatient surgery. In that case, the savings might be thousands of dollars.

There are also doctors called "participating physicians" who *always* accept assignment for every Medicare-covered service.

To find doctors or other providers who accept assignment, see www.medicare.gov/find-a-doctor/provider-search.aspx, or call Medicare at (800) MEDICARE (800-633-4227). Or simply ask your doctor.

Three Pathways

Now let's examine the three pathways for filling Medicare's gaps. The pathways are summarized in Figure 6.12 and detailed in the following sections.

Note that every pathway assumes you already have Medicare Parts A and B.

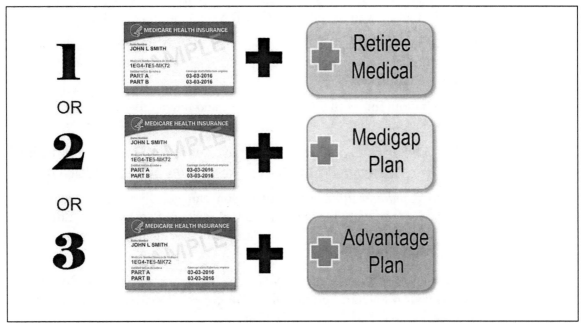

*Figure 6.12. Three pathways for health insurance **while on** Medicare. Note that every pathway assumes you have Medicare Parts A and B. (A few exceptions are covered in the text, page 154.)*

Pathway 1: Medicare plus Retiree Medical

You might be eligible for retiree health coverage from past work or affiliation with a union or tribe. If so, it might be your best pathway, and well worth exploring.

- *Employer or Union retiree insurance.* Your employer or union may offer retiree insurance. TRICARE, Federal Employee Health Benefits Program, RRB, and other government plans are examples, as are retiree plans from unions or large private employers. Generally:

  o You would enroll in Original Medicare (Parts A and B) and your retiree insurance.

  o Medicare is then your primary insurance and your retiree coverage is secondary, so all medical bills would go to both programs.

- Most retiree plans also provide prescription drug coverage. If not, consider also enrolling in Medicare Part D drug coverage, described on page 164.

- Check with your benefits office for details and advice.

- *COBRA.* Having COBRA coverage does not extend the deadline for filing for Medicare Part B (unlike insurance from *current* work), so don't delay filing for Part B even if you have COBRA.

  - When you enroll in Part B, you have only 6 months of guaranteed enrollment in a Medigap policy (page 159), and you might want to drop the COBRA then.

  - The bottom line is that COBRA won't add much coverage when you're Medicare-eligible.

- *Federal Employee Health Benefits.* Some plans under FEHB do not require Part B. See www.opm.gov/healthcare-insurance/healthcare/medicare/.

- *Veterans Administration.* Find out if you can get all your medical care through VA. If so, you do not need to take Medicare Part B or buy additional coverage. Many veterans enroll in Part B anyway if they ever want to get medical care outside the VA system.

- *Indian Health Service, or tribal coverage.* Medical choices vary. Be sure to discuss your Medicare options with your coverage provider to get the best coverage for you and your family.

Pathway 2: Medicare plus a "Medigap" (Medicare Supplement plan)

Background. Medigap insurance, properly known as "Medicare Supplement" insurance, is private insurance designed to fill the gaps in Medicare. It is time-proven, effective and affordable for many retirees. About 23% of Medicare enrollees have a Medigap.[32]

Medigap policies are widely available from many major insurance companies. Policies that cover fewer gaps are less expensive, while those that cover more gaps are more expensive. Some insurance companies offer several policies at different prices, so you can choose the right coverage for your needs.

Medigap eligibility. All Medigap plans assume you are already enrolled in Original Medicare, Parts A and B. Most Medigaps are for those over 65, but some policies cover disabled people with Medicare before 65.

	Plan									
Basic Benefits	A	B	C	D	F*	G	K	L	M	N
Part A: Hospital coinsurance costs up to an additional 365 days after Medicare benefits end.	✓	✓	✓	✓	✓	✓	✓	✓	✓	✓
Part A: Hospice Care coinsurance or copay	✓	✓	✓	✓	✓	✓	50%	75%	✓	✓
Part B: Coinsurance or copay	✓	✓	✓	✓	✓	✓	50%	75%	✓	✓ ***
Parts A & B: Blood (first 3 pints)	✓	✓	✓	✓	✓	✓	50%	75%	✓	✓
Additional Benefits	A	B	C	D	F*	G	K	L	M	N
Skilled nursing facility care coinsurance			✓	✓	✓	✓	50%	75%	✓	✓
Part A deductible		✓	✓	✓	✓	✓	50%	75%	50%	✓
Part B deductible			✓		✓					
Part B excess charges					✓	✓				
Foreign travel emergency (up to plan limits)			✓	✓	✓	✓			✓	✓
Out-of-pocket yearly limit**							$5,240	$2,620		

*Plan F also offers a high-deductible plan. This means you pay for Medicare covered costs up to the deductible amount ($2,240 in 2018) before your Medigap plan pays anything.

**After you meet your out-of-pocket yearly limit and your yearly Part B deductible ($183 in 2018), the Medicare Supplement plan pays 100% of covered services for the rest of the calendar year. Out-of-pocket limit is the maximum amount you would pay for coinsurance and copays.

***Plan N pays 100% of the Part B coinsurance except up to $20 copays for office visits and up to $50 copays for emergency room visits (emergency room copay is waived if you are admitted to hospital).

Figure 6.13. The ten standard Medicare supplement benefit plans. See text for explanation of terms.[33]

Types of Medigap plans. Medigap policies are standardized into ten policy types, lettered A, B, C, etc., summarized in Figure 6.13. (*Note:* in Massachusetts, Minnesota, and Wisconsin, policies are standardized in a different way. See www.medicare.gov/Pubs/pdf/02110-Medicare-Medigap.guide.pdf and contact your state's SHIP for details—see page 157.)

Every Medigap Plan A has the same specific coverage as every other Plan A, all Plan B's are the same, and so on. The only differences between several policies with the same letter designation are the premiums and the customer service you get from the companies.

Not counted as Medigap policies are:

- Medicare Advantage plans (Medicare Part C)

- Medicare Prescription Drug plans (Medicare Part D)

- Medicaid

These will be covered separately below.

Note that neither original Medicare nor Medigaps cover long-term care (for example nursing home care), most outpatient prescriptions, dental care, hearing aids, eyeglasses, or private nursing care.

Changing plan lineups. Occasionally plans are added or removed from Medigap offerings:

- Effective January 1, 2020, Plans C and F will no longer be available to new subscribers. If you already own a Plan C or F, you'll be able to keep it. (Note that Plan D is similar to Plan C, and Plan G is similar to Plan F, except D and G don't cover the small Part B deductible.)[34]

- Effective June 1, 2010, Plans M and N were added.

- Also effective June 1, 2010, Plans E, H, I, and J were no longer available to new subscribers. However, if you already owned one of those plans, you could keep it.

Definitions. Here are explanations of the terms used in Figure 6.13.

Basic Benefits, included in all plans, cover the following:

- *Part A hospital coinsurance.* This provides a full year of hospitalization, eliminating the costs for long hospital stays.

- *Part A hospice care.* This covers the copayments or coinsurance costs of outpatient prescriptions and inpatient respite care while in hospice care. Plans K and L will cover the portion shown in Figure 6.13.

- *Part B coinsurance or copay.* This covers your 20% share of the Medicare approved charge for doctor bills—the middle cost block in Figure 6.11. Plans K and L cover the portion shown.

- *Blood.* Pays all charges not covered by Medicare for the first 3 pints of blood for transfusion. Plans K and L cover the portion shown.

Additional Benefits, available in some plans, may cover the following:

- *Skilled Nursing Facility coinsurance.* Pays for up to 100 days of SNF care, compared to 21 days under Part A. Plans K and L cover the portion shown.

- *Part A deductible.* Covers your deductible for each hospital stay ($1,340 in 2018). Plans K, L, and M cover the portion shown.

- *Part B deductible.* Pays your annual deductible ($183 in 2018) for doctor bills. (Not available after January 1, 2020; see page 156.[34])

- *Part B excess charges.* Covers the amount your doctor charges above the Medicare allowable fee, if the doctor does not accept assignment (page 152). This is the topmost block in Figure 6.11.

- *Foreign travel emergency.* Pays for medically necessary emergency care during the first 60 days of foreign travel. You pay the first $250 per calendar year of such care, then the Medigap covers 80% of costs, up to a lifetime maximum of $50,000.[35]

Shopping for the right Medigap. It won't be hard to find insurance companies that sell Medigap policies. As you near 65, your mail will be stuffed with offers. The hard part will be narrowing your choices to the right policy.

You can organize your Medigap shopping by following these two steps: first, choose the type of coverage you want (A, B, C, etc.) from Figure 6.13. Second, find an insurance company that can deliver that coverage at a reasonable price.

Joan is shopping for a Medicare supplement policy. She studied the ten policy types available and decided she wanted either type "C" or "D" coverage. Then she called four insurance companies and asked for prices on type C and D policies.

Just to be sure, she checked with her state's SHIP on the two lowest-priced policies, to make certain the companies were reputable.

Helen took an easier path. She started with Medicare's Medigap Policy Search online, and reviewed the chart of all policies sold in her area. She quickly narrowed the field to two choices, then called her SHIP office to check on the complaint record of those two companies.

Insurance companies selling Medigaps are required to offer at least Plan A, then may or may not offer other plans. Any company that sells other plans must offer at least either Plan C or Plan F. Each state's insurance commissioner has authority to accept or reject any policies offered, so selections will vary from state to state.[36]

Multiple policies. Companies and agents are prohibited from selling you multiple Medigaps.[37] Instead of buying multiple policies, buy one policy that gives you the coverage you need and can afford. *Exception:* you should consider Medicare Part D drug coverage (page 164) in addition to your Medigap policy. Part D policies do not count as Medigap policies.

💡 Tips For Results: Medicare shopping aids

You have powerful allies when shopping for Medicare information or supplemental insurance.

For local focus, start with your state's "**SHIP**." All 50 states have a SHIP—a Senior Health Insurance Program. They provide publications, educational seminars, and individual help with Medicare decisions, including Medigaps, Advantage plans, and Part D drug plans. Many even list all insurance products sold in your state, with their prices. To find your state's SHIP, go to www.shiptacenter.org, or call 1-800-MEDICARE.

For Medigap information, also explore Medicare's online "**Medigap Policy Search**" at www.medicare.gov/find-a-plan/questions/medigap-home.aspx. Input your zip code to get a chart of available Medigap policies with price ranges and estimated annual out-of-pocket costs. Click on "View companies that offer" to get links to the companies selling those policies. Contact the companies directly (or consult your SHIP) for more detail.

For Advantage plans and Part D drug plans, the **Medicare Plan Finder** at www.medicare.gov/find-a-plan/questions/home.aspx is an outstanding shopping tool. Input your zip code (and optional information like your prescription needs and your favorite pharmacy) and the Plan Finder generates a list of plans that meet your criteria. The list shows coverage, prices, estimated annual out-of-pocket costs, and more, along with links to more information, options to compare plans side-by-side, and even instant enrollment in the plan you choose.

More help. If you need further help making your selection, there are several excellent sources of information:

- See the free booklet *Choosing A Medigap Policy: A Guide to Health Insurance for People With Medicare* at www.medicare.gov/Pubs/pdf/02110-Medicare-Medigap.guide.pdf. You can also obtain it by phoning (800) 633-4227. The booklet explains the gaps in Medicare and what insurance options can fill the gaps. It's also an excellent guide for changing policies.

- AARP has excellent online information on Medicare and Medigap policies. See www.aarp.org/health/medicare-insurance/.

- The Medicare Rights Center has good educational material. See www.medicareinteractive.org/index.php.

With guides like these, you will have an easier time understanding and comparing the features of various Medigap policies available to you.

As you shop, check to see if you can get a Medigap policy for free or at reduced cost from your work or your spouse's. Some employee benefits include this benefit for retired employees, and this could save you time and money.

Medicare and Medigap plans are individual-only—there are no family plans. If you and your spouse or partner are each Medicare-eligible, you'll each purchase your own Medigap policy. Your policies might be different plan types, and from different companies. The two of you might even be on different pathways—one with a Medigap policy and one with an Advantage plan, as shown in Figure 6.18 (page 171).

Medigap costs. Premiums for Medigap policies range from about $50 to about $300 per month, per person. Premiums depend on your state, the insurance company, and which Medigap plan you want. The policies assume you are enrolled in Medicare Part B, so to figure your total cost, add the Part B premium (Figure 6.1, page 136).

Joan found that her chosen Medigap policy would cost $150 per month. She will also pay $134 per month (in 2018) for her Medicare Part B premium. Her total health insurance bill will be $284 per month.

You'll also pay any medical bills not covered by Medicare and your Medigap. Find estimates of your total annual expenses at the Medigap Plan Finder at www.medicare.gov/find-a-plan/questions/medigap-home.aspx.

When to buy a Medigap. There are complex rules about when to buy your Medigap policy.[38] The best time to buy is the Medigap *guaranteed enrollment period,* which lasts 6 months. This period starts when *both* of the following are true:

- You are at least age 65, and

- You are enrolled in Medicare Part B

For most people, that's the first 6 months after their 65th birthday. If you or your spouse work past 65 and have health insurance from that work, guaranteed enrollment starts when you stop work and file for Part B (see "Special Enrollment Period" on page 139).

During the Medigap guaranteed enrollment period, your Medigap insurance company cannot do any of the following:

- Refuse to sell you any policy it offers

- Delay the start of your coverage

- Charge you more because of a pre-existing condition

Exception: If you have a pre-existing condition, the company can refuse to cover *that condition* for the first 6 months you're enrolled, or the first 6 months after diagnosis, whichever comes first. After that, you would be fully covered. Even during this "waiting period," Medicare would cover your pre-existing condition, and your Medigap would pay any covered costs not related to that condition. If you had health insurance coverage before your Medigap enrollment, the waiting period may be shortened or completely waived; check with the Medigap insurer.

Aside from the Medigap open enrollment, you also have a *guaranteed issue right* to buy a Medigap plan without restrictions if your previous insurance ends under certain circumstances, like if you move to a new service area or your existing coverage ends.[39]

Changing Medigap policies. Choose your Medigap carefully. After your 6-month guaranteed enrollment period, it can be hard to change policies, either within an insurance company or to a different company. There's no federal law to allow changing policies, but some states allow periodic changes.[38] Learn the rules in your state by contacting your SHIP (p. 158).

How to enroll in a Medigap. You enroll directly with the insurance company offering the policy you choose.

Pathway 3: Medicare plus a Medicare Advantage plan

Background. The third pathway to fill the Medigap is to enroll in Medicare plus a Medicare Advantage Plan, also called MedAdvantage, MA, Medicare Health Plan, or Medicare Part C. In effect you would replace your Medicare coverage with a private plan that gives you comprehensive coverage in one package.

These plans are offered by private companies and must provide all the services of Original Medicare (Medicare Parts A and B), plus additional benefits.

Many Advantage Plans include prescription drug coverage. Additional benefits can include vision, hearing, dental, or preventive care.

Advantage Plans have a geographical service area, such as a county or state, where care is covered. There may not be an Advantage Plan in your area, so check availability early in your shopping. Outside the service area, care is usually limited to urgent care or emergency care only, including overseas emergency.

Advantage Plans usually have a network of doctors, hospitals, and other medical providers. Make sure their network meets your needs.

Advantage Plans are not considered Medigap plans, but an alternative way to pay for and receive all your Medicare services. You need a Medigap or an Advantage Plan, but not both.

Advantage plans have been increasingly popular, and now 33% of Medicare enrollees have an Advantage plan.[40]

Eligibility. To be eligible for an Advantage Plan, you must:[41]

- Enroll in Medicare Parts A and B, including paying your Part B premium (Figure 6.1)

- Live in the plan's service area

- Not have End-Stage Renal Disease (ESRD) (some exceptions apply)

- Be a US citizen or legal resident

- Pay the plan's premium, if any.

Types of Advantage Plans. It used to be that Advantage plans were all HMOs. Now there are several different types. The types available to you depend on your geographical area. Each arrangement works with you and your medical providers in different ways:[42]

- *Health Maintenance Organizations (HMOs)* are health-care networks of doctors, clinics, and hospitals which offer comprehensive health care for a single monthly fee plus co-pays. You must get all your medical care in-network, with few exceptions. Generally, you name a Primary Care Physician (PCP) who directs all your care. A referral from your PCP is usually needed to see a specialist.

- *Preferred Provider Organizations (PPOs)* are like traditional, fee-for-service insurance. You can see any doctor, even out of network, but you will pay more for out-of-network care. You do not need to name a PCP, and you don't need a referral to see a specialist.

- *Private Fee For Service (PFFSs)* are networks of doctors, clinics, and hospitals that agree to treat you according to the terms of the plan. Like PPOs, you might pay more for out-of-network care. You do not need to name a PCP, and you don't need a referral to see a specialist.

- *Medical Savings Account Plans (MSAs)* are similar to the Health Savings Account plans available to some workers, but for Medicare beneficiaries instead. You enroll in a high-deductible insurance plan, plus you establish a Medical Savings Account to pay for non-covered costs.

- *Special Needs Plans (SNPs)* are limited plans for special populations, such as people living in institutions, on Medicaid, or with specified medical conditions like diabetes or HIV/AIDS.

Shopping for an Advantage Plan. As you approach age 65, offers for Medigaps, Advantage Plans, and Part D policies will stuff your mailbox. Your two best resources for sorting out the offers are the Medicare Plan Finder and your state's Senior Health Insurance Program (see "Tips for Results," p. 157).

Bill is searching for a Medicare Advantage plan. He goes to the Plan Finder and inputs his zip code and the two prescription drugs he takes. He narrows his search to plans with prescription drug coverage.

The Plan Finder lists four plans available. Bill reviews their coverage, premiums, estimated annual costs, out-of-pocket maximums, and quality rating. He narrows his choice to one, and clicks "Enroll" on the Plan Finder.

Mary has narrowed her search for a Medicare Advantage plan using the Medicare Plan Finder. She can't decide between three possibilities. She calls her state's SHIP to discuss the three plans. When she has a clear choice, she enrolls through the Medicare Plan Finder.

In urban areas you'll find many Advantage Plans to choose from. In rural areas there are fewer or no choices.

Like Medigaps, Advantage Plans are individual-only—there are no family plans. If you and your spouse or partner are each Medicare-eligible, you'll each purchase your own policy. Your choices might be completely different; you may choose an Advantage Plan, and your partner might choose a Medigap, as shown in Figure 6.18 (page 171.)

Advantage Plan costs. In an Advantage Plan, you will pay Medicare for your Part B premium, and you might pay a premium to the plan as well. Once enrolled, all your health bills, claims, and appeals will be handled by your plan, not Medicare.

All Advantage plans have an annual *out-of-pocket maximum* for Medicare-covered services to limit your expenses.

Advantage Plan premiums range from $0 up to about $250 per month, per person. Costs vary with the breadth of services covered, and your location.

How can some Advantage plans be *premium-free* while providing all Medicare services and additional services? Because Medicare pays the Advantage plan directly for every person enrolled.

Like Medigap insurance, your Advantage Plan premiums might be subsidized by your former employer or your spouse's. Be sure to check with your employee benefits office.

When to buy an Advantage Plan. You can join an Advantage Plan at these times:[43]

- When you first become eligible for Medicare.

- During the annual Open Enrollment, October 15-December 7.

- If you move from your plan's service area, or if your plan leaves the Medicare program.

- You can change *at any time* to a plan that earns a 5-star quality rating from Medicare, once per year. See the quality ratings on the Medicare Plan Finder (page 158).

Open Enrollment is open to anyone on Medicare, so it's easy to switch from a Medigap plan to an Advantage plan. There are no restrictions for pre-existing conditions.

Once enrolled, you are generally enrolled throughout the calendar year.

Reform Target: The Affordable Care Act (ACA, or "Obamacare") reduced Medicare payments to Advantage Plans starting in 2012. Before that, the government was sometimes paying more for medical care through Advantage Plans than they paid for care through Original Medicare.

Even though these "overpayments" ended, Advantage Plans are still widely available, with low premiums and generous benefits.

Repeal of ACA would have unknown impact on Advantage plan cost and availability.

Changing Advantage Plans. You can switch Advantage Plans at any of the "when to buy" times listed above.

Note that Open Enrollment lets you switch Advantage plans each year. One strategy is to take a less expensive plan early in retirement when you're younger and healthier, and switch to a more expensive plan if your medical needs change.

In addition, if you're enrolled in an Advantage Plan, you can drop it and return to Original Medicare in a special period, January 1 to February 14. You will also have an option to enroll in a Medicare Prescription (Part D) Drug Plan at that time. Note that there is no federally guaranteed enrollment in a Medigap plan at that time, so make sure you can get Medigap coverage before you drop your Advantage Plan.

How to enroll in an Advantage Plan. You can enroll in two ways: through the plan or through the Medicare Plan Finder at www.medicare.gov/find-a-plan/questions/home.aspx. You can also enroll by calling Medicare toll-free at (800) 633-4227.

To learn more about Medicare Advantage Plans and the options open to you, see "Medicare and You" at www.medicare.gov/Publications/Pubs/pdf/10050.pdf, or contact your state's SHIP (page 158).

Adding prescription coverage: Medicare Part D

Background. A Medicare Part D policy can help pay the costs of prescription drugs, lowering your cost of medications. You can add Part D coverage to any of the three pathways. Part D policies are also called "PDPs" for Prescription Drug Plans. Coverage is provided through private companies that are approved by Medicare. 70% of Medicare enrollees have a Part D plan.[44]

Here's how Part D works with the three pathways:

1. *Retiree health care* usually includes drug coverage that's comparable to Part D coverage *("creditable coverage").* If it doesn't, you can add a stand-alone Part D policy.

2. *Medigap policies* don't cover prescriptions. You should consider enrolling in a stand-alone Part D plan to get drug coverage.

3. *Advantage Plans* often include Part D drug coverage as part of their insurance package. If so, they're called "MA-PDs." If not, you can add a stand-alone Part D policy.

Don't buy more than you need. *If you enroll in a stand-alone Part D plan when you're already in an Advantage Plan that includes Part D coverage, you'll be disenrolled from your Advantage Plan and put back on Original Medicare.*[45]

Bottom line: if you have a retiree health plan from employment, make sure it includes prescription coverage comparable to Part D ("creditable" coverage). If you're enrolling in a Medigap plan, be sure to consider a Part D policy in addition. If you're enrolling in a Medicare Advantage plan, consider a plan that includes Part D coverage.

You should enroll promptly, since there are late fees for late enrollment; details appear below (page 166). You should enroll even if your prescriptions aren't currently expensive, since drug costs can escalate as we age. Many older people face drug costs of $1,000 to $2,000 a month, or more—costs that could largely be covered by insurance.

Part D eligibility. To be eligible for Part D, you must:

- Have Medicare Part A and/or Part B. To get Part D through a Medicare Advantage plan, you must have *both* Parts A and B

- Live in the service area of the Part D plan you're considering

Types of Part D plans. Part D plans can either be standard or enhanced. All plans must meet at least the standard design. Enhanced plans may offer different additional coverage, such as a lower deductible or better donut hole coverage (defined below).

As noted above, Part D plans can be stand-alone (mainly to supplement Medigaps) or can be included in an Advantage Plan.

Shopping for Part D. Computers make selecting your Part D plan easy. See "Tips for Success" on page 158.

In most areas, there are many plans to choose from. In my urban county, for example, there are 22 stand-alone Part D plans, plus another 36 Advantage plans that include drug coverage.

Part D plans are not created equal. Each plan covers different drugs differently, has different pharmacy outlets, and different costs.

You'll want to consider three "C's" and a "Q": Coverage, cost, convenience, and quality:

- *Coverage.* Focus your search on the plans that cover your prescriptions best.

- *Cost.* Review the plans with the right coverage with an eye to costs. Remember, in addition to premiums you'll pay deductibles, copayments, and more. See if there's a zero deductible, donut hole coverage, or other "enhanced" features. The Plan Finder provides an estimate of your total annual costs for each plan.

- *Convenience.* Some plans fill prescriptions only through mail order or only through "in-network" pharmacies. Find the plans that offer pharmacy choices that you like.

- *Quality.* Medicare gives each plan a quality rating, from one to five stars, based on claims data and patient complaints. You can also check for quality with your state's SHIP (page 158).

Part D costs. Costs begin with the monthly premium, and can include an income adjustment and/or late fees:

- *Monthly premium.* Premiums vary from plan to plan. In my state, for example, 2018 monthly premiums for stand-alone Part D plans vary from about $15 to $150, with many around $30-$60 per month. Premiums for Advantage plans that include prescription coverage range from $0 to $300 in my county, with many in the $0 to $100 range. Depending on your plan, premiums can be paid by check, or be deducted from your bank account, charge card, or Social Security payment.

- *Income adjustment.* You may have to pay a higher premium for your Part D plan if you are a higher-income retiree, similar to the higher premium you pay for Medicare Part B. You would pay your Part D premium plus an income-related adjustment amount. See Figure 6.14 for details; the amount in the last column would be added to your regular policy premium. The income used, from two years previous, is the same MAGI used to determine your Part B premium (see page 136). Note that the income-related adjustment would also apply to Part C plans with prescription coverage.

2016 Yearly Income (MAGI)			2018 Part D Income-Related Monthly Adjustment Amount
Single Individual	Married, Filing Joint Tax Return	Married, Filing Individual Tax Return	
$85,000 or less	$170,000 or less	$85,000 or less	$0.00*
$85,001 - $107,000	$170,001 - $214,000	Not Applicable	$13.00*
$107,001 - $160,000	$214,001 - $320,000	Not Applicable	$33.60*
$160,001 - $214,000	$320,001 - $428,000	$85,001 - $129,000	$54.20*
Above $214,000	Above $428,000	Above $129,000	$74.80*
*This amount is added to your regular policy premium. Does not include late penalties. See text, page 166.			

Figure 6.14. Your Medicare Part D monthly premium may be increased based on your income level. The income used (MAGI) and the income brackets are the same as those for Medicare Part B premiums—see Figure 6.1 on page 136. (2018 amounts shown.)[46]

- *Late Fees.* Avoid late fees—enroll timely. You have a grace period of 63 days if you don't have Part D or creditable coverage when you could. After that, late fees will apply. Late fees in 2018 are $0.35 for each month you're late.[47] That amount is added to your monthly Part D premium for life. The late penalty is recomputed each year, so expect your late penalty to grow in future years.

Part D coverage. Your prescription costs will be shared between you and your Part D plan. The costs are split differently as you pass through four stages in the calendar year: the Deductible Period, the Initial Coverage Period, the Coverage Gap ("Donut Hole"), and the Catastrophic Period.

- *Deductible Period.* As the year starts, you pay 100% of drug costs up to the deductible. The maximum allowable deductible is $405 (2018) for *Standard* plans.[48] *Enhanced* plans can have deductibles as low as $0.

- *Initial Coverage Period.* Once your deductible is met, you enter the Initial Coverage Period. Here your plan shares costs with you. Your portion is your *copayment* or *coinsurance*—typically 25% of covered costs.[49]

- *Coverage Gap ("Donut Hole").* Once you reach total shared expenses of $3,750 (in 2018), including the deductible, you enter a *Coverage Gap* where you must pay more of prescription costs. This is commonly called the *Donut Hole,* because it's a gap or "hole" in your drug coverage. Standard plans have a Donut Hole; enhanced plans may eliminate it. In 2018, you'll pay no more than 35% of the plan's cost of brand-name drugs in the Donut Hole, and no more than 44% for generic drugs.[50] (See "Reform Target" below.)

- *Catastrophic Period.* You continue to pay higher prescription costs until your total out-of-pocket costs reach $5,000 (in 2018). Then you enter the Catastrophic Period, when your plan pays most or all of your prescription costs for the rest of the calendar year. Expect to pay about 5% of your drug costs in the Catastrophic Period.[51]

Costs for "standard" Part D plans are illustrated in Figure 6.15.

Reform Target: The Affordable Care Act—ACA or "Obamacare"—phases out the Donut Hole by 2020. The phase-out is on schedule.[52] Repealing ACA would increase consumer costs by reestablishing the donut hole.

Help with costs. If paying these costs is a problem, there's help available. Programs called "Extra Help" can help pay Part D premiums, deductibles, and co-payments. In 2018, the resource limits are $13,820 (individual) or $24,360 (couple). Annual income limits are $18,090 (individual) or $23,895 (couple), with some help possible even for higher income.[53] To apply for Extra Help, contact Social Security at their offices, https://secure.ssa.gov/i1020/start, or (800) 772-1213.

When to buy a Part D plan. You can and should enroll when you're first eligible for Medicare to avoid late fees (page 166).

After you enroll, you can change your plan annually during Open Enrollment, which occurs from October 15 through December 7, the same as Open Enrollment for Advantage plans.

Your enrollment is effective for the calendar year. In limited circumstances, you can change plans mid-year (for example, if you move out of your plan's service area). In addition, *at any time* you can change to a plan that earns a 5-star quality rating from Medicare, once per year.

When changing plans, whether at open enrollment or mid-year, you don't need to cancel or notify your old plan. When your new plan starts, your old plan automatically stops.[54]

Deductible Period First $405	Initial Coverage Period $405-$3,750	Coverage Gap ("Donut Hole") $3,750-$5,000	Catastrophic Period Over $5,000
You pay 100%	You pay ~25%	You pay 35% (brand name) or 44% (generics)	You pay ~5%

Figure 6.15. Typical Part D drug costs. You pay monthly premiums throughout the year, in addition to the drug costs shown. 2018 "standard" amounts shown.

How to enroll in Part D. You can enroll in three ways: through the plan, through the Medicare Plan Finder at www.medicare.gov/find-a-plan/questions/home.aspx, or by calling Medicare toll-free at (800) 633-4227.

Sorting your options

With dozens of insurance options for most people, how can you decide which pathway is best for you?

If you have access to a retiree health plan, be sure to check it out. It has been pre-screened by your employer or union and might be your best option.

Otherwise the one big decision you need to make is if you prefer the Medigap pathway or the Advantage pathway. Once you make that decision the other decisions, like which policy to buy and whether you need a Part D plan, flow easier. See the decision guide at www.medicare.gov/sign-up-change-plans/decide-how-to-get-medicare/your-medicare-coverage-choices.html.

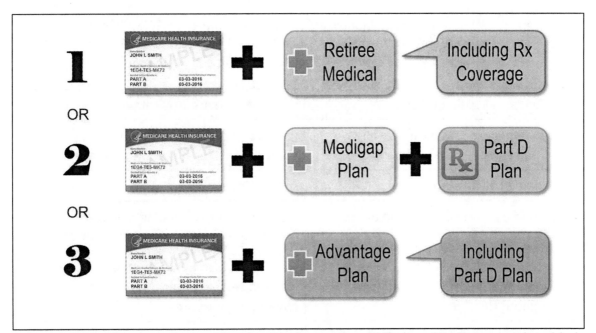

*Figure 6.16. Three pathways for health insurance **while on Medicare**, with added prescription coverage. Retiree and Advantage plans usually include prescription coverage. Medigaps don't cover prescriptions, so consider an added Part D plan.*

Learn the options in your area. After all, if there are only one or two Advantage plans and they're not attractive, you know you'll be on the Medigap pathway.

Figure 6.17 gives general guidelines to compare pros and cons of the Medigap and Advantage pathways.

Remember that there are no family plans under Medicare, so every plan is individual. If you are married, you and your spouse may not only have different supplemental insurance plans, you may even be on different pathways. See Figure 6.18 for an example.

Shopping resources appear in "Tips for Success" on page 158.

Other ways to get Medicare and gap coverage[55]

- *Medicare Cost Plans.* Medicare cost plans, available in some areas, are a type of HMO. The difference is that you can obtain care out-of-network through Original Medicare, although you must then pay all deductibles, coinsurance, and other non-covered costs.

- *Demonstrations/Pilot programs.* Occasionally, research studies are conducted to test improvements in Medicare. Enrollment is usually restricted to a particular population in a limited region.

- *Programs for All-Inclusive Care for the Elderly (PACE).* These programs provide intensive medical, social, and long-term-care services for frail people who would otherwise need to live in a nursing home.

Medigap Plans	Medicare Advantage Plans
Plans *supplement* Medicare by filling specified gaps.	Plans *replace* Medicare with comprehensive, all-in-one coverage.
Available in all 50 states.	Availability varies with zip code.
Accepted by any provider who accepts Medicare.	Network of providers, with limited coverage or higher charges for out-of-network care.
No geographical service area; good throughout the U.S.	Defined service area with limited coverage out of area.
Guaranteed enrollment only in first 6 months of Medicare Part B eligibility; after that, enrollment can be refused, especially with pre-existing conditions.	Open enrollment every Oct. 15-Dec. 7. No pre-existing condition limitations.
Switching plans after enrollment is limited; not guaranteed by law (but some states or companies allow switching).	Able to switch plans annually during Open Enrollment. Able to enroll in a 5-star plan anytime, once per year.
Limited opportunities to switch from Advantage pathway to the Medigap pathway; such path-switching is guaranteed by law only in a few instances (but some states or companies allow switching).	Can switch from a Medigap plan to an Advantage plan during Open Enrollment (or anytime for 5-star plans).
No outpatient drug coverage; must purchase separate Part D plan.	Many plans include Part D coverage.
Claims and appeals must be submitted separately through Medicare, Medigap plan, and possibly Part D plan.	All claims and appeals processed by the Advantage plan (including prescriptions if plan includes Part D coverage).
Premiums are paid through separate billing.	Premiums can be deducted from Social Security payments.

Figure 6.17. Comparing general characteristics of Medigaps vs. Advantage plans.

Sam Older than Sally	Both under 65	Sam turns 65	Sally turns 65
Sam	Individual Plan	Medicare + Medigap + Part D Plan	Medicare + Medigap + Part D Plan
Sally	Individual Plan	Individual Plan	Medicare + Advantage Plan (Includes Part D)

Figure 6.18. All Medicare plans are individual-only, with no family plans. John turns 65 first and chooses the Medigap pathway. Marsha turns 65 later and chooses a totally different pathway and company.

Long-Term Care Insurance

A final way to fill Medicare's gaps is with Long-Term Care (LTC) insurance.

LTC is often thought of as nursing home care. However, there are other LTC options, including home health care, adult family homes, assisted living, adult day-care facilities, respite care, and hospice care.

Medicare does not cover most long-term care. Its Skilled Nursing Facility (SNF) coverage helps with medical care but offers no coverage for typical personal care ("custodial care") that many need (see page 144). Some say this is Medicare's largest gap, and the one most likely to drain your retirement savings.

Today, many LTC costs are borne by individuals or their family members. Medicaid (an aid program for the needy, not Medicare) pays most of the country's LTC bills. Private LTC insurance is assuming a small but growing role in paying these costs.

Many large insurance companies offer LTC insurance. It's also offered by some employee benefits plans, or you might have options like VA or other programs. Explore your options at www.longtermcare.gov.

Costs of LTC insurance vary depending on how much coverage you buy, whether benefits are adjusted for inflation, your age at purchase, and, in most cases, your current health. The less expensive policies have fewer covered services, no inflation protection, and are sold to younger individuals, e.g. in their 40s or 50s. Average premiums in 2017 were $100 to $150 per month per person for 60-year-olds, according to a recent survey.[56]

A great resource for learning about LTC insurance is "A Shopper's Guide To Long-Term Care Insurance," published by the National Association of Insurance Commissioners. Download a free copy at www.naic.org/documents/prod_serv_consumer_ltc_lp.pdf. You can also learn from insurance companies, your state Insurance Commissioner, or AARP.

To summarize:

- You must enroll in Medicare promptly when eligible. Contact SSA to learn when and how to enroll.

- Medicare will cover the bulk of your medical bills once you enroll.

- You are expected to obtain additional insurance to fill Medicare's gaps.

- You can and should obtain supplemental insurance when you enroll in Medicare. Nearly all supplement options assume you already have Original Medicare—Parts A and B.

- Wise supplement choices are summarized in Figure 6.16 and here:

  - Enroll in retiree insurance from an employer or union, if available to you, or

  - Purchase a Medigap policy plus a Part D drug plan, or

  - Join a Medicare Advantage "Part C" plan that includes Part D drug coverage, if available in your area.

  - Long-term-care insurance is also worth investigating.

FOR MORE INFORMATION...

"Medicare"
www.ssa.gov/pubs/EN-05-10043.pdf

"Getting Started With Medicare"
www.medicare.gov/people-like-me/new-to-medicare/getting-started-with-medicare.html

"Medicare and You" (handbook for beneficiaries)
https://www.medicare.gov/Pubs/pdf/10050-Medicare-and-You.pdf

"Your Medicare Benefits"
www.medicare.gov/Pubs/pdf/10116-Your-Medicare-Benefits.pdf

"Are You a Hospital Inpatient or Outpatient? If You Have Medicare—Ask!"
www.medicare.gov/Pubs/pdf/11435.pdf

"Medicare Coverage of Skilled Nursing Facility Care"
www.medicare.gov/Pubs/pdf/10153.pdf

"Medicare and Home Health Care"
www.medicare.gov/Pubs/pdf/10969-Medicare-and-Home-Health-Care.pdf

"Medicare Hospice Benefits"
www.medicare.gov/Pubs/pdf/02154-Medicare-Hospice-Benefits.PDF

"Medicare and Your Mental Health Benefits"
www.medicare.gov/Pubs/pdf/10184-Medicare-Mental-Health-Bene.pdf

"Choosing a Medigap Policy"
www.medicare.gov/Pubs/pdf/02110-Medicare-Medigap.guide.pdf

"Things to Think About When You Compare Medicare Drug Coverage"
www.medicare.gov/Pubs/pdf/11163-Compare-Medicare-Drug-Coverage.pdf

AARP's website on Medicare and other insurance:
www.aarp.org/health/medicare-insurance/

"A Shopper's Guide to Long-Term Care Insurance" free download at
http://www.naic.org/documents/prod_serv_consumer_ltc_lp.pdf

Chapter Endnotes

1. https://www.cms.gov/Research-Statistics-Data-and-Systems/Statistics-Trends-and-Reports/Dashboard/Medicare-Enrollment/Enrollment%20Dashboard.html
2. https://www.cms.gov/Research-Statistics-Data-and-Systems/Statistics-Trends-and-Reports/CMSProgramStatistics/2015/Downloads/MDCR_ENROLL_AB/2015_CPS_MDCR_ENROLL_AB_21.pdf
3. https://www.cms.gov/Outreach-and-Education/Medicare-Learning-Network-MLN/MLNProducts/Downloads/MedQtrlyComp-Newsletter-ICN909435.pdf, p. 2
4. https://www.medicare.gov/your-medicare-costs/part-a-costs/assignment/costs-and-assignment.html under "limiting charge"
5. https://www.medicare.gov/supplement-other-insurance/medigap/whats-medigap.html
6. https://www.medicare.gov/part-d/index.html
7. https://www.medicare.gov/sign-up-change-plans/medicare-health-plans/medicare-advantage-plans/medicare-advantage-plans.html
8. https://www.ssa.gov/pubs/EN-05-10043.pdf
9. https://secure.ssa.gov/apps10/poms.nsf/lnx/0600801006 B.

10. Ibid, second bullet. Note use of "eligible" rather than "entitled," i.e. meet all requirements but not necessarily have applied.
11. https://secure.ssa.gov/apps10/poms.nsf/lnx/0600801191, C.2.
12. https://secure.ssa.gov/apps10/poms.nsf/lnx/0600801131, A. and B.
13. https://secure.ssa.gov/apps10/poms.nsf/lnx/0600801170
14. https://www.medicare.gov/your-medicare-costs/costs-at-a-glance/costs-at-glance.html, under "Part A premium"
15. https://www.medicare.gov/your-medicare-costs/costs-at-a-glance/costs-at-glance.html. Under "Part B premium"
16. https://www.medicare.gov/your-medicare-costs/costs-at-a-glance/costs-at-glance.html under "Medicare Part B"
17. *Medicare and You 2018,* p. 19, available at https://www.medicare.gov/Pubs/pdf/10050-Medicare-and-You.pdf
18. Ibid, p. 21
19. Ibid, pp. 21-22
20. Ibid, pp. 22
21. https://www.medicare.gov/your-medicare-costs/costs-at-a-glance/costs-at-glance.html, under "Part A hospital inpatient deductible and coinsurance"
22. Ibid
23. https://www.medicare.gov/Pubs/pdf/10153.pdf
24. https://www.medicare.gov/Pubs/pdf/10969-Medicare-and-Home-Health-Care.pdf
25. https://www.medicare.gov/Pubs/pdf/02154-Medicare-Hospice-Benefits.PDF
26. *Medicare and You 2018,* p. 33
27. *Medicare and You 2018,* p. 57
28. *Medicare and You 2018,* p. 35
29. https://www.medicare.gov/your-medicare-costs/help-paying-costs/get-help-paying-costs.html
30. https://www.genworth.com/corporate/about-genworth/industry-expertise/cost-of-care.html
31. *Medicare and You 2018,* p.64
32. https://www.kff.org/medicare/issue-brief/an-overview-of-medicare/, Figure 4
33. https://www.medicare.gov/supplement-other-insurance/compare-medigap/compare-medigap.html
34. https://medicare.com/medicare-supplement/is-medicare-supplement-plan-f-going-away/
35. https://www.medicare.gov/supplement-other-insurance/medigap-and-travel/medigap-and-travel.html
36. https://www.medicare.gov/Pubs/pdf/02110-Medicare-Medigap.guide.pdf, p. 10
37. https://www.medicare.gov/Pubs/pdf/02110-Medicare-Medigap.guide.pdf, p. 29
38. https://www.medicare.gov/supplement-other-insurance/when-can-i-buy-medigap/when-can-i-buy-medigap.html
39. https://www.medicare.gov/supplement-other-insurance/when-can-i-buy-medigap/guaranteed-issue-rights-scenarios.html
40. https://www.kff.org/medicare/issue-brief/medicare-advantage-2017-spotlight-enrollment-market-update/
41. https://www.medicare.gov/sign-up-change-plans/medicare-health-plans/medicare-advantage-plans/who-can-join-medicare-advantage-plan.html
42. https://www.medicare.gov/sign-up-change-plans/medicare-health-plans/medicare-advantage-plans/types-of-medicare-advantage-plans.html
43. https://www.medicare.gov/sign-up-change-plans/when-can-i-join-a-health-or-drug-plan/when-can-i-join-a-health-or-drug-plan.html
44. https://www.kff.org/medicare/fact-sheet/the-medicare-prescription-drug-benefit-fact-sheet/

45. https://www.medicare.gov/sign-up-change-plans/get-drug-coverage/get-drug-coverage.html, last section
46. https://www.medicare.gov/your-medicare-costs/costs-at-a-glance/costs-at-glance.html
47. https://www.medicare.gov/part-d/costs/penalty/part-d-late-enrollment-penalty.html
48. https://www.medicare.gov/part-d/costs/deductible/drug-plan-deductibles.html
49. https://www.medicare.gov/part-d/costs/copayment-coinsurance/drug-plan-copayments.html
50. https://www.medicare.gov/part-d/costs/coverage-gap/part-d-coverage-gap.html
51. https://www.medicare.gov/part-d/costs/catastrophic-coverage/drug-plan-catastrophic-coverage.html
52. https://www.medicare.gov/part-d/costs/coverage-gap/more-drug-savings-in-2020.html
53. http://www.q1medicare.com/PartD-ExtraHelp-Low-Income-Subsidy-LIS.php
54. https://www.medicare.gov/sign-up-change-plans/get-drug-coverage/switch-drug-plans/switch-drug-plans.html
55. https://www.medicare.gov/sign-up-change-plans/medicare-health-plans/other-health-plans/other-medicare-health-plans.html
    http://www.aaltci.org/news/long-term-care-insurance-association-news/costs-for-new-long-term-care-insurance-policies-show-nominal-increase

CHAPTER SEVEN

LEARN WHERE YOU STAND

 Chapter in a Nutshell

- Social Security planning begins with your "My Social Security" Account and your Social Security Statement.

- SSA's online calculators give you power to run "what-if" retirement scenarios.

"MY SOCIAL SECURITY" ACCOUNT AND STATEMENT

Remember the Social Security Statement?

You used to get a personalized annual statement in the mail that showed where you stood with the program. Statements were suspended in the spring of 2011, saving millions of dollars in printing and postage costs, then partially reinstated in 2012, then further restricted. Now statements are mailed only to workers over 60, and only if they haven't created a "My Social Security" online account or filed for payments.[1]

Now your Social Security information is available online, just like your bank and investment accounts. Go to www.ssa.gov/myaccount and set up your own "My Social Security" account. Once you establish your identity and create a username and password, you can log in anytime.

Welcome to the 21st Century.

Before you get Social Security, you can:

- Review your earnings history for accuracy

- Get estimates of your retirement, survivors, and disability benefits

- See the amount of Social Security and Medicare taxes you've paid

- Request a replacement Social Security card

- Check the status of a pending claim

- Get a benefit verification letter saying you're not currently getting payments, and

- Obtain the traditional Social Security Statement

Your Statement comes as a PDF so you can save it, print it, or email it to your financial advisor to use in your financial planning.
Note the assumptions the Statement makes:

- Its estimates are in current dollars, not inflated.

- It assumes you will continue to work at last year's level (or the last year posted) until the ages shown.

If you're not planning on working until 62, Full Retirement Age, or 70, or expect your earnings to decline or increase, or prefer to see your estimate in inflated dollars, see "Social Security Calculators" below.

Already getting Social Security? You'll still want a My Social Security account so you can, without visiting or calling SSA:

- Change your address and phone number

- Change your direct deposit information

- Get replacement Medicare or Social Security cards

- Get a replacement SSA-1099 for tax reporting

- Get an official benefit verification statement to prove your income, for example to loan officers or public benefits officials

- Review your earnings record and benefit payments

- Report your earnings if getting disability payments

In short, everyone should have a My Social Security account to keep tabs on their status with SSA.
And when you do, say goodbye to the old mailed Statements. They end when you have the online account.

SOCIAL SECURITY CALCULATORS

Social Security offers both online and downloadable calculators to help you learn where you stand and plot your course toward retirement.

Retirement Estimator

This online program knows your past earnings, and, unlike the Social Security Statement, you can specify your future earnings and retirement date. You can use it if you have enough work credits to be eligible and haven't applied for Social Security.

Go to www.ssa.gov/retire/estimator.html. Then click the "Estimate Your Retirement Benefits" button.

Once you fill in your request, you'll get an estimate based on actual past earnings and the future earnings you post.

To model additional scenarios, click the "Add a New Estimate" button. You can run "what-if" scenarios by changing your stop-work age and future earnings estimates. You can view these estimates online or print them out for your records.

The Estimator cannot take into account railroad pensions, WEP, or GPO. Also, it can only estimate retirement benefits, not survivor or disability benefits. If WEP or GPO applies to you, see the next two sections, "AnyPia calculator" and "More calculators."

Find detailed instructions on using the Estimator at www.ssa.gov/pubs/10511.html. There's additional background on the Estimator at www.ssa.gov/pubs/10510.html.

Quick Calculator

If you don't yet have 40 Work Credits (see page 35), the Retirement Estimator won't work. But you can get a quick online estimate at www.socialsecurity.gov/planners/benefitcalculators.htm by clicking on "Quick Calculator." You simply input your date of birth, this year's earnings, and your expected retirement date. The output is a rough estimate of your retirement, disability, and survivor benefits.

The calculator simply projects your current earnings backwards and forwards to perform the estimate. That would be accurate only if you've had steady earnings for your whole life at today's level. But you can fine-tune the earnings amounts.

From the estimate page, click on "See the earnings we used" to input your actual earnings rather than the projected amounts. The resulting estimate will be closer to your actual future benefits.

You can find your actual past earnings from any previous Social Security Statement you saved, from your tax records like W-2s, or by calling Social Security at (800) SSA-1213 and requesting your earnings record.

AnyPIA calculator

For even more forecasting ability, download the AnyPIA calculator. Go to www.ssa.gov/planners/benefitcalculators.htm and click on "Detailed Calculator." If you're a Mac user, note the link to the Mac version.

Once downloaded, AnyPIA can compute retirement, disability, or survivor benefits for any earnings history and birthdate you input. It also can perform WEP calculations (see page 52). Furthermore, it provides the numbers behind these calculations in detail. AnyPIA was used to generate the sample computation in Appendix A. In short, it's the ultimate wonky calculator.

The only caveat is that the user interface is, well, kludgy. It helps if you have a background in Social Security computations.

More calculators

Finally, you'll find a variety of additional charts and calculators at www.ssa.gov/planners/benefitcalculators.htm. Included are calculators for earnings limits while you get Social Security, payments at various retirement ages, WEP and GPO, and more.

Paper and pencil

If you are at least 62 and prefer the time-tested tools of paper and pencil, there are manual forms you can use to calculate your benefit. Go to www.ssa.gov/pubs/index.html, and enter "How It Is Figured" in the search box. Click on "PDF" and select the proper birth year in the drop-down box. You'll get a form and instructions to manually compute your benefit. It's a great way to get a "behind-the-scenes" feel for how benefits are computed. Sharpen your pencil and have a go.

RETIREMENT PLANNING WITH ONLINE CALCULATORS

The SSA calculators are valuable planning tools. With them, you will know what your Social Security income will be in retirement. In addition, if you have a pension plan and a pension estimate, you can quickly calculate your total income in retirement. At that point, it will be easy to figure out what you will need from savings to support your retirement lifestyle.

These tools are even more powerful if you request two (or three, or more) estimates. You can use multiple estimates to compare several different retirement options such as early vs. late retirement, or part-time vs. full-time work until retirement. This section suggests some uses of the online calculators. Your imagination can add to the uses here.

Will I draw on my own record or my spouse's?

Getting the answer from SSA is easy—just get an online estimate for yourself, and have your spouse do the same. With the estimates in hand, check to see if your own benefit is less than the payment you could get as a spouse (32.5% to 50% of your spouse's full retirement benefit, as shown in Figure 3.2, page 67).

If you are widowed, divorced, or separated, call Social Security (1-800-SSA-1213) and explain that you might be eligible on your spouse's record and need an estimate. In many cases, the SSA representative can give you an estimate over the phone.

There is a related question: *Should I keep working to secure a higher benefit on **my own** record? Or am I going to draw a **spouse** payment anyway?*

To determine where you stand, try this:

- Get one estimate showing little or no future work.

- Get another estimate showing your current wages continuing.

Reviewing the estimates, see if stopping work keeps your benefit below what you would receive as a spouse. Also, see if continuing work boosts your payment above what you would receive as a spouse. Consider whether postponing your own payment to age 70 would make a difference. If your spousal payment will always exceed your own payment, continuing to work will not raise your Social Security. Together with other financial factors (pension, savings, need for current income, etc.) and your personal preferences, this information can help you decide whether to continue working.

When should I retire?

This is one of the most frequently asked questions. A variation of the question is *"I want to retire early, at age 58 (or 55, or 60), but how much will my Social Security be reduced because of early retirement?"*

The SSA calculators can give you the answer:

- Get one estimate assuming a late retirement date, say age 66.

- Get a second estimate assuming an early retirement date, say age 58.

With the estimates in hand, compare the Social Security amounts. How big is your "penalty" for early retirement? Can your personal finances afford the difference? These considerations will help you determine your best retirement date, especially if you consult with a financial planner.

What about part-time, "phased" retirement?

Phased retirement is becoming a very attractive option for many. In phased retirement, you reduce your work to part-time to "ease into" retirement during your last few years at work, thus splitting the difference between working steadily to retirement age and retiring early. A similar strategy is to change work to something that pays less but you love more. The question then becomes, "How much will my Social Security be reduced because of lower earnings in the last few years before retirement?"

To answer this, get two estimates:

- On one, show your projected retirement age and show your *current full-time earnings* as your future earnings.

- On the other, show the same retirement date, but make your future earnings about half (or 1/3, or 2/3, etc.) of your current earnings.

Reviewing the estimates, you can quickly compare your future Social Security payments under each option.

Don't overlook more exotic strategies like Voluntary Suspension or Spousal-Only payments, if you qualify. See Chapter 10, "Maximizing Your Social Security."

To summarize:

- The My Social Security account and the online calculators are informative, flexible tools.

- They provide personalized information about your projected Social Security payments.

- By requesting multiple estimates, you can answer "what if" questions about many retirement options.

In the next chapter, we will get to the nuts-and-bolts level of dealing with SSA: How to file your claim.

FOR MORE INFORMATION...

SSA "Benefits Planner":
www.ssa.gov/planners/

"Plan For Your Retirement"
www.ssa.gov/planners/retire/index.html

Chapter Endnotes
1.   https://www.ssa.gov/myaccount/statement.html

FILING YOUR CLAIM

 Claiming in a Nutshell

- You must file a claim to get most Social Security or Medicare benefits.

- You can file 3 months early for most benefits.

- In some cases, your claim can be retroactive, generating back payments.

- You can file in person, by phone, or online.

- The appeals process lets you get a new decision on your claim if you are not satisfied.

GENERAL INFORMATION ON FILING YOUR CLAIM

The big day has finally come. You are ready to start drawing your Social Security payments or enrolling in Medicare. Now—how to apply?

This chapter examines how to file your Social Security or Medicare application. You will learn when and how to claim your benefits, what documentation may be needed, and what to expect when talking with a Social Security representative.

The purpose of the claims process is two-part: to make sure you meet the requirements for payments, and to establish a computer record which will pay you properly.

Your role in filing your claim

Your role in filing your claim is to initiate the claim, to provide accurate information to SSA, and to provide proper documentation, each in a timely manner.

If you start the claim on time, the other tasks are not difficult since a Social Security representative will be providing verbal or written instructions or requests every step of the way. For the typical retirement claim, filing for Social Security is easier than renewing your driver's license. A more involved claim, especially a disability claim, will be more difficult.

The process can be easier than you think for two reasons:

- First, by reading this book, you are an informed claimant with knowledge of SSA policies and practices. You understand your rights and benefits better than the average claimant, and can confidently navigate the claims process.

- Second, the typical Social Security representative will handle your claim with expertise and sensitivity. The staff at SSA consistently receives top ratings in surveys of public service delivery.

The role of your Social Security representative

Your Social Security representative has a unique role. She is the liaison between you and the government, and acts as a translator and "go-between." She works for SSA and must represent the agency to you. On the other hand, she must also represent your interests in your claim to the government. Her job is very different from the old stereotype of government workers "out to get you."

Her many roles include:

- Assisting you to file your claim,

- Helping you obtain necessary documentation,

- Explaining the program so you know where you stand,

- Explaining your options and the short-term and long-term effects of each decision you make,

- Processing your claim as efficiently as possible, and

- *Paying you as much as possible.*

That last line is correct. If a representative fails to explore every possible avenue or option that could result in a higher payment for you, she hasn't done her job. She could be charged with an error that could lead to a low evaluation or worse.

The point is, your representative is trained in the technicalities of SSA. Her job is to pay you the proper amount at the proper time—not too much or too little, and not too early or too late.

Are Social Security representatives perfect? Of course not. They're human, have good days and bad, and make inadvertent mistakes. But because of the background you have gained from this book, you will be in a better position to spot errors before they become problems.

How And When To Contact SSA

When to file your claim

Contact Social Security *early* to file your claim. The following guidelines will give you a good idea of when to contact SSA:

- For a *retirement or Medicare* claim or a claim for *family benefits,* file three months before you want your payments or eligibility to begin. That would be three months before your retirement date, your 62nd birthday, your 65th birthday, your Full Retirement Age, or other key date as appropriate.

   Sam wants his retirement payment to begin in April. He could contact SSA as early as January to start the claim.

   Marsha will turn 62 in August. She wants to file for spouse benefits as early as possible. She should contact SSA in May.

- For a *survivor* claim, file in the month of death if you are immediately eligible, or within 6 months to avoid loss of benefits. For later eligibility (for example, as you approach age 60 or your retirement date), follow the suggestions under retirement claims in the paragraph immediately above.

   Harold died in November at age 28. His widow Hannah needed to contact Social Security to file for survivor benefits for herself and the children. Her brother called SSA in November to start the claims process.

   Fran will turn 60 in June. She can apply for her widow's payment in March.

- For a *disability* claim, contact SSA as soon as possible after the onset of disability—definitely within 18 months. Your onset is generally the date your impairment makes you unable to work.

   Sheila stopped work due to disability on January 10. She should apply as soon as possible for Social Security—definitely within 18 months to avoid a loss of benefits.

The reason for filing as soon as possible is to avoid any loss of benefits. One of the changes in the 1983 overhaul of Social Security was to severely limit retroactivity of claims.[1] Many claims are now effective with the month of filing, so if you file late, you are losing valuable payments. Retirement claims are filed early to allow time for normal processing (usually only a few days) and for unforeseen delays such as problems obtaining proof of your age.

Three ways to file

There are three different ways to file your claim:

1. *In the office.* You can visit any Social Security office to file your claim in person.

2. *By phone.* You can call SSA and file over the phone, then complete the claim by mail.

3. *Online.* You can complete an online application, then complete the claim by mail.

1. Filing in the SSA office

You can file your claim the old-fashioned way, face-to-face in an SSA office. It can be the best bet for a complex claim like Disabled Adult Child (page 117). In-office is the least popular and most inconvenient way to file. However, a few steps will streamline the process:

- *Find your local office.* There are SSA offices in or near most towns and cities. Offices are assigned to geographic areas by zip code. Go to www.ssa.gov/locator/ and input your zip code. Or call (800) SSA-1213 and ask for your office location. See the tips in the next section to avoid a long wait on SSA's phone line.

- *Make an appointment.* You don't need an appointment to file, but it will shorten your wait at the office and smooth your visit. Call the 800 line (above) a month or two before you want to file. Don't be surprised if you're offered a telephone application instead, right on the spot. See below, "Filing by phone," to see if you'd prefer the phone route.

- *Take your proofs.* For a typical retirement claim, you'll usually need proof of age, possibly your latest W-2, and possibly your DD-214 military discharge form, if applicable. Don't delay filing just to locate proofs. For more on proofs, see "Documenting your claim" below.

- *Be patient.* You might have a wait, so a magazine or other pastime could be helpful.

Once at the office, things should go smoothly. A retirement application usually takes less than 20 minutes and you'll be on your way. A disability claim takes about an hour. For details, see "The Claims Process, Step By Step" below.

2. Filing by phone

Your entire claim can be completed over the phone. To start the application process, call Social Security at their national toll-free number: **1-800-SSA-1213**.

The good news is that you can call any time of day from anywhere in the country. The bad news is that when you do, you'll likely have to wait in line. Here are the details and some strategies for cutting the wait.

The SSA phone lines are staffed from 7 AM to 7 PM every workday, no matter what time zone you call from. To avoid the backups, try these ideas:

- Avoid the busy hours of 10 AM to 3 PM. Call during non-core hours, e.g. at breakfast or dinner time.

- Call at night and leave a message. SSA is committed to call-backs the next business day.

- Avoid calling at the beginning of the month. Many payments are delivered on the first of the month (SSI payments) or the third (regular Social Security payments). Any delivery problems turn into phone calls to SSA during the first week of the month.

You'll find that by using these strategies, you will usually reach an SSA representative quickly. Still, it's a good idea to have a magazine or other pastime handy when you call, just in case of delay.

Once you're connected, tell the representative that you want to file a claim.

A typical retirement claim takes under 20 minutes to complete on the phone. Disability can take an hour. For details, see "The Claims Process, Step By Step" below.

The rest of the application, including proofs, will be handled by mail.

THE INSIDE STORY

Who am I talking to?

When you call Social Security's toll-free number, you reach a *Service Representative* (called an "SR" inside the agency) or more specifically a *TeleService Representative* ("TSR"—an SR specializing in telephone calls).

SRs and TSRs are trained to provide a variety of front-line client services, such as answering general inquiries and scheduling appointments. They are also experts on Medicare and at solving problems with existing Social Security payments. TSRs work in TeleService Centers, collectively handling thousands of calls per day. SRs work in Social Security field offices, meeting face-to-face with hundreds of visitors per day.

The person who takes and processes your claim is called a *Claims Representative* (or "CR"). CRs also provide front-line client services, but of a more complex and technical nature. Examples include processing claims, writing appeals determinations, and troubleshooting stubborn computer problems.

The CR may have more in-depth training than the SR and rises to a higher pay grade, but make no mistake: when it comes to solving Medicare problems or certain Social Security issues, a CR will ask an SR for expert help.

---

3. Filing online

Filing online is the most popular way to apply. Most retirement claims are filed online.[2] One benefit to online filing is that you can do it quickly and easily any time it's convenient for you. You also can save a partially-completed application and finish it later.

Online filing is available during these hours (Eastern Time):[3]

Monday-Friday:	5 AM until 1 AM ET
Saturday:	5 AM until 11 PM ET
Sunday:	8 AM until 11:30 PM ET
Federal Holidays:	Same hours as the day of the week the holiday occurs

To start, go to www.ssa.gov/forms/apply-for-benefits.html and click on the type of claim you'd like to file. Then follow the on-screen instructions. Note that you cannot file a survivor's claim online.

For guidance, there are general instructions at www.ssa.gov/benefits/retirement/ and www.ssa.gov/pubs/EN-05-10523.pdf, with more information nearby on each webpage.

Once you complete the online application, the rest of your claim will be handled by phone and mail.

THE CLAIMS PROCESS, STEP BY STEP

The process of filing your application will follow certain steps. Let's walk through the typical retirement phone application.

Your initial call to Social Security

The day you've been waiting for has arrived. It is three months before your scheduled retirement date, so you pick up the phone to call SSA's toll-free number, (800) SSA-1213. Because you follow the calling guidelines above (under "Filing by phone"), you reach a Service Representative in a few minutes. You tell him that you want to file for retirement benefits.

He asks whether you would rather go into a Social Security office or file the entire application by phone. Like 80% of people filing non-internet claims, you decide to skip the trip and ask for a phone interview. You might be routed directly to a teleclaims unit. More likely, the representative gets your contact information, makes an appointment for the claims interview, and says that a Claims Representative will call you at that time.

You can skip this step if you file online.

The claims interview

At the appointed time, your Claims Representative calls you, ready to complete your retirement application. She starts by introducing herself. Then she checks your identifying information and asks some general background questions about your work and planned retirement. Once this preliminary information is clear, your Claims Representative starts completing your application.

The application is a series of questions about you, including:

- *Identification*—your name and Social Security number, along with any other names or numbers you may have used. Your name and Social Security number are needed to confirm your identity and to associate your SSA records properly.

- *Age*—your date of birth, place of birth, and whether there is a civil or religious record of your birth made at an early age. These questions provide information about your age and how to prove it.

- *Work history*—where you worked this year and last, how much you earned, and an estimate of future earnings if you continue working. Your recent work will be manually added to your earnings record and may increase your payment. Current earnings, if any, will also be evaluated to see whether they will reduce your Social Security payments.

- *Special factors*—information about railroad work, Civil Service employment, foreign work, military service, and any pensions related to such work. Your railroad or government work history allows SSA to take such work into account in computing your payment, whether the effect is to limit your payment or increase it.

- *Family data*—your family members, including your current and former spouses and your children, if any. These questions explore whether someone might be paid on your work record, or whether you might be paid on someone else's record.

- *Payment information*—where you would like your payments sent. SSA no longer issues paper checks. The default is direct deposit into your bank or credit union. If you have no bank account, your benefits can be loaded onto a prepaid Direct Express Debit MasterCard. For details on Direct Express, see www.usdirectexpress.com/. SSA has switched to direct deposit and Direct Express because of the much lower loss and error rates, and to save millions in printing, postage, and processing lost checks.[4]

- *Signature*—in signing, you certify that you have told the truth, and that you will report any changes and return any incorrect payments. If you file online, checking the electronic signature block suffices. No physical signature is required.

Completion of your retirement application will typically take 20 minutes or so. As mentioned above, more complex applications—survivor or disability claims or complex retirement claims—will take longer.

If you file online, you'll input all this information yourself, with on-screen instructions. You'll get an application number for follow-up and a receipt for your claim. There's a great preview of the online retirement process at www.ssa.gov/pubs/EN-05-10523.pdf.

Documenting your claim

After the phone application is completed, your Claims Representative will send a copy of the application to you for your records. She will also ask for certain documentation, or "proofs," of facts on the application.

The documents you supply should always be original documents, not photocopies of originals. *Certified copies*, identified by the stamp, seal, or signature of the official record-keeper, are always acceptable. Notarizing is not needed.

Here are some kinds of documentation that might be requested:

- **Proof of age.** Proof of age is usually required for retirement claims and most other Social Security business, since every computation is based on your exact age. Preferred proof is a civil or religious record of birth made before you were age 5 (such as your birth certificate or baptismal certificate). If one of these is at all available, SSA will require it. Social Security representatives in any office and at the toll-free phone service can help you obtain your birth certificate from any state and from most foreign countries. If such proof is absolutely unavailable, secondary proofs such as census records, U.S. entry records, school records, etc. will be accepted. Your Claims Representative will help you establish your age in the simplest acceptable way, and help you obtain the documentation. If SSA has already seen proof of your age and posted it to their computer, you won't have to re-submit it.

- **Last year's wages.** You may be asked to prove your recent earnings with last year's W-2 (for employees) or tax return (for self-employed individuals). Manually posting these earnings to your earnings record could increase your payment if last year has not yet been posted automatically. (If you are unable to provide this proof, your payments will automatically be recomputed anyway, when your earnings record is updated every year; see "AERO" on page 211.)

- **Military service.** If it will increase your payments, you will be asked to prove your 1951-1967 military service (see page 219). Your DD-214 discharge form is the usual documentation.

- **Marriage.** If you will draw benefits on a former spouse's record, you will need to prove you were married for at least ten years. Your marriage certificate and divorce decree are the usual proofs requested. Spouses filing together don't generally need to prove their marriage.

- **Death.** If you are applying for survivor benefits, you may have to supply the death certificate of the worker.

- **Other public pensions.** If your public-employment or military pension affects your payments, you may be asked to provide detailed award letters from the issuing agency, so that their exact effects can be assessed.

Other proofs are sometimes needed, but the ones described above are the most common.

Documentation requirements are usually modest. When you apply for retirement, you might be asked for just your birth certificate and *perhaps* last year's W-2.

Your Claims Representative will request that you mail in the required proofs. But what if you don't want to send your original documents away in the mail?

Your documents will be returned to you. It's extremely rare to lose a document in the mail. Still, rather than risk a loss, you can take the proofs to your local Social Security office in person—delivering valuable papers is a very common reason for visiting an office. In that case, the receptionist will probably move you to the head of the line, so you can submit your papers. It can help if you call ahead for an appointment; your Claims Representative's telephone number is included with the request for documentation.

What is your Claims Representative doing when she takes your documents for a few minutes? She is *photocopying them,* after she told you not to do so!

 THE INSIDE STORY

Applicant, Claimant, Beneficiary, Appellant

Depending on your precise status with Social Security, staffers will refer to you in different terms.

Before you file a claim for Social Security, you are called a *Number Holder*. This means that you are the person who was issued your Social Security number.

When you file a claim, you are referred to as a *claimant.*

When the claim is approved, you become a *beneficiary* (or "bene," pronounced "bennie," for short).

If you file an appeal, you are called an *appellant.*

In some cases, the person filing the claim is not the claimant. For example, you may file and sign a claim for your minor child, who legally cannot sign his own claim. In that case, your child is the *claimant* and you are called the *applicant.*

Actually, she is examining your original document to be sure it is authentic (perhaps inspecting with ultraviolet light, for example), and she must certify the photocopy by affirming that she examined the original and that the copy matches the original. In other words, she is *creating a certified copy* of your original.

After examination, your original documents will be returned to you either in person or by mail.

Paying your claim

There is only one step remaining in your claims process: posting a payment decision to your computer record. The computer record was established by your Service Representative back when you first called about applying for payments. It has been expanded as you answered the application questions and supplied the necessary documentation. Now your Claims Representative examines the entire claim—your application, documents, and earnings record—and decides whether you meet all "eligibility factors" required for payment.

If you do meet all requirements, an allowance is posted to your computer record and your first payment is triggered. You will receive an *award letter* describing when and how much you will be paid, including any back pay due. (You'll get to know these computer-generated Social Security letters well. They're sometimes a bit indecipherable, but they mean well. Save them all.)

Payments will continue at the same level every month until a change is posted. For example, you might call in to change your address or report a new job; then the new facts would be posted to the computer and appropriate changes made in your payment. In addition, the computer will *automatically* detect certain changes that could affect your payments. For example, an annual cost-of-living-adjustment (COLA) could be posted to all Social Security records, increasing your payment. Or new earnings could be detected on your earnings record, which could increase or decrease your payment.

If (1) your claim shows that you do not meet all requirements for payment, or (2) *if it fails to show either way that you do or do not meet the requirements,* your claim must be denied. An example of the first would be a birth certificate that shows you are not yet old enough for retirement payments. An example of the second would be no proof of age in file. In other words, the burden of proof of eligibility is yours.

If your claim is denied for any reason, you will be sent a *denial letter* explaining why the claim was denied. The denial letter also informs you that you have the right to file an *appeal* of the denial. The appeals process is described in the next section.

THE APPEALS PROCESS, STEP BY STEP

Sheila's disability claim has been denied. The letter explaining the denial says there is no medical evidence to establish her disability.

Sheila believes this denial is wrong. Where does she turn to reverse the denial?

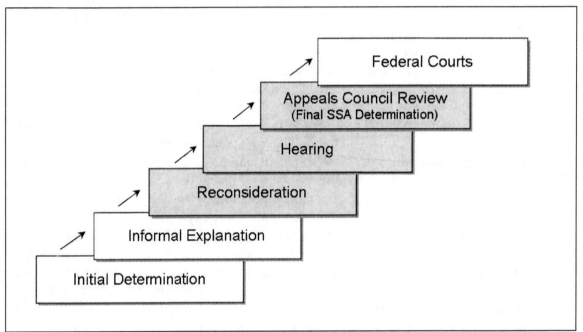

Figure 8.1. The appeals "ladder." Shaded boxes are part of the formal administrative appeals process.[5]

Social Security is dedicated to making decisions and payments that are fair, timely, and accurate. But to err is human, so mistakes happen.

The appeals process recognizes the possibility of errors and offers a way to correct them as quickly and inexpensively as possible. The process is built like a ladder, with lower levels of appeal to correct simple errors, and higher, more complex levels of appeal available if needed (see Figure 8.1).

In a nutshell, the idea behind the appeals process is that if you are dissatisfied with a decision that SSA makes, you can request a new decision by a different person or persons.

The adverse initial determination

The seed of the appeals process is the *adverse initial determination.* This is the "bad news" you get from Social Security which sparks your disagreement. An *initial determination* is a decision about your payments which is subject to the appeals process. An *adverse* initial determination is one which in some way harms you or is unfavorable to you.

Some examples of initial determinations which could be adverse:[6]

- Entitlement or continuing entitlement to benefits. Your claim might be denied, or your continuing payments stopped.

- The amount you are paid. Your payments could be reduced.

- Revision of your earnings record. Posted earnings could be reduced or deleted.

- Deductions from your benefits because of work. Your payments could be reduced because you returned to work.

- Termination of your benefits. Your payments could be stopped.

- Whether your impairment meets the definition of disability. Your disability claim could be denied because your impairment is not severe enough.

- Adjustment or recovery of an overpayment you received. Your payments may be stopped because you were previously paid too much.

In cases like these, you may initiate an appeal to get a new determination on the issue.

However, there are Social Security decisions which are *not* initial determinations and are *not* subject to the appeals process. Some examples:[7]

- Withholding part of your monthly payment to recover an overpayment you received. SSA can reduce your payments if previous payments were too high. SSA has the final decision on how much to withhold.

- Extending or not extending the time to file a report of earnings. SSA's deadlines are firm.

- The amount of fee payable to an attorney representing you before SSA. By law, only SSA can determine the attorney's fee.

- Disqualifying a person from representing you before SSA. SSA may decide that your chosen representative is not capable of doing so.

In decisions like these, there is no appeal possible. SSA's decision is final.

When SSA makes an initial determination, you are notified in writing. The notice tells you about the determination and informs you of your *appeal rights*. The determination becomes *final* 60 days after you receive the notice (assumed to be 5 days after the notice date). Once a determination is final, you cannot appeal it, although Social Security will "reopen" the decision if a mistake is discovered within a specified time, usually within a year.

In other words, if you are dissatisfied with a decision made by Social Security, you have 60 days to request a formal appeal. After that, it is too late.

When you are dissatisfied: the first step

The first step in handling an adverse determination is to simply contact Social Security and ask for an explanation. Call the toll-free number (1-800-SSA-1213) or visit the office and say you got a letter that you need explained. Perhaps you will be satisfied by the explanation, or perhaps your Social Security representative will readily see the mistake and correct it on the spot.

At this stage, a confrontational attitude is unproductive. Whether the problem is a lack of understanding, a simple error, or a major disagreement between you and SSA, there are procedures to handle it. By *working with* your SSA representative, you may solve the problem immediately without escalating it unnecessarily.

Sheila calls SSA to ask about the denial of her disability claim. She learns that the decision was proper because Dr. Smith, her cardiologist, did not supply two important test results.

No one suggests that you relinquish your rights. If you are not satisfied by this first step of explanation and discussion, you should request an appeal. At this point, the appeal is called a *reconsideration*.

The reconsideration level

The first level of appeal is called a *reconsideration* (or "recon" in SSA-speak).[8] It reviews only *initial determinations* with which you are dissatisfied.

Exception: if the issue is the waiver of an overpayment or cessation of your disability, the first level of appeal is a *hearing*, described below.

A reconsideration is a new decision on your case made by a new person. You will have an opportunity to review your file and present new evidence or point out important features of evidence already submitted.

Issues addressed by the reconsideration are not limited to the point of disagreement. Occasionally, a reconsideration opens a whole new can of worms—it could reveal another error in your case which must then be corrected. In rare occasions, you may win a higher payment on the point of disagreement, but end up with a lower overall payment because of another adjustment.

You must request the reconsideration *in writing*. Initiating the request is as simple as calling SSA and asking for the form—a one-page form requesting the new decision with space for you to explain the disagreement. Remember, the request must be *signed and submitted to* SSA within 60 days of the initial determination, or it is too late (a postmark before the deadline is acceptable).

Exception: If the issue is a medical denial of a disability claim, you may file an *iAppeal,* an online alternative to the written request for reconsideration. Start your iAppeal at https://secure.ssa.gov/iApplsRe/start.

The time frame for a reconsideration, from request to decision, is usually between one week and several months.

Sheila files for a reconsideration and makes sure Dr. Smith provides the needed tests. A new decision is made by a different evaluation team, taking the new information into account.

When all evidence is in, the new decision-maker writes a fresh determination on your case. You will receive written notice of the new decision. The *reconsidered determination* becomes final 60 days after the date of the notice (plus five days for mail time).

If you are still not satisfied with the decision, you or your appointed representative can request a *hearing* on the decision. Remember, you must request the hearing within 60 days of the date of the reconsideration decision. This keeps your appeal open and raises it to the next level.

The hearing level

Sheila's reconsideration decision arrives. It says that her claim must be denied even though the new test results were considered. What is Sheila's next step?

The second level of appeal is called a *hearing.*[9]

Exception: if a decision has been rendered at the reconsideration level or above, and you wish to challenge the constitutionality of the law governing the decision, you may request the *Expedited Appeals Process* (EAP). If SSA agrees, under the EAP you would skip any further SSA administrative appeals and go straight to federal court, described below.

You must request a hearing *in writing* within 60 days of the reconsidered determination. Like a reconsideration, the paperwork is a one-page form requesting the hearing with space to state your disagreement. (If the issue is a medical denial of a disability claim, you will be offered an online *iAppeal,* described above under "Reconsideration.")

The hearing is conducted almost like a legal proceeding, although it is less formal. The typical site is a hearing room in a federal courthouse, or by video connection. Presiding is an Administrative Law Judge (ALJ) assigned to your case.

The ALJ is not a "regular" judge; he or she works for SSA and makes decisions only on Social Security cases. The ALJ's background is impressive: a minimum of 7 years' experience as a trial lawyer, plus years of specialized training in Social Security law and in making medical determinations.[10]

The judge will thoroughly review your case file and consider any additional evidence you wish to present. During the hearing, she may ask you questions about your side of the story. An expert may attend to offer expert opinion. For instance, a vocational expert might attend, to talk about possible jobs you could hold despite your impairment. You will also have a chance to have witnesses support your side of the story.

*Sheila's impairment is a combination of three impairments: heart disease, breathing difficulty, and arthritis. She points out to the judge that although no **one** of the impairments would be disabling by itself, in combination they are disabling.*

The judge asks Sheila for examples of her work limitations and consults with a vocational expert about Sheila's abilities and limitations.

After the hearing, the judge will write a determination on your case. It may be partly or wholly favorable to you, or it may be adverse. Another course is that the judge can send the case back to a lower level for a new decision because the earlier procedure was flawed.

The time frame for a hearing, from request to decision, is averaging 600 days.[11]

The ALJ writes a decision favorable to Sheila, allowing her claim of disability. Sheila's award letter arrives one month after the hearing date. Because she filed timely requests for the reconsideration and hearing, her claim has been considered active since her first application date. She is awarded disability payments with full back payments.

The hearing decision becomes final 60 days after you receive the written notice, unless you appeal to the next higher level, the Appeals Council.

Appeals Council Review

If you disagree with the hearing determination, you may request a review by the Appeals Council.[12] This is a panel of three ALJs near Washington, D.C. who review hearing decisions. There is no provision for your attending the review, but you can provide evidence in writing. Time frame from request to decision is months to years.

The only possible issue at "AC Review" is whether the hearing followed proper procedures.

If a flaw is found, the AC will send the case back to the hearing judge for further consideration. The hearing judge might then find in your favor, but occasionally, the procedural flaw is corrected, and the decision remains adverse to you.

If the AC upholds the hearing decision, it becomes the *final* decision of the Social Security Administration. At this point, the *administrative* appeals process is exhausted. However, you can still appeal the decision outside the administrative process, by using the court system.

Suing in Federal court

Once all administrative avenues of appeal have been completed, you can still bring civil suit against the Social Security Administration in federal district court.[13]

Your suit must be filed within 60 days from the date you receive notice of the Appeals Council decision. The court may decide on your case or "remand" (return) the case to Social Security for further development.

If you are dissatisfied with the district court decision, you could appeal to higher courts like the Appellate Court and, eventually, the Supreme Court.

Interestingly, many of the changes in Social Security law and practices come not from the Administration or Congress, but from the court system. An example was a 1992 district court decision that SSA needed to simplify the procedure for workers to correct erroneous earnings records. SSA agreed to simplify evidence requirements and improve communication links with IRS, the source of earnings information.

The point is, don't believe the old saw that "you can't fight city hall." You can, and you could win, leading to better conditions for all.

Let's move now from the "ladder of appeal" to a question raised by many Social Security claimants: should a representative handle the appeal and other Social Security business?

Should an attorney handle my claim or appeal?

You are welcome to have a friend, family member, or professional representative (such as an attorney) handle any Social Security business you may have, including your appeal. The representative you appoint must be an individual, not a corporation or other organization, and must be qualified to represent you.[14]

The decision to appoint a representative is a personal one. Social Security is not in the business of "putting one over" on you. SSA employees normally extend every courtesy to help you make proper choices, and they should make fair decisions on your case. However, Social Security can be intimidating, especially at the appeals level. At the very least, I would recommend that you have a friend or family member accompany you to a hearing or other conference. Many appellants have told me that having a friend along helps calm jittery nerves on the day of the hearing.

Hiring a professional representative can be a reasonable option to consider, depending on the complexity of the case and your ability to present your side clearly and convincingly. It's especially reasonable at the hearing level and above. If you are not represented, the ALJ will go the extra mile to understand your situation and make a fair decision, but having representation puts a knowledgeable professional on your side.

Any time you are dealing with the federal courts, it is strongly advisable to have legal representation.

If you choose to appoint a representative, look for someone who has experience handling Social Security appeals. In many cities, retired ALJs or SSA attorneys have started private practices which specialize in SSA appeals. There are also other attorneys who specialize in Social Security. If fees are a problem, consider getting free or low-cost legal help from your local Legal Aid Society; Social Security is a familiar part of their practice. A call to your local bar association should produce several possible representatives. Or do a computer search for "Social Security attorneys" in your area.

Speaking of fees, your representative cannot charge a fee without written approval from SSA. In many cases, a professional representative will serve in return for a portion of any back pay you receive from a favorable decision. SSA limits such fees to 25% of the back payment, and commonly arranges direct payment for the representative by withholding a portion of your back payment.

To summarize:

- You should file your Social Security claim as early as possible—up to three months before your payments should begin.

- You can file in person, by phone, or online.

- You will be asked to provide certain documents to establish your eligibility.

- The appeals process is a mechanism for reconsidering decisions and correcting errors. You have 60 days to appeal a decision.

- At your option, you may appoint a representative to handle your Social Security business, including an appeal.

FOR MORE INFORMATION...

"Online Services From www.socialsecurity.gov"
www.ssa.gov/pubs/EN-05-10032.pdf

"How To Apply Online For Retirement Benefits" with screen shots
www.ssa.gov/pubs/EN-05-10523.pdf

"How to Apply Online For Just Medicare"
www.ssa.gov/benefits/medicare and
www.ssa.gov/planners/retire/justmedicare.html

"How To Apply Online For Medicare Only" with screen shots
www.ssa.gov/pubs/EN-05-10531.pdf

"The Appeals Process"
www.ssa.gov/pubs/EN-05-10041.pdf

"Your Right To Question The Decision Made On Your Claim"
www.ssa.gov/pubs/EN-05-10058.pdf

"Your Right To Representation"
www.ssa.gov/pubs/EN-05-10075.pdf

Chapter Endnotes
1. https://www.socialsecurity.gov/OP_Home/handbook/handbook.15/handbook-1513.html
2. https://www.socialsecurity.gov/open/data/fy12-onward-rib-filed-via-internet.xlsx
3. https://www.ssa.gov/onlineservices/current.htm
4. See https://www.ssa.gov/deposit/ and related links
5. https://www.socialsecurity.gov/pubs/EN-05-10041.pdf
6. https://www.socialsecurity.gov/OP_Home/handbook/handbook.20/handbook-2002.html
7. https://www.socialsecurity.gov/OP_Home/handbook/handbook.20/handbook-2003.html
8. https://www.socialsecurity.gov/OP_Home/handbook/handbook.20/handbook-2005.html
9. https://www.socialsecurity.gov/OP_Home/handbook/handbook.20/handbook-2006.html, ff., and https://www.socialsecurity.gov/appeals/hearing_process.html with related links
10. https://www.opm.gov/policy-data-oversight/classification-qualifications/general-schedule-qualification-standards/specialty-areas/administrative-law-judge-positions/
11. https://www.ssa.gov/appeals/index.html
12. https://www.socialsecurity.gov/OP_Home/handbook/handbook.20/handbook-2013.html, ff., and https://www.socialsecurity.gov/appeals/appeals_process.html with related links
13. https://www.socialsecurity.gov/appeals/court_process.html
14. https://www.socialsecurity.gov/OP_Home/handbook/handbook.20/handbook-2017.html and https://www.socialsecurity.gov/pubs/EN-05-10075.pdf

CHAPTER NINE

SHORT TOPICS

 Chapter in a Nutshell

- This chapter includes a variety of topics that could affect your payments, or simply satisfy your curiosity.

- Topics include working while getting Social Security, income tax on benefits, military service, living overseas, SSI, and more.

WORKING WHILE GETTING SOCIAL SECURITY

I want to pursue my dream of starting a small business in my retirement. My husband has his eye on his ideal part-time job for his retirement. Can a person work and still receive Social Security retirement payments?

The answer is a *qualified yes*.

There are four sets of rules for working while getting Social Security:

- Working while over Full Retirement Age (FRA, see page 47)

- Working while under FRA

- Working in the year you turn FRA

- Working while getting disability (not covered here; see page 119)

The earnings rules apply to everyone getting Social Security—retired workers, spouses, survivors, even children. (As mentioned, different rules apply to those getting disability.)

Working over FRA

This part is easy. There are no earnings limits or penalties while you are over FRA. You can work all you want and get full paychecks and full Social

Security payments. None of your earnings count against Social Security starting with the month you attain FRA.

Working under FRA

Social Security payments are intended to replace lost earnings. Therefore, SSA needs a way to measure the loss. The solution is an earnings limit which applies to anyone under FRA who works and receives Social Security retirement, family, or survivor payments. Applying the limit is called the *earnings test.*

The annual limit

An earnings limit is specified each year, and increases with inflation. In 2018, the earnings limit for those under FRA is $17,040 per year.

If your earnings are under that limit, your Social Security benefits are not reduced. You would get full paychecks and full Social Security payments.

For example, if you are 64 and getting Social Security, and you earn $14,000 this year, your monthly Social Security payment will not be reduced. In fact, the additional earnings, when posted to your earnings record, may increase the amount of your Social Security payment (see "AERO" on page 211.)

If you earn more than the annual earnings limit

Higher earnings may reduce, but not necessarily stop, your payments, according to a simple formula. $1 is deducted from your Social Security payments for every $2 you earn above the limit (one-half of your "excess earnings").

The amount deducted is called your "work deductions" for the year. Examples appear below.

The monthly limit

Mary wants to retire at 62 in July and then start her Social Security. But her earnings in the first 6 months exceed the annual earnings limit. Will her pre-retirement earnings decrease her Social Security after retirement?

For situations like this, a special monthly rule applies. Under this rule, you can receive a full Social Security payment for any month you are "retired," regardless of your yearly earnings. This rule applies only during your first year of Social Security.

To meet this requirement, your earnings in any particular month must be under the *monthly limit.* The monthly limit is always 1/12 of the annual limit, so in 2018, the limit is $1,420 per month.

Mary learns that if she retires on July 1, she will be eligible for Social Security in July through December—no matter what her earnings in the first half of the year were—because her earnings are under the monthly limit. Her eligibility month is July, with payments starting in August.

Returning to temporary work

Let's change the example a bit:

After Mary retires on July 1, her employer asks her to come back on a temporary basis. In September and October, she earns over the monthly limit, then her earnings drop back to zero.

Mary will be eligible for full Social Security in every month after June except September and October.

The monthly limit and self-employment

It is difficult to compute exact monthly earnings for self-employed individuals, so the monthly limit measures your *hours of work* rather than your earnings. There are two important thresholds:

- Working over 45 hours in a month is generally considered "substantial services" and bars your Social Security for that month.

- Working under 15 hours in a month is not considered substantial.

- Work between 15 and 45 hours is judged on the individual characteristics of your case.

If you perform professional work in your business, like marketing, bookkeeping, or providing professional services, only the 15-hour limit applies.

Applying the proper limit

In your first year of Social Security, SSA will compute your payments using both the annual limits and the monthly limits. You will be paid using whichever method is best for you.

Working in the year you turn FRA

A final set of rules applies in the year you turn FRA. In that year, much higher earnings limits apply, and they apply only to earnings in the *months before you attain FRA.* The annual limit in 2018 is $45,360, and the monthly limit is $3,780 per month.

In addition, a different, more generous formula applies: $1 is deducted from your Social Security payments for every *$3* you earn above the annual limit (one-third of your "excess earnings").

It boils down to this: You might be able to start your Social Security in January of the year you turn FRA, even if working, with little or no penalty.

Income that counts toward the earnings limit

There are only two types of income which count toward your limit while under FRA: gross wages from employment, or net earnings from self-employment. Included in your wages are bonuses, commissions, fees, vacation pay, cash tips of $20 or more a month, severance pay, and noncash compensation such as meals or living quarters.

Other income does not count. Non-work income like investment income, interest, Veterans or other government payments, rental income (unless that is your business activity), or an inheritance, will not affect your Social Security and you do not have to report them as income to SSA.

Basically, then, SSA is interested *if you return to work before FRA,* in either employment or self-employment. If you do return to work after you begin to receive Social Security benefits, you must promptly report such work to SSA. Remember these points:

- SSA counts total yearly earnings, including all wages and self-employment income.

- SSA counts gross wages, not take-home pay.

- SSA counts wages from a job even if you don't pay Social Security taxes.

- You will still have to pay Social Security taxes if they apply to your job. Your new wages will be credited to your earnings record and may increase your monthly Social Security payment. (See "AERO" on page 211.)

If you're self-employed

Special rules apply if you are self-employed or a corporate officer, and under FRA. SSA may investigate your work to see if your stated earnings accurately reflect the true worth of your work. Again, the aim is to determine if you are actually "retired."

For more information on self-employment, see the SSA publications listed on page 211.

Examples of work in retirement

Some examples will make these rules clearer.

Example 1: Age 63, earning $21,040 in 2018.

Earnings	$21,040
Less your limit (under FRA)	—17,040
Excess Earnings	$4,000
x 1/2	x 1/2
Deduction amount	= $2,000

Therefore, $2,000 will be withheld from this year's Social Security payments. You receive full paychecks minus taxes, and full Social Security payments minus the $2,000 deduction. (See below for how deductions are made.)

Example 2: Turning FRA, earning $70,000 in 2018, of which $48,690 is earned before the birthday month.

Earnings before birthday month	$48,690
Less your FRA limit	—45,360
Excess Earnings	$3,330
x 1/3	x 1/3
Deduction amount	= $1,110

Here, $1,110 will be withheld from this year's Social Security payments. Earnings in or after your birthday month will not count. You receive full paychecks minus taxes, and full Social Security payments minus the deduction.

Example 3: Age 68, earning $75,000 in 2018.

There is no limit for those FRA and above, so there is no reduction in Social Security payments. You receive full paychecks minus taxes, and full Social Security payments.

How deductions are made

Impact if the primary worker returns to work

If work deductions apply, some or all of your Social Security payments will be withheld. In Example 1 above, the $2,000 would have to be deducted from this year's Social Security payments. This is done by stopping your payments until the full $2,000 has been held back. If your monthly benefit is $1,200, your entire January and February payments would be withheld. You would receive full payments every month for the rest of the year.

In Example 2, you would have your first payment withheld, then receive full payments for the rest of the year.

Impact on family benefits

In addition to your own payment, any *spouse* or *child benefits* payable on your record can be reduced because of your work. Spreading out the deductions to these other payments will more quickly "pay off" your excess earnings.

There can be negative effects when your work causes an interruption in payments to your spouse and children. Be especially aware that deductions can be imposed on your children being raised by a former spouse. (An exception: your *former* spouse's payments will not be withheld because of your earnings. See page 64 for the reason.)

Impact if a family member works

If someone getting family benefits works, only that person's Social Security payments are affected. The same formulas shown above would apply, based on the age of the working family member.

Credit back for stopped payments: The ARF

If some of your Social Security payments are stopped *due to work,* you get a raise in your future payments. It's called the Adjustment to the Reduction Factor (ARF), and happens automatically when you reach FRA.

Here's how it works: Let's say your FRA is 66 and you start your Social Security at 62. You get a 75% payment because you're 48 months early; you expect 48 early payments. The 48 early months are called your *Reduction Factor.*

Now suppose you get a great job 8 months later, and you earn enough that all the rest of your Social Security payments are stopped, all the way to your FRA.

When you reach 66, SSA looks back and sees that you actually received only 8 early payments, not the 48 early payments expected. SSA will perform an

Adjustment to the Reduction Factor (ARF) and adjust your payments accordingly. Your Reduction Factor of 48 months is changed to 8 months, as if you filed only 8 months early. As a result, you'll get a raise from a 75% payment to a 95.6% payment. Basically, SSA adds about one-half percent to your payment for each month your payment was withheld.

The ARF is automatic. If you forfeited some payments because of work, all you have to do is survive to FRA to get the raise.

Another possible raise: The AERO

Working might increase your Social Security payments in another way.

When you work and pay Social Security taxes, the new earnings are posted to SSA's records. Now you have a new year of work that could change your 35-year earnings average (see page 41). SSA performs an "AERO" (Automatic Earnings Reappraisal Operation) to recompute your payment using the new earnings. If the new computation is advantageous, you get a raise.

As the name implies, it's all automatic. Around November, you get a letter saying your payment has been recomputed due to new earnings, and you get a tiny raise going forward, plus a lump sum to apply the raise back to the previous January.

You can work and draw Social Security at the same time

The bottom line is that you can work and draw Social Security at the same time. Too many people think that if they earn one dollar over their limit, all their Social Security payments will be immediately halted. But as you can see, you would have to earn quite a bit to completely stop your payment. If you are 64 and receiving $1,500 per month from SSA, you would have to earn $53,040 in 2018 to stop all 12 of your Social Security payments.

And anyone reaching their FRA, working or not, should consider filing, since there are no work penalties after your birthday.

More information on working while getting Social Security

"How Work Affects Your Benefits"
www.ssa.gov/pubs/EN-05-10069.pdf

"If You Are Self-Employed"
www.ssa.gov/pubs/EN-05-10022.pdf

INCOME TAX ON SOCIAL SECURITY BENEFITS

General information about taxation of Social Security payments

Part of your Social Security benefits may be included in your taxable income. In general, lower-income retirees do not pay taxes on their Social Security, while higher-income people do, on a sliding scale.

No more than 85% of your Social Security is taxable; so at least 15% of your Social Security is always tax-free. Even if your benefits are not completely tax-free, they are tax-advantaged.

The tax money collected is reimbursed to the Social Security system. It's the third-largest income stream for the system, after payroll taxes and interest from investments (page 258).

Taxation of your Social Security is triggered when certain countable income exceeds a threshold called the "Base Amount." Your IRS Form 1040 instructions will walk you through your individual computation, but here is a preview.

The computation

Determining if taxation applies

To see if your Social Security payment is taxable, follow these two steps:

(1)   Find the sum of these three amounts (your *combined income*):

Your gross income
+
Your non-taxable interest income (e.g. from municipal bonds)
+
Your "countable" Social Security (1/2 of your yearly Social Security)

(2)   Compare to the IRS Base Amount:

Individual:	$25,000
Couple:	$32,000

If the result of Step 1 exceeds the IRS Base Amount, part of your Social Security is taxable.

The taxable amount

The amount that is taxable could be anywhere from 0 to 85% of your Social Security. To determine the exact amount, see "More information on taxation of benefits" just below. Your Form 1040 will guide you at tax time.

The bottom line is that if you are single and your combined income is $25,000 to $34,000, you may have to pay taxes on up to 50% of your Social Security. If your combined income is over $34,000 you may have to pay taxes on up to 85% of your Social Security.

If you file jointly and your combined income is $32,000 to $44,000, up to 50% of your Social Security may be taxable. With combined income over $44,000, up to 85% of Social Security could be taxable.

Note that Social Security continues to be tax-advantaged: under the formula, *at least 15%* of your Social Security is always tax-free.

Withholding taxes from your benefits

Complete a form W4-V form to withhold taxes from your Social Security benefits.

Download the form at www.irs.gov/pub/irs-pdf/fw4v.pdf. You can choose a percentage to withhold. Return the signed form to your SSA office in person or by mail.

More information on taxation of benefits

IRS 1040 online instructions
www.irs.gov/pub/irs-pdf/i1040.pdf

Withholding
www.ssa.gov/planners/taxwithold.html

Appendix D of this book (page 287)

YOUR SOCIAL SECURITY (FICA) TAXES

What "FICA" means

FICA stands for Federal Insurance Contributions Act, the 1935 law which authorizes collection of the tax.

What FICA does

Your FICA payroll deduction pays for your Social Security coverage. Just as Social Security is the foundation of most retirement income, the FICA Social Security tax is the foundation of Social Security.

When you are employed, the tax is deducted from your pay. Your employer matches your contribution, and the combined contribution is credited to the Social Security trust funds by way of IRS, which collects the tax.

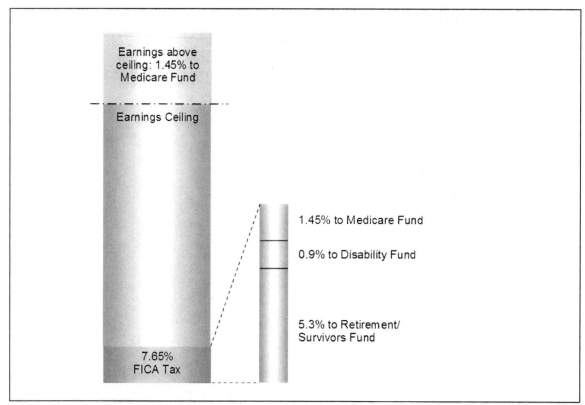

Figure 9.1. FICA taxes and their allocation. (For tax years 2016-2018, the Retirement/Survivors fund will collect 0.235% less than shown here, with the same amount credited to the Disability Fund, to avoid insolvency of the latter. Total tax remains 7.65%.)

The amount of the deduction

The tax is currently 7.65% from you and 7.65% from your employer. If you are self-employed, you pay *both* portions, or a total of 15.3%, on your net earnings from self-employment. In this case, it is called "Self-Employment Tax" rather than "FICA contributions."

The 7.65% is quite a bit higher than the 1% tax rate originally enacted in 1937. However, the original Act provided for automatic rate increases leading to 3% in 1949. Since then, the coverage you "buy" with your contributions has expanded many-fold to include more comprehensive spouse and survivor protection, disability benefits, and the Medicare program.

The taxable earnings ceiling

The tax is collected on all earnings up to a specified ceiling, or maximum. This is called the "taxable earnings base." In 2018, for example, you pay the full 7.65% on all earnings up to $128,400. Above that level, you pay only the 1.45% tax allocated to Medicare. (The 1.45% is technically the "Medicare Tax," not part of FICA.) Earlier ceilings are listed year-by-year in Appendix A, Column 2. Like the tax rate, the taxable earnings base has increased, starting from $3,000 in 1937. Currently it is increased annually to account for inflation.

Where the money goes

The 7.65% is not invested in a lump sum. It is allocated among three trust funds. 5.3% is deposited in the Old Age and Survivor Insurance Trust Fund for retirement and survivor payments, 0.9% is allocated to the Disability Insurance Trust Fund, and 1.45% goes to the Health Insurance Trust Fund for Medicare. These allocations are summarized in Figure 9.1.

Tax years 2016-2018 are slightly different; 0.235% is being temporarily re-allocated from the Retirement/Survivors fund to the Disability fund, to bolster the latter. In 2019 the allocations return to those shown in Figure 9.1.

More information on Social Security taxes

"Social Security Tax Rates"
www.socialsecurity.gov/OACT/ProgData/oasdiRates.html

YOUR SOCIAL SECURITY NUMBER

The reason behind the number

The Social Security Number (SSN) was originally devised to keep an accurate record of each person's earnings.

The number was needed to distinguish your earnings record from all other records. A glance at birth records will show that using traditional identifiers such as your name, birthdate, birth place, and even your parents' names would not always result in a *unique* identifier. Your SSN is not only one-of-a-kind, it is also handier than a more traditional handle such as "Andrew, son of John and Elaine, born in Philadelphia."

The three sections

Take a look at the typical SSN. It looks like this, and each section has a name as shown:

987-65-4320
Area—Group—Serial

Each section has a meaning and a specific job. To understand why this structure was adopted, we need to remember that the numbering system was devised in the 1930's. With modern computers, any 9-digit number will do, but with 1930's office technology, the number needed to "talk" to staff members. As you will see, this gives the SSN a human dimension, and about as much "charm" as a number can have.

The first three digits—area number. These numbers were originally a geographical indicator. Before 1972, the area number specified the Social Security office which issued your Social Security card. From 1972-on, they were issued centrally, but continued to be based on the state of your mailing address. With some exceptions, the "0" group—those numbers starting with zero—were from the far northeast (from Maine to Connecticut), the "100" group, from slightly farther south (New York, New Jersey, and Pennsylvania), and so on up to the 500 group in the far west.

Effective June 25, 2011, SSN "randomization" removed the geographical significance of the area number for new SSNs.

In addition to indicating where your number was requested, the first three digits determine which *Program Service Center* (PSC) will process your payments. Six PSCs handle the record-keeping and payment operations for the six regions of the country reflected in the various SSN area numbers. Two additional Program Service Centers are devoted to international operations and disability operations.

Some 600- and 700-series SSNs are being issued to specific groups of new U.S. residents. And many 700-series SSNs are reserved for railroad workers. They are covered by the Railroad Retirement Board (RRB) rather than Social Security and, in the 1930's, a quick way was needed to recognize them, so the proper agency would handle their retirement.

The reason for the geographic code, as best I can determine, is that some way was needed to distribute Social Security *cards* and the Social Security *workload* across the country in the 1930's. Remember, the cards were actual pieces of paper onto which your name would be hand-typed. They needed to be distributed in a systematic way to workers in every city in the nation in 1936. In 1937, the wage reports started coming in and each report needed to be associated with the proper file—by hand. And once the claims started coming in 1940, each claim had to be associated with the same file and the meticulous payment records kept in that file.

To break all this work down to manageable-sized jobs, the Social Security Board divided the country, and the cards, and all the associated record-keeping tasks, into five areas (now six). In addition, staffers could trace backwards from a person's SSN to the exact office which issued the SSN—a permanent "paper trail" that was easy to trace if necessary.

The middle two digits—group number. These are a "bundling" tool allowing early staffers to store and issue Social Security cards in convenient quantities.

There is also a special sequence code embedded in the group number. As numbers are assigned, the middle two digits advance following a special pattern, not a straight numerical order. First, the odd group numbers from 01-09 are issued, then even numbers 10-98, then even numbers 02-08, and finally odd numbers 11-99. Then, on to a new 3-digit area number, where a similar pattern would be followed.

Why not simply follow numerical order: 01, 02, 03 and so on? Because the middle two digits are a 1930's *security measure*. By scrambling the order, it would be easy to spot counterfeit SSNs. A counterfeiter printing Social Security cards in the 987 series (our fictitious example number above) would print his 64's, then his 65's, then his 67's. But unknown to him, the "odd sixties" might be the *last* 987 numbers to be issued, not due for issue until years from now. His fraud would be quickly detected by anyone who knew the proper sequence.

The last four digits are simply a serial number. They start at 0001 and advance in numerical order until 9999. Then the "middle two" digits advance one step in their scrambled sequence, and the "last 4" start over at 0001.

Incidentally, the 9 digits allow a billion possible SSNs. Since 1936, about 450 million have been used, so we still have quite a bit of breathing space.

Today, the various sections of the SSN are not as critical, except that it is much easier to remember an SSN broken into its component sections than if it came all at once! When you apply for an SSN for the first time these days (generally at birth), your application is typed into a computer, the number is automatically assigned, and the card is mailed to you, usually within 7 days. The computer retains the order the numbers are issued and establishes a wage record for you automatically. Also retained is a "paper trail," including the office which processed your application, the person who helped you, and the person who typed the application into the computer. In other words, the geographic codes and security scrambling are little needed today. Personally, though, I'm glad the number was invented in the 30's and not today—somehow, the old area, group, and serial portions of the number give it a human touch.

By the way, there are still some security measures embedded in the SSN which we haven't discussed here. Counterfeiters beware.

How to get a replacement card

Obtain a form SS-5 from SSA at (800) SSA-1213, any SSA office, or www.ssa.gov/forms/ss-5.pdf. Or use your My Social Security account (page 176) to request the card online.

The form is short; the instructions long. Be sure to pay close attention to the documentation requirements, especially your identification.

You will get the same Social Security *number*. There is a short list of exceptions at https://faq.ssa.gov/link/portal/34011/34019/Article/3789/Can-I-change-my-Social-Security-number.

More information on the Social Security Number

"The SSN Numbering Scheme"
www.ssa.gov/history/ssn/geocard.html

"The Story of the Social Security Number"
www.ssa.gov/policy/docs/ssb/v69n2/v69n2p55.html

MILITARY SERVICE AND YOUR SOCIAL SECURITY

Your military service affects your Social Security in several ways, some favorable and some not. Here is a summary of the major provisions related to your military service.

Your military service: 1940 through 1956

Manual earnings posting

You did not pay Social Security taxes for military service during this period, because military pay was not subject to FICA taxes until January 1, 1957. That means your military service in those years does not appear on your Social Security earnings record.

To recognize your service, SSA manually posts a special $160 wage credit to your earnings record for every month you were in active duty (or active duty for training) between September 16, 1940, and December 31, 1956. This is extra credit on your Social Security record which could increase your Social Security payment. The following conditions apply:

- You must have been honorably discharged after 90 or more days of service, or released because of a disability or injury received in the line of duty, or

- You must still be on active duty, or

- If you are applying for survivor benefits, the veteran must have died while on active duty.

How to get the credits

To receive the manually-posted credits, you must prove the exact months of your military service. Your military discharge form (DD-214) is the usual proof. If you have trouble locating your DD-214, Social Security will help you obtain another from the military.

You might not be asked for proof of military service if adding the $160 monthly military credit does not raise your Social Security payment. Your military years may not be among your best 35 years even with the additional credit. In that case, there is no point to having you prove your military service, and no proof is requested.

Your military service: 1957 through 1977

Manual extra credit

Beginning January 1, 1957, your military pay was subject to FICA taxes just like most other jobs. Therefore, your military service automatically appears on your Social Security earnings record and will be used to compute your payment.

You are also credited with $300 in additional earnings for each calendar quarter in which you received active duty basic pay. These extra earnings may help you qualify for Social Security or increase the amount of your Social Security payment.

This *deemed credit* of $300 per quarter does not automatically appear on your earnings record for years before 1968. Therefore, to receive this credit for service prior to 1968, you will need to submit proof of your service dates—usually your DD-214 discharge form. After 1967 the credit is automatic.

Your military service: 1978-2001

More extra credit

Again, your military pay is subject to FICA taxes, appears on your Social Security earnings record, and influences your Social Security payment computation.

You are also automatically credited with $100 in additional earnings for every $300 in active duty basic pay you received, up to a maximum of $1,200 a year in additional earnings. If you enlisted after September 7, 1980, you need to complete at least 24 months of active duty or your full tour, to get the additional earnings.

After 2001 your military service earns no special Social Security credit.

Your military pension and Social Security

You can receive both Social Security benefits and military retirement. Normally, your Social Security benefits are not reduced because of your military retirement. But watch for these effects:

Veterans Administration payments called "pension" are considered aid payments—other income you receive will reduce the amount of your VA pension payment. Therefore, your Social Security payment could affect your VA pension payment. Other VA payments such as "compensation" are not affected by Social Security payments.

If you receive military *retirement*, SSA's special wage credits for 1951 through 1956 cannot be granted to you unless you have active duty after 1956.

If you receive a military *disability* pension and apply for Social Security disability payments, your total compensation from these programs *plus workers' compensation* is limited to 80% of your average current earnings before you became disabled.

Wounded Warriors

If you became disabled while on active military service on or after October 1, 2001, your Social Security disability claim gets expedited processing. The same is true if you have a VA compensation rating of 100% Permanent and Total (P&T). The expedited process means you get a decision on your disability claim much quicker.

To summarize:

- In most cases, your military service increases your Social Security payments.

- In a few isolated instances, you may not get the usual advantages or may have limits on your payments because of your military service.

- If you were disabled on active duty, your Social Security disability claim can get expedited processing.

More information on military service

"Retirement Planner: Military Service"
www.ssa.gov/planners/retire/veterans.html

"Military Service and Social Security"
www.ssa.gov/pubs/EN-05-10017.pdf

"Information for Wounded Warriors and Veterans Who Have a Compensation Rating of 100% Permanent and Total (P&T)"
www.ssa.gov/people/veterans/

GETTING SOCIAL SECURITY PAYMENTS OVERSEAS

Citizens of the U.S. and allies

In most cases, there is no problem receiving your Social Security overseas. If you are a citizen of the U.S. or a qualifying country friendly with the U.S., your payments can usually be sent directly to you for as long as you are eligible.

Any Social Security business that comes up can be handled at the nearest U.S. Embassy or consulate, or directly with SSA's headquarters in Baltimore.

You can even have your U.S. Social Security directly deposited to a foreign bank, in over 80 countries. And, in many cases, your Social Security payment will have much more purchasing power overseas.

Other citizenship

If you are not a citizen of the U.S. or other qualifying countries, your payments will stop after you have been outside the U.S. for 6 full calendar months. (There are many exceptions to this rule—for example if you are in the U.S. military or if you reside in a country with special treaty privileges.)

If the exceptions do not apply, your payments will stop after you have been outside the U.S. for 6 months, and cannot be started again until you are again in the U.S. for one full calendar month.

Where payment is barred

There are several countries where you cannot receive Social Security. U.S. Treasury regulations require your payments to be withheld while you are in Cuba or North Korea. If you are a U.S. citizen, your withheld payments are issued to you when you leave those countries. If you are not a U.S. citizen, you *forfeit* your Social Security payments while you live in Cuba or North Korea.

Social Security regulations prohibit payments while you are in many of the former members of the USSR. There are exceptions, for example if you receive your payments at the U.S. embassy in person.

Working overseas

Special work rules apply when you are overseas. If you are under Full Retirement Age and outside the U.S., your monthly Social Security benefit is withheld for each month you work more than 45 hours. This applies whether you work in employment or self-employment. Furthermore, if other people receive payments on your work record, *their* payments will stop when your payment stops.

The foreign work rule is strict, but is understandable when you consider how difficult it would be to establish individual earnings limits for each foreign nation.

An exception applies if you are a U.S. citizen or resident, and your foreign work is covered by the U.S. Social Security program. In that case, you are subject to the same annual earnings limits that apply to people in the U.S. (see page 205).

Income tax on Social Security while overseas

Your Social Security payments continue to be taxable while you are outside the U.S. If you are a U.S. citizen or resident, you are subject to the same tax rules as people inside the U.S. (see page 212). If you are not a U.S. citizen or resident, Federal income taxes will be withheld from your Social Security. The withholding is 30% of 85% of your payment amount.

In addition, many foreign governments tax U.S. Social Security payments. You should contact the embassy of your foreign host country for information.

Medicare while overseas

Your Medicare covers medical treatment only in the U.S.

You could keep your Medicare Part A active, usually without premium, and it would be effective when you re-enter the U.S.

You would need to pay the Part B premium to keep it active. You could cancel the Part B to save the premium. But if you re-activate your Part B, you would be subject to late fees of 10% of the premium for each 12-month period you could have had Part B but didn't. (See page 141.)

Reporting to Social Security while outside the country

Because of the special rules while you are outside the U.S., you are required to notify Social Security promptly if you move overseas, work overseas, or experience other changes that could affect your eligibility. While you are outside the U.S., you will periodically receive a questionnaire to fill out and return to the U.S. Embassy, consulate, or SSA. Based on your answers, SSA will determine whether your eligibility continues.

Brief foreign trips are normally not a problem. When in doubt, contact Social Security.

To summarize:
- You can usually receive Social Security when you travel overseas or even live overseas.

- Your Medicare does not cover foreign medical treatment.

- Many special rules and reporting requirements apply to foreign travel, residence, and work.

More information on eligibility overseas

"Your Payments While You Are Outside The United States"
www.ssa.gov/pubs/EN-05-10137.pdf

REPRESENTATIVE PAYMENT

Amy's 6-year-old daughter will be eligible for Social Security. Amy wonders how the payments will be issued—in the name of a child?

Abe's mother is in a nursing home and has Alzheimer's. She is not aware of her Social Security payments or other financial arrangements for her care. Abe wonders if the payments should continue to be sent directly to his mother.

Situations like these call for *representative payment.* Representative payment means that a *representative payee* other than the beneficiary receives the Social Security or SSI payments and uses the money for the beneficiary. (The SSI program is described on page 227.)

When a representative payee is needed

A representative payee is needed when a beneficiary is not capable of managing or directing the management of his or her own funds in his or her own best interest.

This does not mean that the beneficiary is *physically unable* to pay bills or go to the bank. For example, an individual may be bedridden but able to direct family members to properly handle financial affairs. In that case, no representative payee would be needed. However, a physical impairment can be so severe that the individual cannot manage funds.

Indications of inability to manage funds include confusion about financial matters, mishandling or losing Social Security payments, inability to care for oneself, unconsciousness (e.g. coma), or other signs of financial difficulty.

How Social Security determines capability or incapability

SSA assumes an adult can manage funds unless the facts indicate incapability. There are three different determinations for three different situations:

- Minor children generally need representative payees, since they are not legally competent. An exception is made if the child is over 15, has no legal guardian, and is independent (e.g. self-supporting, serving in the military, a head of household, etc.).

- An adult beneficiary who has been legally determined to be *incompetent* is considered incapable of managing funds. Incompetence can be determined only by a court of law.

- A legally competent adult can be determined by SSA to be incapable of managing funds. The SSA determination of incapability is normally based on a physician's written opinion.

Choosing a representative payee

SSA guidelines indicate that the best payee is one who will best represent the beneficiary's interests.

This usually means the payee should be a close and trusted family member. The parent is the usual choice for a minor child.

If no family member can serve, a friend or institution may be named as the payee. For example, a nursing home may receive payments for a resident who cannot manage funds.

Safeguards

Representative payment is a serious matter. Generally, a physician or court must determine that representative payment is in the individual's best interest.

Before representative payment is started, the beneficiary and family members are notified of the proposed change. Any party to the decision may file an appeal of the change. The beneficiary may apply for direct payment at any time.

A representative payee must account for the money entrusted to him or her. Mishandling Social Security or SSI funds is a federal offense.

If capability returns (as after treatment for a serious illness), then direct payment to the beneficiary is reinstated.

How payments are issued

The payment legend shows the representative payee's name *for* the beneficiary. For example, if Mary Jones is the payee for John Smith, the payment would show:

Mary Jones for
John Smith
(Mary's address)
(Mary's city, state, zip)

Only Mary Jones could cash or deposit the payment.

Duties of the representative payee

- The representative payee acts as a substitute for the beneficiary in all Social Security business.

- The payee is responsible for all reports to SSA, and for signing all SSA documents.

- The payee receives all notices and payments from SSA (copies of notices are also sent to the beneficiary).

- The payee is responsible for managing the Social Security funds in the best interest of the beneficiary. This usually means opening a separate bank account to receive, hold and disburse the Social Security funds.

- Finally, the payee must make periodic reports on the use of the benefits and, if requested by SSA, the payee may have to provide a detailed accounting.

More information on representative payment

"A Guide for Representative Payees"
www.ssa.gov/pubs/EN-05-10076.pdf

Supplemental Security Income (SSI)

About SSI

If you have low income and resources, the SSI program may be able to help.

Many people become disabled or retired only to discover that they have little or no income from Social Security or other sources. SSI was created with these people in mind.

SSI basics

SSI's full name is *Supplemental Security Income for the Aged, Blind, and Disabled.* It is part of the "safety net" of public assistance or welfare programs for the needy.

The purpose of SSI is to provide a subsistence level of income to aged or disabled people in need, together with incentives to develop other sources of income such as wages. SSI establishes a "floor level" of income, below which aged or disabled people will not drop. In addition, everyone receiving SSI is also eligible for Medicaid medical assistance.

SSI's funding

Since SSI is part of the public assistance program, its funding is separate from Social Security funding.

Some people mistakenly believe that part of their Social Security taxes are used to fund "welfare." In fact, Social Security payroll taxes fund only the Social Security insurance programs—the retirement, family, survivor, disability, and Medicare programs. SSI is funded from federal *general revenues* provided by federal income taxes, excise taxes, etc. Some states also contribute state monies to augment SSI's payments. Nothing in the SSI program, not even the overhead such as payroll and office space, is funded by Social Security FICA taxes.

SSI provides supplemental payments to over 8.1 million individuals, 2.5% of the U.S. population. Federal SSI payments totaled $54.6 billion in 2016. Administrative costs were $4.3 billion, or 7.9%. The total cost was 0.29% of GDP. (See www.ssa.gov/oact/ssir/SSI17/ssi2017.pdf.)

SSI's history

SSI was created and brought under SSA's umbrella in 1974. Before 1974, similar assistance was provided by three separate programs, one providing aid for aged individuals, one for blind individuals, and one for disabled individuals. The three pre-1974 programs were administered by local public assistance offices, like the Food Stamp program, Medicaid, and other aid programs are administered today.

In 1973, Congress merged the three programs into one, and simultaneously transferred administration of the new SSI program to the Social Security Administration.

The merger made sense, since many of the rules of the three separate programs were identical. The transfer to SSA also made sense because most income programs for aged, blind, and disabled individuals could be housed in one office. After all, SSA was already providing Social Security for many people in the SSI program (though certainly not all SSA recipients got SSI, and vice versa).

The transfer made SSI the first—and still only—federally-administered public assistance program. Part of SSI's success results from its close ties to the Social Security program. For example, the SSI and Social Security computers are linked so that changes in Social Security income are automatically incorporated in SSI payment computations. And proof of age or disability for Social Security is proof for SSI as well, eliminating duplicated efforts.

Who qualifies for SSI

To be eligible for SSI you must meet all the following:

- Be a U.S. citizen or legal permanent resident

- Be aged, blind, or disabled

- Have low income

- Have low resources

"Aged" means that you have attained age 65. There is no provision for "early retirement," unlike regular Social Security payments.

"Blind" is defined just as it is for Social Security disability insurance: either visual acuity no sharper than 20-200 corrected vision, or a visual field no wider than 20° (tunnel vision), in your better eye.

Similarly, "disabled" is defined the same as for Social Security disability.

SSI for children

Disabled children can receive SSI, even newborns. If the child lives with the parents, the parents' income and resources are counted in determining eligibility and payment amount.

Once the child reaches age 18, the parents' income and resources are no longer counted. Only assets in the child's own name count.

Income: definition and impact

Income refers to money coming into your ownership during a month. Examples include cash gifts, Veterans payments, wages, and even Social Security payments. Income can also include non-cash items such as free or reduced rent, free food, or free clothing you receive during a month.

To oversimplify a bit, you are considered *low income* if your total income is lower than these standards (2018):

- For a *single individual:* $750 per month

- For a *couple:* $1,125 per month

In some states, standards are higher because the state subsidizes the SSI program with state funds. Also, *earned income from work* is largely exempted, allowing higher income for workers.

Again, to oversimplify, your SSI payment is determined by subtracting your income from these standards. In effect, SSI supplements you up to the income standard—thus the name *Supplemental* Security Income.

In practice, part of your outside income is not counted—there are *deductions* and *disregards* from your income. Thus, your total income, including your SSI payment, can be slightly higher than the payment standard—typically $20 higher. In the case of *earned income* such as wages, the discounts are significantly higher, creating a substantial raise if you work. This serves as a work incentive, with higher and higher total income as the reward for working.

Resources: definition and impact

Your *resources* are composed of all the things of value that you own on the first of the month (as opposed to income, which you obtain *during* the month). Examples include cash on hand, bank accounts, and non-cash items such as your car or house—basically anything you could convert to cash to live on.

To be eligible for SSI, your *countable* resources cannot exceed $2,000 for an individual, or $3,000 for a couple. Countable resources include all cash and liquid resources. Not counted are your residence, one vehicle of reasonable value, and some other assets. If your resources exceed these standards on the first of the month, you are ineligible for SSI throughout the month. The idea is simple: if you own resources above the standard you should live on the resources that month instead of SSI.

To summarize:

- SSI has two roles. It guarantees a living income to aged, blind, and disabled people, so it serves as an important safety net for needy individuals.

- In addition, with its efficient operation, it is a model for effectively administering other aid programs.

If Social Security is the foundation of income security for retirees, survivors, and disabled individuals, SSI is the bedrock that underlies the foundation.

More information on SSI

"Supplemental Security Income (SSI)"
www.ssa.gov/pubs/EN-05-11000.pdf

"Benefits for Children With Disabilities"
www.ssa.gov/pubs/EN-05-10026.pdf

"Supplemental Security Income (SSI) for Noncitizens"
www.ssa.gov/pubs/EN-05-11051.pdf

CHAPTER TEN

MAXIMIZE YOUR SOCIAL SECURITY

 Maximizing in a Nutshell

- Various tools and tactics can help you maximize your Social Security payments.

- Simpler techniques include maximizing your earnings and delaying your Social Security.

- You can "undo" a claim error by withdrawing your claim and starting over.

- You can increase retirement payments by suspending payments for some or all months from FRA to 70.

- If you are dually eligible for your own retirement payments and widow(er) benefits, or (in some cases) spouse benefits, you can time your claims strategically to maximize payments.

- Several free or fee-based tools can guide you to the best pathway.

BACKGROUND

For most people, Social Security is simple. When they retire (or when they reach 62, if already retired), they file for retirement payments. If married, their spouse also files at retirement. They receive payments every month for life, with annual Cost-of-Living Adjustments (COLAs).

But Social Security is like a new smartphone or computer: there's a lot more to it than just turning it on. There are numerous "hidden features" to make it do more for you, to personalize it.

For some people, it's important to maximize their lifetime Social Security payments. This may be for financial reasons—needing to pay the bills—or it may be for personal reasons like wanting to get the most from the system they paid into for so many years.

In this chapter, we will explore different approaches to optimize your Social Security, from the simple to the exotic.

MAXIMIZE YOUR EARNINGS

The Social Security system rewards higher lifetime average earnings, as measured by your best 35 years of earnings (page 41). If you increase your lifetime average earnings, you get more Social Security.

There are two ways to do this: increase your earnings per year (earn more), or increase the number of years you work (work longer).

The first makes sense if you have a choice between higher or lower earnings in a given year. If Social Security is your only criterion (doubtful!), take the higher earnings.

The second approach is more practical. If you have less than 35 years of earnings, every extra year of work will increase your Social Security. The new earnings will replace a "zero" year from the past, increasing your lifetime average.

More work years can help even if you already have 35 years of work. New work might replace a previous "low" year, i.e. when you were in school or just starting out.

This works even if you have a long career of steady high earnings. That's because recent earnings are weighted slightly heavier in the computation, even after earlier years are indexed for inflation. The index used is the *increase in average earnings*. That increase has been lower than either Consumer Price Index (CPI) increases or increases in high earnings in the overall economy.

For example, maximum taxable earnings in 1980 were $25,900. Even after inflation indexing for a 2017 age-62 application date, only $99,456 will be used in the computation.[1] That's quite a bit less than the $127,200 maximum in 2017. Thus, new high earnings in 2017 would replace high earnings in 1980, increasing the Social Security computation.

Bottom line: continuing to work generally increases your Social Security, at least modestly. More work could increase not only your own payments, but also family or survivor benefits based on your work. To quantify the effect of additional work, use SSA's online Retirement Estimator (page 179).

Get Social Security while maximizing your earnings

You can even draw Social Security payments while you maximize earnings.

Recall that if you return to work before Full Retirement Age, some of your Social Security payments may be stopped (page 205). Recall also that you will get credit back for the missing payments when you reach FRA, when you get an *Adjustment to the Reduction Factor (ARF, page 210)*.

In addition, any time you work, SSA recomputes your payment every year, with the *Automatic Earnings Reappraisal Operation (AERO, page 211)*.

The ARF allows you to draw early Social Security, continue working, and eliminate some of the reduction for early filing. It provides a safety net for the early filer who wants to return to work. The AERO further increases your payment by raising your 35-year average.

This is especially helpful if job loss forces you to file for Social Security:

John was laid off at 61 and was unsuccessful in finding a new job. He had always intended to file for Social Security at FRA but now he needed income. He reluctantly applied at 62 for a 75% payment. John was thankful for the Social Security—a lot of his younger friends had it harder—but he regretted the steep "permanent" reduction in his payments.

6 months later, John landed a great job. His Social Security stopped due to his earnings.

At 66, his Social Security automatically restarted because John's current work no longer affected his payments. Because of the ARF, John's payments were raised from 75% (48 months' reduction) to 96.7% (6 months' reduction). His steep reduction for early filing wasn't so permanent after all.

John's payments got a second boost, the AERO: his new earnings increased his 35-year computation a small amount, further raising his Social Security payments.

The bottom line here is that if you're temporarily unemployed and seeking work, you can tap into your Social Security early with little permanent damage, if you return to work. You'll get an ARF for every month payments are stopped, plus and AERO every year you pay FICA taxes.

THE DELAY STRATEGY

Quite simply, the later you apply for retirement payments, up to age 70, the higher they'll be for the rest of your life. You'll get a higher total payout if you live at least to average life expectancy. And the higher payments might continue even longer, for your spouse after you pass away—it's the gift that keeps on giving, for two lifetimes. Perhaps the simplest strategy for maximizing your Social Security is to postpone filing until age 70, or at least until FRA. Call it the *Delay Strategy*.

Break-even points for the Delay Strategy

If your FRA is 66, there are a couple of "break-even" points you need to know: age 78 and age 82-1/2. (Breakeven points for different FRAs are slightly different.)

Obviously, filing at 62 gives you the earliest retirement benefit but also the lowest monthly payment for the rest of your life. Filing later gives a higher monthly payment but fewer payments.

Using simple dollars (ignoring inflation, COLAs, taxation of benefits, additional work, and return on invested money), filing at 62 instead of 66 puts you "money ahead" until age 78. Those four years of early payments pay off for a good number of years. But at age 78, the age-66 filer has caught up, and from then on is ahead, with higher monthly payments for the rest of his or her life. The bottom line is that if you just want the most dollars from SSA and expect to live past age 78, file at 66, not 62.

Again, using simple dollars, filing at 66 instead of 70 puts you money ahead until age 82-1/2. After that, the age-70 filer is ahead for the rest of his or her life.

Sally's full payment amount at her FRA of 66 is $1,000 per month. Therefore, if she files at 62, she would get $750 per month; filing at 70, she would get $1,320 per month—an increase of 76%. Sally wants to know which choice yields the highest lifetime payments.

First, Sally compares filing at 62 vs. 66. If she files at 62, by the time she is 66, she has gotten $750 per month x 48 months = $36,000, a great head-start.

However, if she filed at 66 she would get $250 per month more ($1,000 vs. $750). At $250 per month, it will take $36,000/$250 = 144 months or 12 years to recoup the head start. That's age 78. After that, she will be $250 ahead every month for the rest of her life because she waited until age 66.

To check the break-even point, Sally considers that, at age 78, she will have received either $750 per month x 192 months (16 years) = $144,000. Or she will have received $1,000 per month x 144 months (12 years) = $144,000. This calculation confirms the age 78 break-even point.

Next, Sally compares filing at 66 vs. 70. Her head-start is $1,000 per month x 48 months = $48,000 by age 70.

However, if she files at age 70, she gets $320 per month more. That would recoup the head-start in $48,000/$320 = 150 months (12.5 years), at age 82-1/2. After that, her $320 raise is hers to keep forever.

To check the break-even point, Sally calculates that at 82-1/2 she will have received either $1,000 x 198 months (16.5 years) = $198,000. Or she will have received $1,320 x 150 months (12.5 years) = $198,000, confirming the age 82-1/2 break-even point.

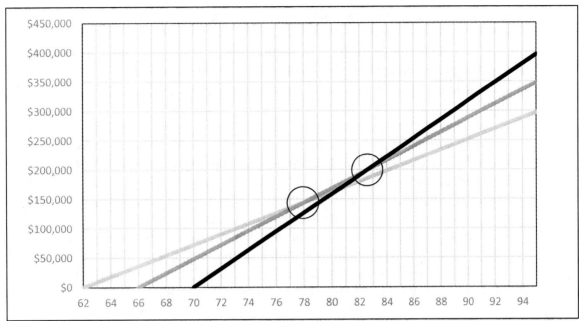

Figure 10.1. Lifetime payouts to age 95 with payments starting at 62, 66, and 70, along with break-even points (circles). FRA is 66, with payment amount of $1,000/month at 66. (Different dollar amounts do not change the break-even points. Different FRAs change the break-even points slightly.)

The same break-even points hold true regardless of the full payment amount. The bottom line: if you expect to live a shorter life, file early. If you expect to live longer, file later.

My friend and colleague Steve Vernon, President of Rest-of-Life Communications and a career actuary, has pleasingly clear analyses to pick the right application date based on simple dollars. Find his article, "How to maximize your Social Security payouts" at www.cbsnews.com/news/how-to-maximize-your-social-security-payouts/. Find more of his informative articles at www.cbsnews.com/search/author/steve-vernon/. Vernon concludes that you should file at 62 if you expect to live only to age 70; file at 66 if you expect to live to 80; and file at 70 if you expect to live to 90.

Life expectancy and the Delay Strategy

Clearly, the question of when to file depends on your life expectancy. If you know your death date, you know exactly when to file to maximize your Social Security. Since we don't know that date, we need to rely on averages.

You can calculate your average life expectancy at www.ssa.gov/OACT/population/longevity.html. For a broader view, a table of average life expectancy for all ages from birth to 119(!) can be found at www.ssa.gov/OACT/STATS/table4c6.html. (Note that web addresses are case-sensitive; use capital letters as shown.)

Life expectancy tables show median age at death—the age when one-half of a given group will have died. The other half lives longer. Thus, you have a 50% chance of out-living the table age, and an even better chance if you're in good health.

If you are a member of a couple, you should know that *joint* life expectancy—the median age at the *second* death—is longer than individual life expectancy. For example, IRS estimates 21.0 remaining years of life for a 65-year-old individual, but 26.2 years for a 65-year-old couple.[2] That's age 91 for the longer-living spouse. And remember, if you are married, your spouse may receive widow(er)'s benefits after you pass away, for the rest of his or her life.

These long life expectancies argue for taking Social Security as late as you possibly can, especially if you're the higher earner in a couple.

All of this is based on *average* life expectancy. Be sure to take other factors into account, like your family longevity and personal health.

Present-Value and the Delay Strategy

The complete story is not as straightforward as simple dollars and life expectancy. Remember the old saying, a bird in the hand is worth two in the bush? The same is true with money. Money today is worth more than money tomorrow. Money today has today's dollar value; tomorrow's money may be inflated and worth less. Money today could be invested and earn interest; money tomorrow cannot be invested now.

To account for the time value of money, financial planners perform a *present-value* computation, considering inflation, taxes, and interest on savings or potential investment gains. Figure 10.2 shows some of the present-value considerations of drawing Social Security early vs. making withdrawals from tax-deferred savings like a traditional IRA.

Your financial advisor might recommend drawing Social Security as *early* as possible after retirement and postponing or minimizing savings withdrawals. (This assumes, of course, that you're already retired. You'll normally be money ahead by staying on the job.)

The bottom line is that every case is individual, and maximizing your Social Security is only one part of your retirement picture. An expert decision considers your current and future tax rates, your current and future income sources, your assets and how they're characterized (taxable, tax-deferred, or tax-free), and of course your own goals and desires. It takes a financial planner to do that.

Factor	Drawing Social Security	Drawing from tax-deferred savings
Inflation	Annual COLAs make Social Security inflation-proof. No disadvantage for drawing early.	Need to draw more each year to keep up with inflation. Increasing drain on savings.
Tax rates	Always tax-advantaged. At least 15% will be tax-free.	100% taxable when withdrawn from tax-deferred accounts.
Savings growth rates	Savings stay relatively intact, allowing further compounding. Or part of Social Security payments can be saved and earn interest.	Withdrawals deny compounding power of each dollar withdrawn.

Figure 10.2. Financial implications of drawing living expenses from Social Security vs. from tax-deferred savings (e.g. traditional IRA, 401(k)).

"Bridges" to later filing

Say you want to delay filing until FRA or age 70. The problem is what to live on while you delay Social Security. You need a "bridge" to help you get to a later filing age. Here are some ideas:

Work strategy. The classic bridge to later Social Security. By working, you have some income to pay your bills. You're probably paying FICA or Self-Employment taxes on your ongoing work, possibly increasing your future Social Security payment. You can beef up your retirement savings on your own or through a workplace savings program. You might be earning a pension or retiree medical coverage. Even part-time work can allow you to delay Social Security.

Draw-down strategy. Blessed with some retirement savings? It can be worth it to draw down savings to postpone Social Security.

Think about it. Delaying Social Security from age 62 to 70 yields a 76% increase, above the inflation rate, with lifetime inflation adjustments and tax benefits, all guaranteed by the government. Which of your investments guarantees that kind of performance?

A problem with the draw-down strategy is it's hard to use savings to pay your bills when the Social Security alternative is so tempting. Here's an exercise that might help: compute how much it would cost to use your savings to *replace* your Social Security payments.

Say you're 62 and eligible for $1600 per month at 66, $1200 at 62 (75% of $1600), or $2112 at 70 (132% of $1600). To get from 62 to 66 would cost you

$57,600 ($1200 x 48 months). To get from 62 to 70 would cost $115,200 ($1200 x 96 months).

That's a lot of money, but if you can afford the "investment," it pays huge dividends in the long run—an extra $912 per month for the rest of your life (and possibly your spouse's life too) by delaying from 62 to age 70. That's a 9.5% return, guaranteed for life. It helps, at least psychologically, to set aside the dollars, earmarked for Social Security replacement.

Be sure to discuss your draw-down strategy with a financial professional.

File and Suspend strategy. If you have a spouse, and suspended your Social Security before April 30, 2016, your spouse might be able to draw spousal payments. The spousal payments act as your bridge from FRA to age 70.

Restrictions apply. See the description of Voluntary Suspension below (page 241).

Restricted Application strategy. Are you eligible for Social Security spousal or widow(er)'s payments? You might qualify to draw *only* the spousal or widow(er)'s payments from FRA to age 70, then switch to your own payments at 70 at the 132% level. The spousal or widow(er)'s payments act as your bridge, giving you smaller income in the first four years so you get higher income after age 70.

There are restrictions. For example, you must be born before January 2, 1954, to use the Restricted Application for spousal payments. See the description of Restricted Application below (page 249).

Combination strategy. The above strategies can be combined to fit your needs. For example, you could work while receiving spousal benefits, with no benefit reduction once you're over FRA.

THE "UNDO"

When you make a mistake on your computer, you hit the "undo" command. It reverses the process and puts you back where you were before. Guess what: Social Security has an undo also. It's called "withdrawal" of your claim.

Normally, the "Undo" is a way to correct mistakes, like filing too early, or for the wrong benefit. But it also offers another way to draw Social Security early without a permanent reduction. It's a way to have your cake and eat it too, since you get the benefit of early Social Security payments *plus* higher payments later in life, as if you delayed filing.

Anyone can take advantage of the Undo if they recently took Social Security any time before age 70, but there are some limitations:

- You must have some savings available to make it work.
- You can only use the Undo in the first 12 months you get Social Security.
- You can execute the Undo only one time in your life.

Officially, the Undo is called *application withdrawal and refiling*. The first step is to *withdraw* your earlier Social Security claim. You can withdraw at any SSA office using Form SSA-521, Request for Withdrawal of Application.

When you withdraw your application, it's like you never filed for Social Security. That means every dollar you received must be repaid. This is where your savings come in—or rather, go out. You will have to pay back thousands of dollars in a lump sum to SSA.

Why would you do that? Because once your withdrawal is approved, you refile for Social Security. Now that you're up to a year older, you will get a higher monthly payment. You've "undone" your claim and restarted your Social Security with new Reduction Factors or Delayed Retirement Credits.

The procedure goes like this:

1. File for early Social Security, and draw the reduced payments for up to 11 months.

2. Withdraw your claim. Dependents will also have to approve the withdrawal.

3. Repay all benefits received, including dependents' payments. No interest is charged.

4. Refile for Social Security. Your new claim will be based on your current age, and will yield a higher benefit.

SSA's description of the Undo can be found at www.ssa.gov/planners/retire/withdrawal.html.[3]

Brian's FRA is 66. His full payment amount is $1,000. He starts his Social Security at 62, getting $750 monthly payments.

At 63, Brian withdraws his application. At that point he has received $750 x 11 months = $8,250 (ignoring COLAs for this example). He draws $8,250 from his retirement savings and repays it to SSA. He does not have to pay interest on the $8,250.

Then, Brian refiles for Social Security. Since he is now 63, he gets an 80% payment, or $800, for the rest of his life.

Brian's $8,250 "investment" in Social Security results in a raise of $50 per month, (from his previous monthly benefit of $750 to his new amount of $800), or $600 per year. He calculates that this is a government-guaranteed 7.3% return on investment. He also discovers that he gets a tax credit for that year since he received "negative" Social Security. In *addition, he has secured a higher widow's payment for his wife if he dies before her.*

> *Mary's FRA is 66. She starts Social Security at 66 to get her full payment amount of $1,000 a month.*
>
> *At 67, Mary withdraws her application. At that point she has received $1,000 x 11 months = $11,000 (ignoring COLAs). She repays the $11,000 to SSA without interest.*
>
> *Then Mary refiles for Social Security. Now 67, she gets a 108% payment, or $1,080, for the rest of her life.*
>
> *Mary's $11,000 "investment" yields a raise of $80 per month, or $960 per year. That's an 8.7% return, guaranteed for life by the government, plus a possible tax credit.*

Since Mary is over FRA, she should consider *suspending* her payments instead of withdrawing (see page 241).

Note that you don't pay interest when you repay SSA. Some call the early Social Security payments a free loan.

Normally claims are withdrawn only to undo a mistake. For example, you file on your own record at 66, and then discover that you could instead draw benefits on your former spouse's record, then switch to your own at 70 for a higher payment. You would withdraw the first claim to make way for the second.

But the undo can also be a strategy for those who want early payments from Social Security but also want the higher payments of later filing—a tactic to maximize their lifetime payments.

The undo is often framed as "withdraw and refile," as if you would immediately refile. In fact, you might not refile for years.

> *Ken filed for Social Security at 62 because he was desperate for income after he lost his job. Eight months later he got a great job. He understood about work offsets and the ARF (see page 210), but he still wished he had never drawn the first 8 Social Security payments.*
>
> *Ken withdrew his claim, repaid the eight payments, and did not refile until he was age 70 for a full 132% payment.*

Remember, the catch is that you must repay SSA. All payments must be repaid, including dependents' payments, and dependents must approve the withdrawal. And you can only do it once, in the first 12 months of your Social Security.

Be sure to check all of this with SSA. You might drop this reference from their internal Program Operations Manual System: POMS GN 00206 ff.

There are risks involved:

- SSA may eliminate the provision before you exercise it.

- You may die before completing the Undo, locking your survivor into your original lower payments.

- You may not have the money to repay when needed, again locking you and your survivor into the original lower payments.

- You may die before your "investment" pays you back, reducing or negating the benefits of the Undo.

- Later, you may have an even better opportunity to withdraw, but you're allowed only one per lifetime.

VOLUNTARY SUSPENSION OF PAYMENTS

Voluntary Suspension of payments (or simply "suspending") is an incredibly powerful tool for maximizing Social Security. Anyone can suspend any or all of their payments from FRA to 70. One use of the tool is called *File and Suspend* or *Claim and Suspend.*

Under the Bipartisan Budget Act of 2015 (BBA 2015), there are two sets of rules for suspension. The old rules govern suspension requests from 2000 through April 29, 2016. The new rules govern suspension requests after April 29, 2016.

Old rules: If you requested suspension before April 30, 2016, including any suspension already in effect on that date, you secured three benefits:

1. *Increased payment.* Your suspended payments gain Delayed Retirement Credits (DRCs, see page 49) for every month they are suspended, and so are growing in the background at the rate of 8% per year. Your payments could rise to as much as 132% at age 70. The increased payment could be passed on to your surviving spouse as a widow's payment.

2. *Family payments.* Your spouse (and/or children) can receive family payments on your record while your payments are suspended.

3. *Contingency fund.* You can voluntarily "unsuspend" (resume) your payments at any time. Furthermore, you can unsuspend *retroactively* back to the month of suspension. SSA would immediately pay you every payment you suspended, up to 4 years' worth. In effect your suspended payments have created a contingency or hedge fund. (More details below.)

New rules: If you request suspension after April 29, 2016, you gain only the first benefit. Benefits 2 and 3 would be unavailable:[4]

1.   *Increased payment.* Your payments will increase while suspended, just like the old rules (above).

2.   *Family payments.* Family benefits are stopped while your benefits are suspended. Exception: divorced spouse payments continue.

3.   *Contingency fund.* You cannot resume payments retroactively. Payments would begin the month after you requested resumption, with no retroactivity.

In short, under the new rules, there are no retroactive or current payments during suspension, for the worker or anyone else on that record, except a former spouse.

Features of the old rules vs. new rules are summarized in Figure 10.3.

Feature	Old Rules	New Rules
Effective Date	Must be FRA **and** request suspension before 4/30/16	Must be FRA; suspension requested after 4/29/16
Payment increases while suspended	YES	YES
Family payments available	YES	NO
Retroactive unsuspension possible	YES	NO

*Figure 10.3. Summary of Voluntary Suspension "old rules" vs. "new rules." Note that the rules governing suspension depend completely on **request date**.*

Voluntary Suspension applies in these situations:[5]

•   You can suspend only your own retirement benefits. You can't suspend family, survivor, or disability benefits you get.

•   You can suspend benefits only between FRA and age 70.

•   If you took Social Security early, you can suspend any or all payments from FRA to age 70 to erase part of the payment reduction for early filing.

•   *Old rules only.* If you are married (and/or have eligible children), and requested suspension before April 30, 2016, your spouse (and/or children) can draw family benefits from your suspended record.

•   *Old rules only.* If you suspended payments before April 30, 2016, you can unsuspend retroactively to access the "contingency fund."

Voluntary Suspension/New Rules

Anyone can suspend some or all their own retirement payments, from FRA to 70, even under the new rules. Here are two examples that illustrate ways to use it.

Voluntary Suspension/New Rules Example 1: Suspending Existing Payments (Start-Stop-Start)

You can suspend payments that have already been in effect, under either the old rules or new rules:

Loretta files for Social Security at 62 because she needed the income. She gets a 75% payment.

By the time she reaches her FRA of 66, her financial situation has improved. She wishes she had never taken the early Social Security and the reduced payment.

At 66, Loretta suspends her Social Security payments. She works part-time and draws down savings a bit to bridge to age 70. While suspended, her Social Security is growing at the rate of 8% per year, computed monthly.

At 70 her payments automatically resume. The payment rate is 132% of her original 75%, resulting in a 99% payment. She has virtually erased the reduction for early filing. Her 99% payment will continue for life.

The "Start-Stop-Start" strategy can be used anytime from FRA to 70. Let's say you start your Social Security, then come into some money at 68 (e.g. an inheritance, a new job, lottery winnings, etc.). You could suspend your Social Security until 70, living off your new money, and when your Social Security starts at 70, it would be 16% bigger for life (8% per year x 2 years).

Voluntary Suspension/New Rules Example 2: Start-Stop-Start to "Front-Load" Family Payments

Under the old or new rules, you can start payments early to collect child benefits, then suspend payments to recoup some of the reduction for early payments.

Steve retires at 62. His FRA is 66. His wife Michaela is 60, and his daughter Lisa is 14.

Steve claims his Social Security at 62 and gets $1,500 (75% of his $2,000 PIA, reduced because of early filing).

Lisa gets Social Security child payments of $1,000 (50% of $2,000) until she graduates from high school.

Michaela is working and therefore cannot get spousal payments.

After four years Steve is 66 and Lisa's payments stop due to graduation.

*During the first four years of Social Security, the family has received a total of $120,000 (Steve's $1,500 per month + Lisa's $1,000 per month x 48 months). Call it **front-loading**—collecting as many payments as possible while child payments are available. The $120,000 is theirs to keep.*

Steve suspends his payments from 66 to 70. At 70 he gets $1,980 (132% of his original $1,500), virtually erasing the reduction for early filing.

Under the new rules Michaela cannot draw spousal benefits while Steve's payments are suspended, even if she's over FRA or not working. She can draw her own Social Security when she chooses, or wait for spousal payments when Steve's payments resume.

Whoever survives the first death will get the $1,980 for life, assuming it's the larger Social Security payment.

Voluntary Suspension/Old Rules

This section applies only if you *already suspended your payments before April 30, 2016*. Then you are under the old rules, with all three benefits shown in Figure 10.3.

The old rules will continue to apply until you unsuspend, or potentially until your age 70, when your payments automatically unsuspend. That gives you the following capabilities.

File and Suspend (old rules)

A common use of Voluntary Suspension under the old rules is *File and Suspend,* a tactic to maximize Social Security payments, especially for married couples.

The procedure is as follows, assuming "you" are the primary worker:

1. At FRA (or more), you filed for your own retirement benefit. However, you immediately suspended your payments. (As noted above you can also suspend already-existing Social Security payments, a "start-stop-start." For example, you could file at 62, draw payments from 62 to FRA, then suspend payments for some or all months from FRA to age 70.)

2. Your spouse (and/or children) can receive up to 50% spouse (and/or child) payments on your suspended record.

3. At 70 your payments automatically resume. Or, you can voluntarily re-start your payments any month before 70.

   a. At 70, your payment could be up to 132%, plus up to 50% for your spouse, for a total payment of 182%.

   b. Contingency fund: Before age 70, you may specify any start-payment date all the way back to suspension date, with resulting immediate back payment.

4. The long-term effect is that the 182% payments continue until the first death. After that, the survivor will get the 132% payment for life no matter who dies first, so the augmented payment will continue for the joint life of the couple, assuming it's the higher of the two.

SSA's description of File and Suspend is here: www.ssa.gov/planners/retire/suspend.html.[6]

Voluntary Suspension/Old Rules Example 1: Classic "File and Suspend" Strategy

Bill and Barb both turned 66, their FRA, in 2015. Barb is not eligible for Social Security on her own. Bill is eligible for $1,000 a month at FRA.

*At 66, Bill filed for Social Security retirement but immediately suspended payments. Because he did so in 2015, the **old rules** apply.*

Barb filed for spouse payments on Bill's record at her age 66. Because she was FRA, she gets a $500 payment, 50% of Bill's full payment amount. That's all the Social Security they expected for the next four years.

Bill and Barb work intermittently from 66-70 to supplement their income. Since they are over FRA the Social Security is not reduced due to work.

At 70, Bill's payments will automatically start at $1,320 (his $1,000 x 132%). Barb's $500 payments continue, for total income of $1,820.

Whether Bill or Barb dies first, the survivor's payment will be $1,320 for the life of the survivor.

Figure 10.4 summarizes this example.

	Full Payment Amount	Age 62	Age 66	Age 70	Survivor, After First Death
Bill	$1,000	$0	$0 Bill files but suspends payments	$1,320 Bill's own	$1,320 Bill's own
Barb	$0 Not Eligible	$0	$500 As Bill's spouse	$500 As Bill's spouse	$1,320 As Bill's widow

Figure 10.4. Summary of Bill and Barb's classic File and Suspend strategy, Example 1, available only under the old rules for suspending payments.

Voluntary Suspension/Old Rules "Contingency Fund"

Since you suspended before April 30, 2016, you have some remarkable flexibility on unsuspending (resuming) your payments.

First, you can "unsuspend" (start payments) any month up to age 70, any time you need them. At 70, your suspended payments automatically unsuspend.

Second, when you unsuspend, you can specify *any start-payment date back to the date of suspension.* An earlier start-payment date will trigger back pay. Your suspended payments create a "contingency fund" or hedge fund that you can tap into if needed, anytime from FRA to age 70.

All this applies because you suspended before April 30, 2016, and are thus under the **old rules.** Under the new rules, your payments resume the month *after* you request them.

Voluntary Suspension/Old Rules Example 2: Contingency Fund

Suspended payments automatically unsuspend at age 70, and are paid at the age-70 rate. Just before age 70 you can re-assess your options and choose a different outcome:

When Bill (Example 1 above) approaches 70, he discovers that he can specify any start date for his monthly payments. He considers three options:

He could start payments effective with age 70. He would receive no back pay but would receive ongoing payments of $1,320 (his full age-70 payment with 48 months' DRCs).

Or he could start payments effective with, say, age 68. He would receive a $27,840 lump sum (2 year's back pay) plus ongoing payments of $1,160 per month (his age-68 payment with 24 months' DRCs).

Or he could start payments effective with his original claim at age 66. He would receive a $48,000 lump sum (4 years' back pay) plus $1,000 a month for life (his original age-66 payment amount).

The first option was always Bill's "Plan A," but depending on his current vs. long-term needs, Bill can choose a larger lump sum with smaller monthly payments, or a smaller lump sum with greater monthly payments. Being a long-term planner, Bill chooses to start payments at age 70 to ensure the greatest security throughout his lifetime and Barb's.

Voluntary Suspension/Old Rules Example 3: Contingency Fund

Under the old rules, you can unsuspend with back pay any time from suspension to age 70. Here are Bill and Barb again from Example 1, but with this change:

At 68, tragedy strikes. Barb passes away, and Bill learns that he has a terminal illness. He decides that the whole idea of File and Suspend was to maximize payments in the long run, but now he doesn't have a long run. He wishes he had the money now, not later. In fact, he wishes he had never suspended his payments.

Bill unsuspends his payments retroactively, effective age 66. SSA immediately deposits $24,000 in Bill's bank account, representing 24 months at $1,000 per month, Bill's age-66 payment amount. He gets ongoing payments of $1,000 per month for life. The net effect is as if he filed at 66 and never suspended payments.

Voluntary Suspension/Old Rules Example 4: Contingency Fund, then Re-Suspend

You can voluntarily suspend, unsuspend, and re-suspend, with or without back pay, like turning a tap on and off. You receive DRCs for any months your payments were suspended and never paid out:

Jennifer's age-66 payment is $2,000 per month. Her FRA is 66. She planned to delay Social Security until 70 to maximize future payments. But she wanted to keep open the option to file for retroactive payments—she wanted the Social Security contingency fund under the old rules.

Jennifer filed and suspended before April 30, 2016, at 66. She planned to bridge to age 70 with a combination of work and savings.

Unfortunately, at age 68 she has a financial emergency and needs money quickly. She unsuspends her payments retroactively, effective age 66. SSA immediately deposits $48,000 to her bank account in a lump sum, representing 24 months of payments at her age-66 payment of $2,000 per month.

Jennifer doesn't need the ongoing Social Security payments, so she immediately re-suspends her payments.

Her Social Security automatically resumes at 70 at $2,320 per month. That's 116% of her $2,000 age-66 payment, representing the 24 total months from age 68-70 that her payments were suspended.

*Note that Jennifer's second suspension (after the lump sum payment) will be under the **new rules**, because it is requested after April 29, 2016.*

Even under the new rules, Jennifer can start and stop payments for any months before 70. She will not be able to retroactively unsuspend again, and no family payments are available during any new-rules suspension.

RESTRICTED APPLICATION FOR "DUALIE" SPOUSES

You are a "dualie" (my own term, not Social Security's) if you are *dually eligible* for both your own retirement payments and spousal payments (page 68).

If so, here's a way to "get paid to wait" from 66 to 70, if you qualify. File a *Restricted Application for "Spousal-Only" payments,* also known as "claim now, claim more later." It's a powerful tool for working couples. It also works if you're divorced and eligible on your former spouse's record. (See below for different rules for dualie widow(er)s.)

The general idea is to take a small Social Security payment at FRA and a bigger one later. To do so, you take a lower Spousal-Only benefit at FRA, and wait until age 70 to apply on your own record. By then, Delayed Retirement Credits (DRCs) will have increased your own payment. The aim is to use the spousal payment as a bridge to get the higher 132% payment at age 70.

The strategy works because of an exception to SSA's *deemed filing* rules (page 68). Under deemed filing, applying for your own retirement payments means you are *deemed* (assumed) to claim spousal payments too, and vice versa. Deemed filing does not apply if you were born before January 2, 1954, *and* first file for benefits at FRA. Figure 10.5 summarizes these rules.

Feature	Old Rules	New Rules
Effective Date	Birthdate before 1/2/1954	Birthdate after 1/1/1954
Can file Restricted Application before Full Retirement Age	**NO** Deemed Filing applies below FRA	**NO** Deemed Filing applies at all ages
Can file Restricted Application at/after Full Retirement Age	**YES**	**NO** Deemed Filing applies at all ages

*Figure 10.5. Summary of Restricted Application "old rules" vs. "new rules" for **spousal benefits**. The rules governing RA depend completely on **birthdate**. Note that **widow(er)'s benefits** have different rules allowing Restricted Application for any birthdate, before or after FRA.*

You can use the Restricted Application in these situations:[7]

- You must be born before January 2, 1954.

- You must be at least FRA when you first file.

- You are eligible for a spousal payment (either current or former spouse).

- You have not received a reduced retirement or spousal payment before.

- Your own payment at 70 is higher than your spousal payment at FRA.

- You, your spouse, or both, may be working or retired after FRA.

Spousal-Only Application procedure

The procedure is as follows, assuming "you" are the one filing the Restricted Application:[8]

1. For you to get a spousal payment, your spouse or ex-spouse must claim their "own" Social Security.

    a. Your spouse or ex-spouse may be receiving monthly payments, or have requested suspended payments before April 30, 2016 ("old rules" suspension; see page 241).

    b. Exception: if you have been divorced over 2 years, your ex-spouse does not need to apply (pages 63-64).

c. He or she may have applied at any age (before or after FRA) for retirement or disability payments.

2. At your age 66 (or more), you file for *spousal* benefits on your spouse's record.

   a. You do *not* file for your own retirement benefits. You do *not* File and Suspend your own benefits. Filing for your own benefits, even if suspended, can eliminate the spousal payments you seek.

   b. You *"limit the scope"* of the application to Spousal-Only benefits, specifically excluding retirement payments. If filing by phone or in-person, make this clear to your Claims Representative. If filing online, it's a simple checkbox near the end of the application.[9]

3. Your spouse should *not* request a new suspension of their own benefit, because that would also stop your spousal payments ("new rules" suspension, page 241).

4. At 70 (or before), you file for your "own" benefits. Delayed Retirement Credits have escalated your retirement payment in the background, up to 132% at age 70.

5. Your spousal payments stop, since your own payment is higher.

6. Your spouse could then file for spousal benefits on your record, if that would be a raise.

7. The short-term effect is that the spousal payments act as a bridge to get you to age 70. The long-term effect is that your 132% payments continue throughout your life, and possibly your spouse's too. (The 132% payment will continue for whoever survives the first death, if your payment is the higher of the two. See page 92.)

Spousal-Only Application Example 1

The Restricted Application is particularly powerful for working couples, as in this example:

Tom and Ann both work and are eligible for their own Social Security retirement payments. They are both turning 66. Tom's full payment amount is $1,000 and Ann's is $2,200.

Tom files online for his own $1,000 payment. Ann also files online, and restricts her application to spousal-only payments by checking the proper box. Her payment is $500 (50% of Tom's $1,000).

Together, Tom and Ann receive $1,500 per month for the next 4 years.

At 70, Ann files for her own retirement payments. DRCs have increased her own retirement benefit every month, so her new payment is $2,904 (132% of her $2,200 payment). That automatically stops her $500 spousal payment.

Also at 70, Tom files for spousal benefits on Ann's record, now that her own benefits have started. His new payment is $1,100 (his $1,000 payment, plus $100 spousal payment, to equal 50% of Ann's $2,200 age-66 payment).

Whoever survives the first death will get Ann's payment of $2,904 for life.

Figure 10.6 summarizes this example.

	Full Payment Amount	Age 62	Age 66	Age 70	Survivor, After First Death
Tom	**$1,000**	**$0**	**$1,000** Tom's own	**$1,100** Tom's own + spousal	**$2,904** As Ann's widower
Ann	**$2,200**	**$0**	**$500** As Tom's spouse ONLY	**$2,904** Ann's own	**$2,904** Ann's own

Figure 10.6. Summary of Tom and Ann's Spousal-Only Application strategy, Example 1.

The bottom line is that Ann and Tom use the spousal payments from 66-70 to increase Ann's payment to 132%, an increase that will last for both lifetimes.

Spousal-Only Application Example 2

The Restricted Application can be used by a single person who is eligible as a former spouse, as in this example:

Madam X (page 77) delays her Social Security until age 66 to get her own 100% payment of $2,000. Then she learns that she could opt for Spousal-Only payments on the record of John, her former spouse, and delay her own.

She files a Restricted Application for Spousal-Only benefits at 66 and receives $500 per month (50% of John's own $1,000). Because her divorce is over two years old, it does not matter whether John files for his own Social Security.

For the next 4 years, Madam X uses the $500 spousal payments as a bridge to get to 70.

At 70 she files on her own record and gets $2,640 (132% of her $2,000 age-66 payment) for life.

Figure 10.7 summarizes this example.

	Full Payment Amount	Age 62	Age 66	Age 70	Survivor, After First Death
John (Madam X's former spouse)	$1,000	N/A	N/A	N/A	$2,640 Potential as Madam X's surviving former spouse
Madam X	$2,000	$0	$500 As John's former spouse ONLY	$2,640 Madam X's own	N/A

Figure 10.7. Summary of Madam X's Spousal-Only Application strategy, Example 2. Note that John could potentially receive $2,640 as a surviving former spouse, if he survives Madam X.

Additional considerations

- You must be FRA or above. Under FRA, *deemed filing* (page 68) would force you to apply for both payments, eliminating the choice to delay your own payment. At FRA, deemed filing ends, opening the door to a Spousal-Only Application. In Example 1, Ann must be FRA to take spousal-only payments.

- You must be born before January 2, 1954. For later birthdates, deemed filing applies both before and after FRA.[7]

- You must have assets (like savings) or income (like a pension or job) to bridge the four years of lower Social Security from age 66 to 70. The spousal payments can be part of the bridge.

- You as an individual or couple should have enough life expectancy to reach the break-even point.

- Note that, with higher monthly payments, all ensuing COLAs would be larger dollar amounts—a nice gift for your later years.

- A failsafe applies: If Ann dies before age 70, Tom can still get widower's payments augmented by DRCs up to Ann's month of death.

- If necessary, assist your SSA representative with the following citations: POMS GN 204.004 B, GN 204.020 D.1.b, and GN 204.035 B.1.[10]

RESTRICTED APPLICATION FOR "DUALIE" WIDOW(ER)S

You can be a "dualie" survivor (page 98), dually eligible as a worker and as a widow or widower. If so, you can maximize your lifetime Social Security payout by strategically timing each benefit.

Deemed filing (page 68) does not apply to widow(er)'s payments.[11] Furthermore, a reduction of one payment will not carry over to the other payment.[12]

That means you could start either your own payments or your widow(er)'s payments early, before FRA, then switch to the other payment later, with no permanent reduction.

The general rule is to take the lower payment first and the higher payment second. Remember that widow(er) benefits maximize at your FRA, while your own benefits maximize at age 70. Be sure to review the Louise, George, and Pam examples on pages 98-99 to understand ways to time your claims.

If you plan to take a benefit before FRA, remember that the work rules on page 205 apply to all retirement, family, and survivor payments, and may preclude payment until you retire or reach FRA.

FINDING YOUR OPTIMAL PATHWAY

If you're trying to find the optimal Social Security pathway for your individual situation, the math can be tedious. Luckily there are computer programs to run the numbers for you and give you simple step-by-step instructions for timing your Social Security claims.

- Start with good old SSA.

  o Establish your *My Social Security* account at www.ssa.gov/myaccount and note the Social Security payment at FRA for you and your spouse (if married). All other planning will need this step.

- To experiment with different future work scenarios like early retirement or part-time work, use SSA's Retirement Estimator at https://www.ssa.gov/retire/estimator.html.

- Call or visit SSA for individual help.

- Run your numbers through a free online calculator. Input your birth dates and your SSA benefit estimates to get advice on your best pathway. My current favorite, updated to the "new" filing rules:

  - Financial Engines: https://financialengines.com/education-center/social-security-planner/. Click the "Edit information" button in Step 2 to personalize the data for you (and your spouse, if married).

- Also check out three private fee-based calculators. Each is updated to "new" filing rules:

  - http://maximizemysocialsecurity.com (Individual consultation available)

  - www.socialsecuritysolutions.com (Individual consultation and free assessment available)

  - www.socialsecuritychoices.com (Individual consultation available)

- Consider financial planning. Social Security is just one part of your retirement finances. You need a strategy that takes into account your taxes, other income, work plans, savings, marital status, and life expectancy, as well as your Social Security. Only a professional financial planner can address your entire financial picture. You can search for planners at www.fpanet.org, www.napfa.org, or www.garrettplanningnetwork.com. The last one, Garrett Planning Network, lists Certified Financial Planners who are available by the hour. Find advisors specially trained in Social Security at www.nationalsocialsecurityassociation.com and click on "Advisors."

Using your deeper knowledge of Social Security, especially with the specialized strategies in this chapter, you can optimize your Social Security. Using a financial professional you can optimize your entire retirement finances.

FOR MORE INFORMATION...

"When Should You Start Social Security Benefits? Do the Math!"
www.cbsnews.com/news/when-should-you-start-social-security-benefits-do-the-math/.

"Life Expectancy Calculator"
www.ssa.gov/OACT/population/longevity.html

"The Social Security Claiming Guide" (e-book)
http://crr.bc.edu/special-projects/books/the-social-security-claiming-guide/
(See additional articles from the Center for Retirement Research at Boston
College at http://crr.bc.edu/index.php.)

"Retirement Planner: If You Change Your Mind"
www.ssa.gov/planners/retire/withdrawal.html

"Retirement Planner: Suspending Retirement Benefit Payments"
www.ssa.gov/planners/retire/suspend.html

Chapter Endnotes

1. https://www.ssa.gov/pubs/EN-05-10070-1955.pdf
2. https://www.irs.gov/publications/p590b/index.html, Appendix B, Tables I and II.
3. See also https://ssa.gov/OP_Home/handbook/handbook.15/handbook-1515.html and https://secure.ssa.gov/poms.nsf/lnx/0200206000 ff.
4. https://www.ssa.gov/planners/retire/suspend.html
5. https://secure.ssa.gov/apps10/poms.nsf/lnx/0202409100 ff.
6. Also see FAQs at https://www.ssa.gov/planners/retire/suspendfaq.html
7. https://www.ssa.gov/planners/retire/applying6.html, second blue box under "How Much Will I Receive?"
8. https://secure.ssa.gov/apps10/poms.nsf/lnx/0200204004, B, second paragraph, and https://secure.ssa.gov/apps10/poms.nsf/lnx/0200204020, D.1.b. and D.2. General rules for deemed filing are at https://secure.ssa.gov/apps10/poms.nsf/lnx/0200204035
9. https://www.ssa.gov/pubs/EN-05-10523.pdf, last question before signature area. Checking this box effectively limits the scope of the application per https://secure.ssa.gov/apps10/poms.nsf/lnx/0200204020, E.6.
10. https://secure.ssa.gov/apps10/poms.nsf/lnx/0200204004, https://secure.ssa.gov/apps10/poms.nsf/lnx/0200204020, and https://secure.ssa.gov/apps10/poms.nsf/lnx/0200204035, respectively
11. https://secure.ssa.gov/apps10/poms.nsf/lnx/0200204035 B
12. https://secure.ssa.gov/apps10/poms.nsf/lnx/0300615150 and https://secure.ssa.gov/apps10/poms.nsf/lnx/0300615160, A.1

SOCIAL SECURITY FOR THE NEXT GENERATION

 Solvency in a Nutshell

- Social Security is financially sound in the short run, but faces shortfalls in the long run (after 2034).

- There are numerous tools to extend solvency, and options are being explored.

- The author offers a plan to achieve near-permanent solvency.

SOLVENT OR BANKRUPT?

Why should I learn about Social Security? It will be bankrupt before I retire, won't it?

Many younger workers believe that the Social Security system is bankrupt and that they'll never get a Social Security payment. "More likely to see a UFO than Social Security" was one poll's finding.[1] Fortunately, the facts are considerably brighter than that.

Here are the facts:[2]

- Social Security is presently running a surplus, and has done so every year since 1984.

- Excess funds are invested safely for future needs, and earn interest.

- Surpluses are projected to continue through 2021. Then, with most Baby Boomers retired, the system will operate at a deficit, drawing from its invested funds.

- Invested funds are projected to be exhausted in 2034.

- After 2034, the system will continue to be about 77% funded for the rest of the century.

- Reforms are needed to fill the 23% shortfall, to continue to pay full benefits after 2034.

- Such reforms are now being considered. Options include cutting benefit payments, raising taxes, changing how excess funds are invested, instituting private individual accounts, providing direct government subsidies, or some mix of these.

Has Social Security ever faced a shortfall before?

Yes. 1983.

Headlines in 1982 stated the exact month that SSA would go broke—July 1983.[3] The system was in a tailspin, running annual deficits despite Congressional attempts in 1977 and 1980 to patch up its financing.

Finally, on April 20, 1983, the 1983 Amendments to the Social Security Act were signed into law. The reforms were successful because the changes were major. On the income side, FICA taxes were increased from 5.4% to 6.2%, and more jobs were brought under the program. On the expense side, computations were lowered, retirement age was raised, some benefit categories were eliminated, and eligibility requirements were stiffened.[4]

The result has been healthy annual surpluses since 1984, with the actual surpluses running close to the amounts forecast by the framers of the Amendments.

The accumulated surplus funds, about $2.8 trillion in 2018 and growing, are invested in U.S. Treasury bonds, widely considered the safest investment in the world.

Income type	2016 income	% of total income
Payroll taxes	$836.2	87.3%
Interest on trust fund bonds	$88.4	9.2%
Income tax on benefits	$32.8	3.4%
General Fund reimbursements	$0.1	0.01%
Total	**$957.5**	**100%**

Figure 11.1. Sources of income for Social Security. (Dollar amounts in billions.)[5]

Surpluses? I heard there were deficits starting in 2010.

In 2010, there was a deficit in only one of Social Security's three main income streams. If you only counted payroll tax income, it *could* be called a deficit, but that would ignore the other two income streams: interest on SSA's treasury bonds and income tax on benefits. Figure 11.1 summarizes SSA's income sources.

Social Security's solvency is a remarkable accomplishment in this era of troubled banks, large insurance companies in receivership, and pension plans in bankruptcy. Social Security is one of the soundest financial systems in the nation and the world. Americans can take pride in this achievement, yet the success is unknown to most citizens. Some remember that Social Security was financially struggling in the late 1970's and early 1980's. Even worse, there has been a massive effort since the 1990's to erode confidence in Social Security. The result is we don't recognize how financially sound Social Security really is.

What about the FICA "tax holiday" in 2011 and 2012? Didn't that reduce Social Security's revenue?

No, the shortfall was made up by general revenues transferred from the federal government to Social Security.[6]

WHY A SURPLUS?

Why should Social Security run a surplus instead of balancing income and expenses?

The need for building a surplus of Social Security funds is twofold. First, any financial system, if it expects to survive in the long term, needs to stay in the black. The second reason is more important, and can be summed up in two words: Baby Boom.

Before 1983, Social Security was a "pay as you go" plan. Almost as soon as the tax money came into the system, it was paid out in the form of Social Security payments. Yes, there were trust funds to hold excess money from month to month, but they contained at most a few months' worth of payments. Social Security functioned more like a pipeline than a reservoir, with tax money coming in one end and payments going out the other end in a steady stream.

But starting with the 1983 Amendments, Social Security started stockpiling funds for future retirees.

Why the change?

Demographics. The "pay as you go" practice worked fine as long as there were enough workers paying taxes at one end of the pipeline to supply the payments for the beneficiaries at the other end. And back then, there were plenty of workers. In the 1940's and 50's, there were 10 to 15 tax-paying workers for every beneficiary of the brand-new Social Security system.

However, with Baby Boomers having fewer children of their own, the ratio is changing. The current ratio is 2.8 workers for every beneficiary, and in 2035, when the Baby Boom generation is retired, there will be only 2.2 workers for every beneficiary.[7] Thus, it gets more and more expensive for those still working to support those on Social Security. As Boomers retire in large numbers, they will have an unprecedented impact on *all* pension systems, Social Security included.

That is why SSA is "stockpiling" Social Security dollars now to pay for retirement benefits later. For the next decade-and-a-half, SSA will act more like a reservoir and less like a pipeline, compared to its earlier years.

Many writers still call Social Security a "pay as you go" system. That ignores the large surpluses and investments of the system. The current system might more properly be called a *modified* pay as you go system.

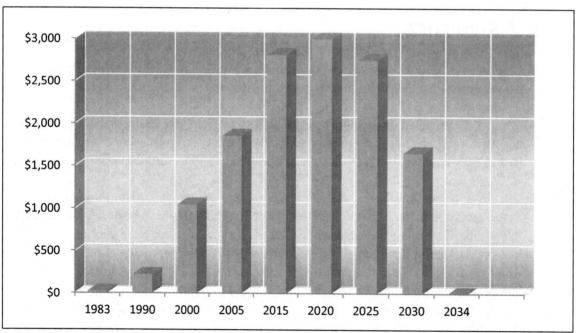

Figure 11.2. OASDI trust fund reserves. Dollar amounts in billions. Actual amounts shown to 2015, projections shown after 2015.[8]

AMOUNT OF THE SURPLUS

How much of a surplus is the system running each year? How long will the surplus last?

In Calendar Year (CY) 2016, the Old-Age, Survivor, and Disability Insurance (OASDI) programs cost $922.3 billion including administrative expenses, but received $957.5 billion, for a surplus of $35.2 billion. Closing balance was $2,847.7 billion.[5]

Surpluses are projected to continue through 2021.[8]

The surplus is invested in two trust funds, the OASI trust fund and the DI trust fund. As noted above, the funds are invested in U.S. Treasury Bonds, considered the safest investment in the world. In CY 2016, interest income alone was $88.4 billion.[5]

Figure 11.2 shows the total trust fund reserves in past years and projected reserves in future years. Note that reserves are now almost at their peak of about $3.0 trillion in 2021. However, don't overlook the last column, labeled 2034. The OASDI trust funds are expected to be depleted at that time, following a period of intense drawing down.

Here are some important dates for understanding Social Security's financing:

2010-2021	Expenses exceed payroll taxes.
	Payroll taxes plus interest exceed expenses.
	Trust Funds continue to grow.
2022-2034	Income from taxes and interest together no longer sufficient to pay benefits.
	Trust Fund principal is drawn down.
	Trust Funds shrinking.
2035 on	Trust Funds exhausted.
	No further interest income since principal is spent.
	Tax income continues.
	Tax income alone is sufficient to pay about 77% of benefits

Thus, Social Security is still expected to run out of money sometime this century. If present trends and laws continue unchanged, *your* retirement may be in good shape, but our children may face another Social Security crisis like the one in 1983.

PROPOSALS FOR EXTENDING SOCIAL SECURITY'S SOLVENCY

What are the options for extending Social Security's solvency past 2034?

Like a family spending more than it earns, getting by with withdrawals from savings, Social Security has only two real options to reach solvency:

- Increase income (in Social Security's case, raise taxes)
- Decrease expenses (cut benefits)

The creative and interesting part is *how* to make these changes, how to have Congress agree on a reform package, and how to make the changes acceptable to the public.

There have been numerous plans proposed to eliminate the funding shortfall:

- In 1997, the *Advisory Council on Social Security,* a bipartisan commission of experts, made a number of proposals. Most of the members agreed to expand coverage to more workers, invest part of the trust funds in the stock market, increase the number of work years in the computation, increase Full Retirement Age, and tax benefits in the same manner as pensions. Altogether, these changes would have eliminated two-thirds of the funding shortfall. The council proposed three different approaches to eliminate the last third of the shortfall.[9]

- In 1999, the Pew Charitable Trusts conducted an extensive public information and polling program, *Americans Discuss Social Security.* The most popular reforms were to raise the earnings ceiling, reduce benefits for high-income individuals, and expand coverage to more workers.[10]

- In 2001, President Bush's *Commission to Strengthen Social Security* proposed three different plans, all based on partial privatization of the system, using individual investment accounts.[11]

- In 2010, President Obama's *National Commission on Fiscal Responsibility and Reform,* also known as Simpson-Bowles, recommended raising the earnings ceiling, changing the benefit formula, increasing the retirement age, and expanding coverage to more workers. The report was supported by most Commission members, but did not gain the supermajority needed for endorsement.[12]

- In 2011, Congress's bipartisan *Joint Select Committee on Deficit Reduction* was formed to reduce the national debt, and Social Security reform was expected to be included in its proposals. It was unable to reach agreement and was dissolved.[13]

- Along the way, virtually every congressional office and interest group has proposed its own plan for reform.

All these proposals share one feature: no action was taken on any of them. Therefore, we're still on the same financial track laid down in the 1983 Amendments.

Analysis

Reforms are grouped around these options:

Changing the Cost of Living Adjustments (COLA). Currently, Social Security benefits are increased annually for inflation, as measured by the Consumer Price Index for Urban Wage Earners and Clerical Workers (CPI-W). Some reform plans suggest a different inflation index like the "chained-CPI" proposal, or giving COLAs smaller than the full CPI-W, like CPI minus 0.5%.

Level of monthly payments. The PIA formula could be changed to produce smaller benefits for everyone, or for targeted groups such as high earners. A related idea is to increase the number of work years used in the computation from the current 35 to 38 or even 40.

Retirement Age. The Full Retirement Age is currently moving from 65 to 67, with early retirement benefits still available at 62. FRA could be moved higher than 67, e.g. 68 or 70, and/or the early retirement age could be raised beyond the current 62.

Family benefits. The current 50% computation for most spouses and children could be reduced to a lower percentage, say 40% or 33%.

Payroll taxes. The payroll tax rate, currently at 6.2% for Social Security, could be raised for everyone or for targeted groups such as high-earners. Or the taxable earnings ceiling, currently $128,400 (2018), could be raised to collect more taxes from high earners.

Coverage of earnings. Currently, about 6% of workers are outside the Social Security system,[14] primarily state and local government workers. Covering them or new hires under Social Security would help long-term solvency. Other earnings, such as the value of employee health insurance, could also be covered by the payroll tax.

Re-investing the trust funds. Investing a modest portion of the trust funds in the stock and/or real estate markets should increase long-term returns while preserving security during market downturns.

Taxation of benefits. Currently, only part of Social Security is income-taxable, and only for higher-income retirees. More benefits could be made taxable or the income thresholds could be phased out.

Individual investment accounts. There are two kinds of individual investment accounts proposed: either a *carve-out* (diverting part of the payroll tax to an individual account) or an *add-on* (leaving the payroll tax as-is but adding an individual account on top of it). Note that, by themselves, neither approach extends Social Security solvency. On the contrary, a carve-out will worsen the solvency problem by reducing Social Security's income.

In practice, it's doubtful that one "fix" will be used to balance Social Security's books. There will almost certainly be a combination of tax increases and benefits cuts, as was done in 1983.

Author's Comments

Background. Social Security is just that: *social*—not individual—and *security*—not risky. With so much of retirement at risk these days, those two features should be retained in any reform package.

It's insurance, not an investment. Specifically, it's insurance with a risk pool spread over the entire workforce, not an individual or a small group. That fits well with the *security* nomenclature.

Individual investment accounts. Individual accounts are the opposite of Social Security. They're not social, they're private. And they're not secure, they're risky.

Individual accounts are fine. Investment is wise. The power of compound interest is astounding. Everyone should save and invest.

However, only a fool would cancel his home insurance or health insurance and invest the premiums, because he can get a "better rate of return" by investing. The wise person buys the insurance *first* and *then* invests above and beyond the insurance.

The same applies to Social Security. It's a starting point, a secure foundation. Individuals should certainly build additional financial security atop it.

Carve-out individual accounts only weaken Social Security and compound its financing problem. Social Security has a long-term cash shortfall. You can't save it by diverting part of its funding into investment accounts. Such a move would obviously just expand the shortfall, causing bigger headaches in the near future and long term.

Carve-out individual accounts make no sense financially, so the aim of proponents must be to shrink or dismantle Social Security on philosophical grounds. My conclusion is that any individual accounts should be funded *in addition to* Social Security (add-on), not *at the expense of* Social Security (carve-out).

I like to say that if you want an individual account, open an IRA or a 401(k). They're available here and now.

Funding Social Security. Full funding of Social Security requires a savings of 2.83% of taxable payroll (2017 Trustees Report[15]). A remarkable document can be found at www.ssa.gov/OACT/solvency/provisions/summary.html. There, SSA actuaries list numerous individual policy proposals and evaluate the impact of each one on Social Security's solvency, as a percent of the shortfall eliminated. You can pick and choose your own reforms to save Social Security.

Below is a modest proposal, a seven-point model that fully funds Social Security for the 21st Century with no benefit cuts and a minimum of disruption. All plan numbers and savings figures are from www.ssa.gov/OACT/solvency/provisions/summary.html:

- *Raise the earnings ceiling (Plan E3.1).* This was the most popular "fix" identified by Americans Discuss Social Security and other polling. It is politically viable and could save a tremendous amount of money for the system. The ceiling can be raised to capture 90% of total compensation, as was the case in 1983, when the current ceiling was adopted. The increase would be phased in by 2027. Retirees would receive increased benefits in line with their increased contributions. Shortfall eliminated: **27%**.

- *Increase the payroll tax rate (Plan E1.5).* An increase from the current 12.4% to 13.3% could be phased in gradually until 2068. Nobody likes a tax increase, but this very modest increase—the employee share would be only 0.45% of payroll—makes a dramatic difference in Social Security financing. Shortfall eliminated: **27%**, and we've already saved over half of the amount needed.

- *Re-invest the Trust Funds (Plan G2).* This is not as popular a fix, but it is an obvious step. 40% of the funds could be put in a broad-based index of stocks between now and 2032. This option assumes a modest 5.2% return on equities. The Trust Funds would still be the most conservative pension fund around, and could weather another Great Depression. Shortfall eliminated: **14%**.[16]

- *Cover newly-hired state and local government employees (Plan F1).* Shortfall eliminated: **6%**.

- *Tax Social Security as pensions are taxed (Plan H1).* This could be phased in by 2027 by lowering the existing taxation thresholds. Shortfall eliminated: **7%**.

- *Adjust the PIA formula (Plan B3.3).* The formula could be modified to protect lower earners and reduce benefits of higher earners. This fits well with increasing the earnings ceiling while still rewarding the higher earner with higher benefits. Shortfall eliminated: **8%**.

- *Increase the computation years in the formula from 35 to 40 (Plan B4.2).* This preserves the principle that benefits should be proportional to lifetime earnings. Shortfall eliminated: **15%**.

Remarkably, these seven reforms *by themselves* would save 104% of the money necessary for *permanent* Social Security solvency. Retirement age remains the same. COLAs are not reduced. Across-the-board cuts are avoided. Cost to the government is zero. Deficit impact is favorable. Changes are focused on a small number of higher-income individuals, most able to afford change. Social Security is sustainable for our children, grandchildren… basically indefinitely.

What could be simpler?

What the reader can do

Social Security will be changed in the next few years, and you will be affected. You owe it to yourself to become involved. Here are some ways you can play a role:

- Learn everything you can about Social Security. You've already taken a big step by reading this book. You already know more about Social Security than most people.

- Think about the value Social Security has for you, your family, and your neighbors. Is disability protection important to you? Survivor benefits? How about spouse or child benefits? Or are retirement and Medicare most important for you?

- Talk with your family and friends about Social Security. Share this book with them to increase their understanding. Start a discussion group at work or your place of worship. Invite a speaker from SSA or AARP.

- Attend an event. Many groups are sponsoring public forums on Social Security: SSA itself, elected officials, AARP, news shows, and others. Listen to other people's ideas and polish your own.

- Use your voice. Call a phone-in talk show, write a letter to the editor, phone your Congressional representatives, email the President.

- Vote. Elect representatives who will strengthen Social Security, not weaken it.

- Elevate the debate. Don't allow misinformation like "the trust funds don't exist" or "Social Security can't work." Tell people that Social Security is valuable, strong, efficient, viable, and affordable.

Social Security's financing problems are solvable. Study after study has published plans to make the system solvent for the next 75 years—straight through the retirement years of the Boomers, Generation X, Millenials, and their children.

It is perfectly reasonable to fine-tune or even redesign the system for the new century. Each generation has adapted the Social Security system for its own needs or desires:

- In the 1930s, Social Security was created as a simple pension system for selected workers and widows.

- In the 1940s, benefits were expanded to other family members.

- In the 1950s, coverage was extended to more workers, disability was added, and early retirement became available for women.

- The 1960s brought the addition of Medicare and early retirement for men.

- In the 70s, COLAs were made automatic and benefits were expanded for former spouses. SSI was added as a safety net.

- The 80s brought a landmark extension of Social Security solvency for 50 years.

- The 1990s and 2000s explored many long-term solutions, gathering financial facts and public opinion.

- Now, it's time for Xers and Millenials to reshape the system for the 21st century.

The next generation needs to look at the "fine print" of reform plans, and really think about what they want their Social Security system to do.

If we do nothing, we get a weaker Social Security. Social Security has never been stronger or more popular. Ironically, it also has never been more threatened by those who would weaken it.

Over the past eight decades, Congress has listened and delivered whatever changes were popular. Let's build a Social Security system that serves us best.

FOR MORE INFORMATION...

"Trust Fund FAQs"
www.ssa.gov/OACT/ProgData/fundFAQ.html

"The 2017 OASDI Trustees Report"
www.ssa.gov/OACT/TR/2017/index.html

"Old-Age, Survivors, and Disability Insurance Trust Funds, 1957-2014"
www.ssa.gov/OACT/STATS/table4a3.html

"Operations of the Combined OASI and DI Trust Funds, In Current Dollars"
https://ssa.gov/oact/TR/2017/lr6g8.html

"The Social Security Fix-It Book"
http://crr.bc.edu/special-projects/books/the-social-security-fix-it-book/

"Summary of Provisions That Would Change the Social Security Program"
www.ssa.gov/OACT/solvency/provisions/summary.html

"Proposals Addressing Trust Fund Solvency"
www.ssa.gov/OACT/solvency/index.html

"CBO Social Security Policy Options 2015"
https://www.cbo.gov/publication/51011

"Social Security Debate in the United States"
https://en.wikipedia.org/wiki/Social_Security_debate_in_the_United_States

Chapter endnotes:

1. http://articles.chicagotribune.com/1994-09-27/news/9409270092_1_personal-retirement-account-ufos-social-security-administration
2. https://www.ssa.gov/news/press/releases/2017/#7-2017-1 and https://ssa.gov/oact/TR/2017/lr6g8.html
3. https://ssa.gov/oact/TR/historical/1982TR.pdf, p. 2
4. https://www.socialsecurity.gov/policy/docs/ssb/v46n7/v46n7p3.pdf
5. https://www.ssa.gov/oact/TR/2017/II_B_cyoper.html#96807
6. https://www.socialsecurity.gov/legislation/legis_bulletin_121710.html

7. https://www.ssa.gov/oact/TR/2017/II_D_project.html#132991, Figure II.D3, including text above
8. https://www.ssa.gov/oact/TR/2017/lr6g8.html
9. https://www.socialsecurity.gov/history/reports/adcouncil/
10. http://www.actuaries.org/Events/Congresses/Cancun/presentations/ICA_19_Rgebhardisbauer. pdf, p. 13
11. http://govinfo.library.unt.edu/csss/reports/Final_report.pdf
12. http://momentoftruthproject.org/sites/default/files/TheMomentofTruth12_1_2010.pdf
13. https://en.wikipedia.org/wiki/United_States_Congress_Joint_Select_Committee_on_Deficit_ Reduction
14. https://ssa.gov/OACT/FACTS/index.html, D.
15. https://www.ssa.gov/OACT/TRSUM/index.html
16. Derived from percent of payroll change from proposal vs. percent of payroll needed to eliminate shortfall, .39%/2.83% = 13.8%

☆ NOTES ☆

☆ A P P E N D I X   A ☆

SAMPLE RETIREMENT COMPUTATION

Our sample computation is performed for Sam Smith, who was born February 15, 1953 and is retiring in 2018 at the age of 65 and 0 months. His earnings have been comfortable for most of his life, with a few lean years due to job changes. He achieved maximum Social Security earnings in some years, with lower earnings in most years.

We will walk through Sam's Social Security computation by referring to the columns in **Figure A-1**. The steps are also described in Chapter 2, pages 37-52.

See Appendix E for other sources of information on Social Security computations and estimates.

Column 1 shows calendar years from 1954 to 2018. 2017 is the last year used for Sam's computation because it is the year before his payments begin. Any wages for 2018 will be added to the computation automatically in 2019, and so on.

Column 2 shows the maximum taxable earnings base for each year. This is the highest earnings level that can be posted to the record each year, and the ceiling for FICA taxes—FICA taxes are paid only on wages at or below this level. Find maximum earnings for any year at www.ssa.gov/OACT/COLA/cbb.html.

Column 3 shows the national average of all wages, as tabulated by SSA for each year. This is used to determine the inflation index factor shown in **Column 4**. Find average wages for any year at www.ssa.gov/OACT/COLA/AWI.html. (2017 was unknown at time of publication.)

Column 4 shows the inflation factor used to make earlier earnings comparable to recent earnings. It is calculated by dividing the average wage for each year into the average wage for your Base Year, the *year you attain age 60*. Sam's Base Year is 2013, so in his case, each year's inflation factor is determined by 2013's average wage of $44,888.16 (from **Column 3**, 2013). Average wages for later years will not affect Sam's computation (but will be used for people with later birth years and Base Years).

The entire set of inflation factors are "locked in" at the year you turn 60. These same factors would be used to compute Sam's payment even if he first filed

Column 1	2	3	4	5	6	7	8
Year	Max. Earnings Base	Average Wage	Inflation Index Factor (2015 elig. yr.)	Sam's Actual Earnings	Sam's Indexed Earnings	High 35 Years	Comp. Earnings
1954	$3,600	$3,155.64	14.2247405	$0.00	$0.00	L	$0.00
1955	$4,200	$3,301.44	13.5965397	$0.00	$0.00	L	$0.00
1956	$4,200	$3,532.36	12.7076968	$0.00	$0.00	L	$0.00
1957	$4,200	$3,641.72	12.3260877	$0.00	$0.00	L	$0.00
1958	$4,200	$3,673.80	12.2184550	$0.00	$0.00	L	$0.00
1959	$4,800	$3,855.80	11.6417242	$0.00	$0.00	L	$0.00
1960	$4,800	$4,007.12	11.2021003	$0.00	$0.00	L	$0.00
1961	$4,800	$4,086.76	10.9838013	$0.00	$0.00	L	$0.00
1962	$4,800	$4,291.40	10.4600270	$0.00	$0.00	L	$0.00
1963	$4,800	$4,396.64	10.2096510	$0.00	$0.00	L	$0.00
1964	$4,800	$4,576.32	9.8087896	$0.00	$0.00	L	$0.00
1965	$4,800	$4,658.72	9.6352990	$0.00	$0.00	L	$0.00
1966	$6,600	$4,938.36	9.0896897	$0.00	$0.00	L	$0.00
1967	$6,600	$5,213.44	8.6100847	$0.00	$0.00	L	$0.00
1968	$7,800	$5,571.76	8.0563700	$0.00	$0.00	L	$0.00
1969	$7,800	$5,893.76	7.6162178	$0.00	$0.00	L	$0.00
1970	$7,800	$6,186.24	7.2561297	$600.00	$4,353.68	L	$0.00
1971	$7,800	$6,497.08	6.9089745	$600.00	$4,145.38	L	$0.00
1972	$9,000	$7,133.80	6.2923211	$650.00	$4,090.01	L	$0.00
1973	$10,800	$7,580.16	5.9217958	$1,000.00	$5,921.80	L	$0.00
1974	$13,200	$8,030.76	5.5895283	$1,200.00	$6,707.43	L	$0.00
1975	$14,100	$8,630.92	5.2008546	$4,000.00	$20,803.42	L	$0.00
1976	$15,300	$9,226.48	4.8651447	$6,000.00	$29,190.87	L	$0.00
1977	$16,500	$9,779.44	4.5900542	$8,000.00	$36,720.43	H	$36,720.43
1978	$17,700	$10,556.03	4.2523714	$5,500.00	$23,388.04	L	$0.00
1979	$22,900	$11,479.46	3.9103024	$9,900.00	$38,711.99	H	$38,711.99
1980	$25,900	$12,513.46	3.5871901	$9,300.00	$33,360.87	L	$0.00
1981	$29,700	$13,773.10	3.2591181	$10,000.00	$32,591.18	L	$0.00
1982	$32,400	$14,531.34	3.0890585	$6,000.00	$18,534.35	L	$0.00
1983	$35,700	$15,239.24	2.9455642	$12,000.00	$35,346.77	L	$0.00
1984	$37,800	$16,135.07	2.7820245	$13,000.00	$36,166.32	L	$0.00
1985	$39,600	$16,822.51	2.6683390	$15,000.00	$40,025.09	H	$40,025.09
1986	$42,000	$17,321.82	2.5914228	$20,000.00	$51,828.46	H	$51,828.46
1987	$43,800	$18,426.51	2.4360641	$22,000.00	$53,593.41	H	$53,593.41
1988	$45,000	$19,334.04	2.3217165	$25,000.00	$58,042.91	H	$58,042.91
1989	$48,000	$20,099.55	2.2332918	$28,000.00	$62,532.17	H	$62,532.17
1990	$51,300	$21,027.98	2.1346872	$31,000.00	$66,175.30	H	$66,175.30
1991	$53,400	$21,811.60	2.0579948	$28,000.00	$57,623.86	H	$57,623.86
1992	$55,500	$22,935.42	1.9571545	$31,000.00	$60,671.79	H	$60,671.79
1993	$57,600	$23,132.67	1.9404660	$33,000.00	$64,035.38	H	$64,035.38
1994	$60,600	$23,753.53	1.8897469	$35,000.00	$66,141.14	H	$66,141.14
1995	$61,200	$24,705.66	1.8169181	$40,000.00	$72,676.72	H	$72,676.72
1996	$62,700	$25,913.90	1.7322040	$45,000.00	$77,949.18	H	$77,949.18
1997	$65,400	$27,426.00	1.6367009	$50,000.00	$81,835.05	H	$81,835.05
1998	$68,400	$28,861.44	1.5552987	$69,000.00	$106,382.43	H	$106,382.43
1999	$72,600	$30,469.84	1.4731997	$74,000.00	$106,954.30	H	$106,954.30
2000	$76,200	$32,154.82	1.3960010	$78,000.00	$106,375.27	H	$106,375.27
2001	$80,400	$32,921.92	1.3634733	$68,000.00	$92,716.19	H	$92,716.19
2002	$84,900	$33,252.09	1.3499350	$67,000.00	$90,445.64	H	$90,445.64
2003	$87,000	$34,064.95	1.3177228	$68,000.00	$89,605.15	H	$89,605.15

Column 1	2	3	4	5	6	7	8
Year	Max. Earnings Base	Average Wage	Inflation Index Factor (2015 elig. yr.)	Sam's Actual Earnings	Sam's Indexed Earnings	High 35 Years	Comp. Earnings
2004	$87,900	$35,648.55	1.2591861	$52,000.00	$65,477.68	H	$65,477.68
2005	$90,000	$36,952.94	1.2147385	$51,000.00	$61,951.67	H	$61,951.67
2006	$94,200	$38,651.41	1.1613589	$51,000.00	$59,229.31	H	$59,229.31
2007	$97,500	$40,405.48	1.1109424	$52,000.00	$57,769.00	H	$57,769.00
2008	$102,000	$41,334.97	1.0859609	$55,000.00	$59,727.85	H	$59,727.85
2009	$106,800	$40,711.61	1.1025887	$58,000.00	$63,950.14	H	$63,950.14
2010	$106,800	$41,673.83	1.0771307	$61,000.00	$65,704.97	H	$65,704.97
2011	$106,800	$42,979.61	1.0444059	$63,000.00	$65,797.57	H	$65,797.57
2012	$110,100	$44,321.67	1.0127813	$65,000.00	$65,830.79	H	$65,830.79
2013	$113,700	$44,888.16	1.0000000	$65,000.00	$65,000.00	H	$65,000.00
2014	$117,000	$46,481.52	1.0000000	$65,000.00	$65,000.00	H	$65,000.00
2015	$118,500	$48,098.63	1.0000000	$67,000.00	$67,000.00	H	$67,000.00
2016	$118,500	$48,642.15	1.0000000	$68,000.00	$68,000.00	H	$68,000.00
2017	$127,200	N/A	1.0000000	$69,000.00	$69,000.00	H	$69,000.00
2018	$128,400	N/A	N/A	N/A	N/A	N/A	N/A

Figure A-1. Retirement computation example (Sam Smith).

for Social Security in 2017 (age 66), no matter how much inflation drove up average wages in the interim. The inflation factor "lock-in" is illustrated in **Column 4** by the inflation factor "1.00000" posted for every year from 2013 on. It will continue at 1.00000 indefinitely. In other words, there is no further inflation indexing of *wages* after age 60. But the Social Security *benefit* is adjusted for CPI inflation, as shown below (see pages 274 and 276). Wages are inflated by average wages; payments are inflated by average prices.

The inflation index factors, and the entire computation dependent upon them, are updated each year for those turning 60. A second retiree, Ms. Jones, who turned 60 in 2014, would have different, higher inflation index factors for every year because they would be compared to the *2014* average wage, which was higher than that of 2013.

You can find the indexing factors for any year at www.ssa.gov/OACT/COLA/awifactors.html. Note that the chart there is tied to the year of eligibility (age 62) rather than the Base Year (age 60).

Column 5 shows Sam's actual earnings. Usually, Sam's earnings were below the Social Security maximum. However, in 1998, 1999, and 2000, his earnings were above the maximum. In practice, only earnings up to the maximum would be posted to SSA's records and used in the computation.

Column 6 displays Sam's *indexed earnings*. These are simply his actual earnings (**Column 5**) or maximum earnings (**Column 2**), whichever is lower, multiplied by the inflation index factor for each year (**Column 4**), to account for inflation.

Column 7 is an analysis of **Column 6**, marking the 35 years with the highest indexed earnings. The 35 high years, also called the Computation Years, are labeled "H." Low years are labeled "L." The low years are sometimes called "dropout years" because they will not be used in the computation. Note that the computation years do not have to be continuous years, as shown by 1977 being an "H" computation year surrounded by "L" years, and 1978 being an "L" year surrounded by "H" years.

Column 8 is a transcription from **Column 6** of the earnings from the 35 highest years. These are the *computation earnings* from the Computation Years. These earnings determine Sam's full payment at his Full Retirement Age, called his *Primary Insurance Amount (PIA)*.

Benefit Computation

Computation of Average Earnings
Dividend:.. $2,380,480.84
Divisor Months (35 years x 12 months):....................................... 420
AIME:...**$5,667**

Computation of full retirement payment, with COLAs
(See text)
Age 62 PIA (2015):...**$2,175.70**
January 2016 COLA (0%):... $2,175.70
January 2017 COLA (0.3%) $2182.20
January 2018 COLA (2.0%) $2,225.80
2018 PIA: **$2,225.80**

Computation of reduced retirement payment
Reduction Months 12
Reduction Factor:.. 0.93333
Benefit before rounding: $2,077.40
Monthly Payment: **$2,077.00**

Figure A-2. Sam Smith's payment computation

Benefit Computation

Computation of Average Earnings
Dividend:.. $2,380,480.84

Figure A-2 summarizes Sam's computation. The first figure, his *Dividend,* is the sum of all indexed earnings from his best 35 years—the sum of **Column 8**. As can be seen, Sam earned over $2.3 million in his career, after accounting for inflation.

Divisor Months (35 years x 12 months): 420

The "Divisor Months" convert Sam's lifetime dividend into a monthly earnings figure. The 420 months shown are the number of months in the 35 Computation Years (35 x 12 = 420).

AIME: $5,667

Dividing the dividend by the 420 Divisor Months results in Sam's *AIME*, or Average Indexed Monthly Earnings. As the name indicates, this is Sam's average monthly earned income after inflation.

Age 62 PIA (2015): $2,175.70

Sam's AIME determines his PIA (his age 66 full payment amount), as of his age 62. Every PIA is determined by a three-stage computation based on the AIME. Sam's computation, based on his year of eligibility, looks like this:

1. 90% of first $826 of AIME   = $743.40
                                                                              (Max $743.40)

2. Plus 32% of next $4,154 of AIME   = $1,329.28
                                                                           (Max $1,329.28)

3. Plus 15% of AIME above $4,980 ($687 x 0.15)   = <u>103.05</u>

The sum of the three stages is rounded down to the nearest dime. That total is the full payment amount at Full Retirement Age, age 66 in Sam's case, *as computed at age 62*. This is his *age 62 PIA*.

4. Sum of 1, 2, and 3 (rounded down to nearest dime)   = $2,175.70

Notice the figures which govern this computation. On the left are the *90%, 32%, and 15% multipliers*. These percentage multipliers stay the same from year to year. Next are the *$826 and $4,980* figures (the $4,154 is the difference between the two). These figures are called the *bend points* in the Social Security computation. They determine *at what levels* the percentage multipliers apply, and how much of your AIME you receive in your Social Security payment. The bend points are updated each year to account for inflation. The bend points used in your computation are the ones in effect in your Eligibility Year, the year you turn 62.

Find bend points for various Eligibility Years at www.ssa.gov/OACT/COLA/bendpoints.html.

You can see that rewards for a low AIME are high (90% return) while rewards for a higher AIME taper off (32% and 15% returns). The 90%, 32%, and 15% multipliers are the mechanism that gives low-income workers a faster payback, while ensuring that high-income workers still get credit for their earnings.

Age 62 PIA (2015):..	**$2,175.70**
January 2016 COLA (0%):	$2,175.70
January 2017 COLA (0.3%)	$2182.20
January 2018 COLA (2.0%)	$2,225.80
2018 PIA:	**$2,225.80**

Next, Sam's Age 62 PIA is adjusted for inflation to a "current" PIA for the year he first draws benefits. In this case, Sam's first benefit is at age 65—three years after his Age 62 PIA. Each January, his PIA will earn the COLA (Cost Of Living Adjustment) based on the inflation rate, whether or not he was actually drawing a payment. COLAs for recent years are posted at www.ssa.gov/OACT/COLA/autoAdj.html. (Note that at that site, the COLAs are posted effective *December* of the year shown. That amount would be applied to payments in *January of the following year.*)

Adding the three COLAs makes his **2018 PIA $2,225.80**, after again rounding down each step to the next lower dime.

Computation of reduced retirement payment
Reduction Months 12

The last few lines in Sam's benefit computation determine his reduced payment for being younger than his Full Retirement Age. If he enrolls in his birth month at age 65, he will have 12 "reduction months" because he is 12 months younger than his FRA of 66.

Reduction Factor:... 0.93333

The reduction factor is computed as follows:

- For the first 36 months of early eligibility, each reduction month causes a payment reduction of 5/9 of 1% (0.00556).
- Each additional early eligibility month causes a reduction of 5/12 of 1% (0.00417).

With 12 reduction months, Sam's total reduction for early retirement is 6.667%, dropping Sam's payment to 93.333% of his full payment amount (PIA).

Benefit before rounding: $2,077.40

The reduction factor of 0.93333 times Sam's full payment amount ($2,225.80) makes Sam's benefit amount $2,077.40.

Monthly Payment:..**$2,077.00**

Sam's actual monthly payment is rounded down to the next lower *dollar*. Thus, Sam's monthly payment at age 65 will be $2,077.00.

Not included in this example are Medicare premiums. Since Sam is retiring at age 65, he also files for Medicare Parts A and B and pays a Part B premium of $134.00, the premium for new 2018 enrollees. This is deducted directly from his Social Security payment, reducing his net payment to $1,943.00.

FOR MORE INFORMATION...

"Your Retirement Benefit: How It Is Figured" go to www.ssa.gov/pubs/index.html, search for "how it is figured," and select your birth year in the drop-down box

"Benefit Calculation Examples" www.socialsecurity.gov/OACT/ProgData/retirebenefit1.html

"Benefit Computation and Automatic Adjustment Provisions" www.socialsecurity.gov/policy/docs/statcomps/supplement/2016/oasdi.html Also see www.socialsecurity.gov/policy/docs/statcomps/supplement/2017/oasdi.html (not available at press time)

☆ NOTES ☆

SOCIAL SECURITY FACTS AND FIGURES

SOCIAL SECURITY'S BUDGET

SSA's budget is one of the biggest in the world. Figures for income, expense, and assets for Social Security programs in 2016 are as follows (all figures are in billions):

	Income	Expenditures	Trust Fund Assets
OASDI	$958	$922	$2,848
Medicare A	291	285	199
Medicare B	313	293	88
Total	**1,562**	**1,500**	**3,135**

The SSA and Medicare budgets are actually separate. Social Security alone is the biggest item in the 2017 federal budget, well ahead of the Department of Defense. If Social Security plus Medicare were an independent nation, it would have one of the world's largest national budgets, and be ranked eleventh in the world according to GDP, between Canada and South Korea. And with over $3 trillion in assets, SSA is one of the world's largest investors.

With annual expenditures of $1.5 trillion, Social Security plus Medicare spend about $125 billion per month, $4.2 billion per day, or about $174 million per hour. This works out to about $48,000 per second. At the same time, the combined trust funds grew $60.4 billion in 2016, or $165 million per day.

---

https://www.socialsecurity.gov/OACT/TR/2015/II_B_cyoper.html#96807
https://www.cms.gov/research-statistics-data-and-systems/statistics-trends-and-reports/reportstrustfunds/downloads/tr2017.pdf

https://www.cbo.gov/sites/default/files/115th-congress-2017-2018/graphic/52408-budgetoverall.pdf
http://databank.worldbank.org/data/download/GDP.pdf

SOCIAL SECURITY BENEFICIARIES

61.8 million individuals receive a Social Security payment each month—over one in six Americans (October 2017). The beneficiaries fall into the following categories:

Retired workers	42.3 million
Spouses of retirees	2.4 million
Children of retirees	0.7 million
Survivors of deceased workers	6.0 million
Disabled workers	8.7 million
Spouses of disabled workers	0.1 million
Children of disabled workers	1.6 million
Total OASDI beneficiaries	61.8 million

In addition, there are about 8.3 million SSI beneficiaries.

www.ssa.gov/policy/docs/quickfacts/stat_snapshot/index.html
www.census.gov/main/www/popclock.html

SSA: THE AGENCY

There are about 66,000 employees of SSA, in Field Offices, Program Service Centers, Teleservice Centers, and Headquarters facilities.

The 1,245 Field Offices cover every major community in the U.S. Their mission is to serve as the face-to-face meeting point between the agency and the public by processing claims, inquiries, and reports of change, all in a neighborhood office setting.

The six Program Service Centers are organized to keep records and issue payments, and to process behind-the-scenes workloads such as record corrections. In addition to the six regular PSCs, the Office of Disability Adjudication and Review serves as a PSC for all disability payments, and an Office of International Operations serves as a PSC for all overseas operations such as payments to foreign residents.

The 27 TeleService Centers handled 72 million calls in 2015, or about 275,000 calls per workday. Average wait time was 10.3 minutes. These calls range from general inquiries and requests for Social Security numbers to filing claims.

SSA Headquarters (located in Baltimore) and its ten Regional Offices (located in major cities throughout the country) coordinate the activities of all branches of the agency and attend to administrative functions such as budgeting, hiring, and training.

The agency's staffing level has dropped from 70,758 total work years in 2010 to 65,798 in 2016, resulting in a lean operation with very low overhead. In 2015, Social Security administrative costs were $6.2 billion, or about 0.7% of total expenses or total income. By comparison, overhead can run much more in private insurance companies, charitable organizations, and mutual funds.

https://www.ssa.gov/policy/docs/statcomps/supplement/2016/2f1-2f3.html
https://www.ssa.gov/policy/docs/statcomps/supplement/2016/2f7.html
www.socialsecurity.gov/OACT/TR/2016/III_A_cyoper.html#147356 Tables III.A.3 and III.A.6

SOCIAL SECURITY CLAIMS, FY 2015

The following claims were filed in Fiscal Year 2015:

Retirement & Survivor	5.3 million
Disability	2.7 million
SSI	2.1 million
Total claims	10.1 million

That is about 39,000 claims per workday, or over 31 claims per field office per workday.

https://www.ssa.gov/policy/docs/statcomps/supplement/2016/2f4-2f6.html

SOCIAL SECURITY TIME LINE

8/14/1935   Social Security Act signed into law. Only industrial workers are covered, with retirement benefits available only at 65.

1/1937   First Social Security taxes collected; 1.0% of first $3,000 earned.

1939   Survivor benefits, spouse benefits, and child benefits added.

1/1940   First Social Security monthly benefits paid.

1951	Work coverage extended to farm labor, domestic service, and some self-employed workers.
1955-56	Work coverage extended to military service, self-employed farmers and most professionals.
1956	Disability benefits added for ages 50-64. Early retirement at 62 available to women.
1960	Disability benefits added for those under 50.
1961	Early retirement at 62 available to men.
1965	Divorced wife benefits added. Work coverage extended to medical doctors.
7/1965	Medicare coverage begins.
1/1974	SSI benefits begin.
6/1975	Automatic cost-of-living adjustments begin.
1977	Divorced husband benefits added.
1/1984	Up to 50% of benefits includable in taxable income. All newly-hired federal employees, plus the President, Vice-President, and members of Congress, are covered by Social Security.
1/1994	Up to 85% of benefits includable in taxable income.
2000	Retirement earnings test eliminated at FRA. Retirees may suspend their benefits from FRA-70 to earn DRCs.
2015	Suspending retirement benefits also suspends family benefits. Retroactive reinstatement of suspended benefits no longer allowed. Filing "spousal-only" claim at FRA eliminated for birth dates after Jan. 1, 1954.

www.ssa.gov/history/
https://www.ssa.gov/policy/docs/statcomps/supplement/2016/2a20-2a28.html

☆ APPENDIX C ☆

2018 REFERENCE DATA

CONTACTING SOCIAL SECURITY

Web: www.socialsecurity.gov or mirror site www.ssa.gov
Telephone: (800) SSA-1213
TTY: (800) 325-0778

Toll-free telephone is staffed workdays from 7 a.m. to 7 p.m. in the time zone you call from. Recorded messages and automated services at all other hours.

CONTACTING MEDICARE

Web: www.medicare.gov
Telephone: (800) MEDICARE (800-633-4227)
TTY: (877) 486-2048

FICA TAX RATES

Social Security and Medicare taxes (2018 earnings ceiling: $128,400*)

Paid by employee	7.65%
(6.20% Social Security, 1.45% Medicare)	
Paid by employer	7.65%
Paid by self-employed individual	15.3%

Medicare only taxes (On earnings over $128,400)

Paid by employee	1.45%
Paid by employer	1.45%
Paid by self-employed individual	2.90%

*Revised from original figure of $128,700 on Nov. 27, 2017

Work Credit/Quarter Of Coverage

Minimum earnings to achieve one quarter of coverage: $1,320

Earnings Limits While Enrolled

Under FRA (age 66):	$17,040/year ($1,420/month) Deduction = 1/2 of excess earnings
Turning FRA:	$45,360/year ($3,780/month) for months prior to birthday only. Deduction = 1/3 of excess earnings
FRA and up:	No earnings limit.

Medicare Facts

Part A premium	
With 40+ Work Credits	$0
With 30-39 Work Credits	$232.00/month
With under 30 Work Credits	$422.00/month
Part B premium	$134/month standard $130/month - $428.60/month (See Figure 6.1, p. 138)
Part A deductible	$1,340/benefit period
Part B deductible	$183/year

Benefit Payments

Total Social Security benefits paid (2016)	$922 billion
Individual monthly benefits (2018):	
Maximum for age 66 retiree	$2,788
Average retired worker	$1,404
Retired couple, both receiving benefits	$2,340
Aged widow(er) alone	$1,336
Widowed parent & 2 children	$2,771
Disabled worker	$1,197

www.ssa.gov/OACT/FACTS/
www.medicare.gov/your-medicare-costs/costs-at-a-glance/costs-at-glance.html
https://www.ssa.gov/news/press/factsheets/colafacts2018.pdf

CRITICAL AGES

Birth
- Receive Social Security number (automatic if US-born). Page 216.
- Eligible for Social Security child's payments. Pages 70, 95.
- Eligible for SSI payments if disabled and needy. Page 227.

16
- Parent's Social Security payments stop when youngest child reaches 16. Pages 62, 64, 65, 88, 90, 91.

18
- Child's Social Security payments stop unless child is in elementary or high school, or disabled. Pages 62, 70, 95.
- Disabled individual can get SSI without counting parent's income and resources. Page 227.

19
- Child's Social Security payment stops even if in elementary or high school, unless disabled. Pages 62, 70, 95.

22
- Must be disabled by age 22 to receive Social Security payments as Disabled Adult Child. Page 117.

50
- Eligible for Social Security payments as a Disabled Widow(er) (reduced payment amount). Page 116.

60
- Eligible for Social Security payments as a Widow(er) (reduced payment amount). Page 87.
- Remarriage after 60 does not bar Social Security Widow(er)'s payments. Page 89.

62	• Eligible for early Social Security retirement or spousal payments (reduced payment amount). Pages 34, 60.
65	• Eligible by age for Medicare. Page 131.
	• Eligible for SSI Aged payments. Page 227.
65-67	• Full Retirement Age (FRA). Exact FRA, currently 66, is determined by birth year and type of benefit. Pages 47, 67, 91.
	• Eligible for unreduced Social Security retirement, spousal, or widow(er)'s payments. Pages 47, 67, 91.
	• Maximum spousal and widow(er)'s payments. Pages 67, 91.
	• Earned income no longer reduces Social Security payment. Page 205.
	• Retirement payments automatically increase if payments were withheld due to work (ARF). Page 210.
	• Able to suspend payments voluntarily to receive Delayed Retirement Credits (DRCs). Family payments will also be suspended if suspension is requested after April 29, 2016. Page 241.
	• Able to draw "Spousal-Only" payments without applying for retirement payments, if born before January 2, 1954. Page 248.
	• Disabled worker payments automatically convert to retirement payments, at the same payment amount.
70	• Maximum retirement payments. P. 49.
	• Voluntarily suspended payments automatically resume. Pp. 243, 245.

INCOME TAX ON SOCIAL SECURITY BENEFITS

BACKGROUND

Part of your Social Security payments may be income-taxable if you have outside income such as a pension, dividends, or interest. See page 212 for background information.

The following worksheet will help you estimate how much of your Social Security will be included in your taxable income. Use actual IRS worksheets for tax filing.

TAX ESTIMATOR WORKSHEET

Estimator: How much of my social security benefits are taxable?
(Tax Returns Filed in 1995 and Later)

1.	Your Social Security Benefits	_____(1)
2.	50% of Line 1	_____(2)
3.	Your gross income[A]	_____(3)
4.	Your tax-exempt interest income	_____(4)
5.	Sum of Lines 2, 3, and 4	_____(5)
6.	Your adjustments to income[B]	_____(6)

7. Is amount on Line 6 less than Line 5?
    If No, stop. None of your Social Security is taxable.

    If Yes, subtract Line 6 from Line 5 _____(7)

8. If you are:
    Married filing jointly, enter $32,000

    Single, enter $25,000

    Married filing separately and lived apart
    from spouse all year, enter $25,000 _____(8)

    (If married filing separately and lived with spouse
    for part of year, skip lines 8-15. Multiply
    line 7 by 0.85 and enter result in line 16.
    Then go on to Line 17.)

9. Is the amount on Line 8 less than the amount on Line 7?
    If No, Stop. None of your Social Security is taxable.

    If Yes, subtract Line 8 from Line 7 _____(9)

10. If married filing jointly, enter $12,000
    If single enter $9,000
    If married filing separately and lived apart
    from spouse all year, enter $9,000 _____(10)

11. Subtract Line 10 from Line 9. If zero or les, enter 0 _____(11)

12. Enter the smaller of Line 9 or Line 10 _____(12)

13. Enter one-half of Line 12 _____(13)

14. Enter the smaller of Line 2 or Line 13 _____(14)

15. Multiply Line 11 by 0.85. If Line 11 is zero, enter 0 _____(15)

16. Add Lines 14 and 15 _____(16)

17. Multiply Line 1 by 0.85 _____(17)

18. Enter the smaller of Line 16 or 17. _____(18)

LINE 18 = TAXABLE BENEFITS. This amount would be included in your taxable income on your Form 1040.

NOTE A. Income BEFORE subtracting itemized deductions and personal exemptions. Include all income from Form 1040, "Income" block, right-hand column.

NOTE B. Include adjustments in Form 1040, "Adjusted Gross Income" block. Do not include student loan interest deduction, tuition and fees deduction, or domestic production deduction.

DESCRIPTION: Starting with tax returns filed in 1995, up to 85% of Social Security benefits must be included in taxable income. The 85% rule applies to marrieds with over $44,000 income and singles with over $34,000. Up to 50% of benefits are taxable for marrieds with income from $32,000 to $44,000, and for singles with income from $25,000 to $34,000.

Note that Line 18 is *not* the amount of tax you must pay on your Social Security. It is simply the amount of your Social Security to be included *in your taxable income* on your Form 1040. It would then be taxable at your tax rate.

You can prepare a computer spreadsheet to perform these computations. You can then use it to compare various income scenarios for you.

Source: www.irs.gov/pub/irs-pdf/i1040.pdf

EXAMPLES OF TAX COMPUTATIONS

Example 1: Single Person James Johnson

Assumptions:

Social Security	13,400
Gross Income	$6,000
Non-taxable interest income:	5,000
Income adjustments	0

Computation:

(1-6)	½ Social Security	$6,700
	+Gross Income	+6,000
	+ Non-Taxable Interest	+5,000
(7)	Total	$17,700
(8)	IRS Base Amount (for individual)	25,000

(9)   Line 8 is greater than Line 7, no Social Security is taxable   0

Example 2: Single Person Mary Smith

Assumptions:

Yearly Social Security	13,400
Gross Income	$12,000
Non-taxable interest income:	10,000
Income adjustments	0

Computation:

Using the worksheet above, Line 18 =	$1,850

Therefore, $1,850 of Mary's Social Security is included in her taxable income on her IRS Form 1040. The remaining $11,550 of her Social Security is tax-free.

Example 3: Married Couple John and Marsha

Assumptions:

Yearly Social Security	$22,000
Gross Income	$20,000
Non-taxable interest income:	15,000
Income adjustments	0

Computation:

Using the worksheet above, Line 18 =	$7,700

Therefore, $7,700 of John and Marsha's Social Security is included in their taxable income on IRS Form 1040. The remaining $14,300 of their Social Security is tax-free.

Example 4: Married couple Bill and Barbara

Assumptions:

Yearly Social Security	$36,000
Gross Income	$43,000
Non-taxable interest income:	26,000

Income adjustments   0

Computation:
    Using the worksheet above, Line 18 = $30,600

    Therefore, $30,600 of John and Marsha's Social Security is included in their taxable income on IRS Form 1040. The remaining $5,400 of their Social Security is tax-free.

SOURCES OF SOCIAL SECURITY INFORMATION AND MATERIALS

ITEM	HOW TO FIND	NOTES
SSA Telephone	(800) SSA-1213	Information, publications, claims.
SSA Website	www.ssa.gov	General information, on-line publications, benefit estimates, claims, and research.
"My Social Security" personal account	www.ssa.gov/myaccount	Anytime access to earnings record and benefit estimates. For those on Social Security, online address or direct deposit changes, benefit verification letters, and more.
Apply for Social Security benefits	www.ssa.gov/applyonline/ or (800) SSA-1213	Apply for Social Security retirement, spouse, or disability payments.
Online Social Security Estimates	www.ssa.gov/estimator/	Instant benefit estimates. • You input identifying data to access the estimator. • Past earnings are automatically included but not posted. • You can alter the retirement date and future earnings fields to model various retirement scenarios.
Online Social Security publications	www.ssa.gov/pubs/	Access to all SSA publications.

ITEM	HOW TO FIND	NOTES
Social Security Benefit Calculators Home	www.ssa.gov/planners/benefitcalculators.html	Links to all benefit calculators: • Retirement Estimator (at link above) • Quick Calculator (rough estimate based on current earnings) • Online Calculator (you input past and future earnings; you need Social Security Statement for past earnings) • Detailed Calculator (downloadable "AnyPIA" program) • WEP & GPO Calculators
"Retirement Benefits" e-booklet	www.ssa.gov/pubs/10035.html	Good summary of retirement benefits, including family benefits.
Private Social Security Online Services	http://corp.financialengines.com/individuals/retirement-readiness.html, http://maximizemysocialsecurity.com, www.socialsecuritysolutions.com, or www.socialsecuritychoices.com	Help with when to apply, especially to optimize timing for married couples. Financial Engines calculator is free; others are fee-based and offer trained advisors
Medicare Hotline & Website	(800) 633-4227 TTY (877) 486-2048 www.medicare.gov	General information on Medicare including costs, deductibles, etc.
Medigap Plan Finder **Parts C & D Plan Finder**	www.medicare.gov/find-a-plan/questions/medigap-home.aspx www.medicare.gov/find-a-plan/questions/home.aspx	Computer assistance to select Medigap, Part C, or Part D plans tailored to your needs and budget.
Information on • **Medicare coverage** • **Supplemental insurance** • **Long Term Care Insurance**	Your state Insurance Commissioner • Find in www.shiptacenter.org • "A Shopper's Guide to Long-Term Care Insurance" free order form at http://www.naic.org/documents/prod_serv_consumer_ltc_lp.pdf	Non-biased publications, information, seminars, counseling on Medigaps, Medicare Advantage plans, Part D drug plans, employer or union plans, and LTC insurance.

☆ GLOSSARY ☆

GLOSSARY OF SOCIAL SECURITY TERMS

Bold face indicates a cross-reference—more information can be found in the glossary under that reference. Also see the index (following this glossary) for further information. See also SSA's glossary at www.ssa.gov/agency/glossary.

A

AERO: Automatic Earnings Reappraisal Operation. Recomputing benefit payments when new earnings appear on the **earnings record** of a **beneficiary.**

AIME: Average Indexed Monthly Earnings. The average monthly earnings of a worker's computation years after adjusting for inflation. The computation years are normally the worker's best 35 years after inflation adjustment.

ALJ: Administrative Law Judge; a judge who presides over **appeals** at the **Hearing** and **Appeals Council** levels.

Appeal: An administrative process to review an adverse decision from Social Security.

Appeals Council Review: The final level of **appeal**, following a **Hearing**. The Appeals Council is a panel of three **ALJs**.

Applicant: The person signing the application for Social Security benefits. May be different from the **claimant**, as when a parent is the applicant for a child claimant.

Approved Charge: The dollar amount approved by Medicare for a medical procedure.

Assignment method of payment: An agreement by a medical **provider** to charge no more than the Medicare **approved charge** for a medical procedure.

Auxiliary benefits: Social Security payments to auxiliaries—people other than the worker. Referred to in this book by the terms **family benefits** and **survivor benefits**.

B

Beneficiary: a person receiving Social Security or Medicare benefits.

C

Claim and suspend: see **File and suspend.**

Claimant: A person for whom a Social Security claim is filed. See **Applicant**.

Claims Representative: A Social Security representative trained to process claims and other complex work.

COBRA (Consolidated Omnibus Budget Reconciliation Act of 1985): the law which requires limited continuation of employee health insurance after leaving employment.

Coinsurance: A portion of a medical bill that must be paid by the patient, typically expressed as a percentage of the total bill. See **Co-payment**.

COLA: Cost Of Living Adjustment. An increase in cash payments to account for inflation. Social Security COLAs are paid in January.

Co-Payment: A portion of a medical bill that must be paid by the patient, typically expressed as a flat dollar amount. See **Coinsurance**.

Covered work: Employment or self-employment which is covered by Social Security—subject to Social Security taxes and posted to the earnings record.

CR: See **Claims Representative.**

Credits: See **Work Credits**

Currently insured: Status of a worker who dies or becomes disabled before earning enough work credits to be **fully insured**, but who does have 6 work credits out of the 13 calendar quarters ending in death or disability. Currently insured status allows limited **survivor payments** and **ESRD** Medicare.

Custodial care: Nursing care providing personal assistance with dressing, eating, bathing, etc. Distinguished from **skilled nursing care**.

D

DDS: Disability Determination Service. The government agency which determines whether a claimant meets the definition of disability, typically a state department of health.

Deductible: A dollar amount set by Medicare which must be paid by the beneficiary before Medicare benefits can begin. For **Medicare Part A,** the hospital deductible is $1,340 per benefit period; for **Medicare Part B,** the deductible is $183 per year (2018).

Deemed filing: The assumption that if you claim retirement or spousal payments, you are simultaneously filing for the other benefit.

Dependent benefits: See **Family benefits**.

DI: Disability Insurance

DIB: Disability Insurance Benefit. Disability payments made to a worker on his or her own record.

Direct deposit: Sending a Social Security payment by wire transfer directly into a bank account, rather than sending a paper check by mail.

Disability: A medical condition which prevents or will prevent the performance of **Substantial Gainful Activity** for at least 12 months or until death.

DRC: Delayed Retirement Credit. A bonus added to a retirement payment because the worker delays payments until after the **Full Retirement Age**.

Dual entitlement: Simultaneous entitlement on two different work records, e.g. as a worker in one's own right and as the spouse of another worker.

Dualie: a person with **Dual entitlement.**

E

Earnings record: The record of all **covered work** performed by a worker.

Eligible: Meeting all legal factors of entitlement except for filing a valid claim. A person may be eligible for payment, but not **entitled**, because he or she has not yet filed for benefits.

Enrollment periods: Specified time periods for enrolling in Medicare or supplemental insurance.

Entitled: Literally, receiving title to (ownership of) payments. This means that a person meets all legal requirements for benefit payments, including filing a valid claim. See **Eligible.**

ESRD: End Stage Renal Disease. Severe kidney disease requiring dialysis treatment or transplant, and qualifying for ESRD Medicare.

F

Family benefits: Payments made to a living spouse, former spouse, or child on the work record of a living worker.

Family Maximum: The maximum payment amount available to an immediate family under one earnings record. Applies to both **family benefits** and **survivor benefits**.

FICA: Federal Insurance Contributions Act. Refers to the 6.2% Social Security tax on wages, and informally refers to the 1.45% Medicare tax as well.

File and suspend: A claiming strategy in which the claimant files for benefits and immediately puts benefits in **suspension.**

FRA: Full Retirement Age. The age at which a retiree can receive 100% benefits (100% of the **PIA**). Currently phasing from 66 to 67.

Fully insured: Status of a worker who has sufficient **Work Credits** for unrestricted eligibility for retirement, disability, or survivor payments.

H

Hearing: The second level of administrative appeal, after **Reconsideration** and before **Appeals Council Review**. Conducted by an **ALJ**.

HI: Hospital Insurance; same as **Medicare Part A**. Also means Health Insurance, especially when used with the acronym **OASDHI** or **RSDHI** to describe SSA's programs.

HMO: Health Maintenance Organization. A pre-payment group medical practice providing medical services through its own (or contracted) hospitals, clinics, etc. Services typically require a flat **Co-payment**.

Hold Harmless: the rule that most Medicare premium increases cannot exceed the Social Security **COLA**.

I

Indexing: Adjusting for inflation. Indexed wages are wages adjusted for inflation.

Insured Status: A worker's status of meeting or not meeting the work requirements for receiving payments, as measured in **Work Credits**.

L

LTC: Long-Term Care. Usually refers to custodial care given at home or in an institution such as an adult family home or assisted care facility. LTC can also include respite care or other ancillaries. Also refers to insurance that pays for such care.

M

Maximum earnings: See **Taxable earnings ceiling**.

Means testing: Requiring low income and/or resources for eligibility, as with public assistance programs. Social Security is not means tested, while **SSI** is.

Medicaid: A medical program for low-income individuals; part of the public assistance program. Included with **SSI** entitlement.

Medicare card: A card issued by Medicare indicating entitlement to **Medicare Part A** and/or **Part B**. It provides your claim number for processing medical claims.

Medicare Part A: The hospital insurance portion of Medicare, primarily covering hospital and **Skilled Nursing** bills.

Medicare Part B: The medical insurance portion of Medicare, covering physicians' services and other medical bills.

Medigap insurance: Private medical insurance intended to supplement Medicare's coverage, filling Medicare's "gaps."

Monthly earnings test: A **Retirement test**, used in the first year of retirement, which considers the retiree's earnings month by month rather than annually.

O

OASI: Old-Age and Survivor Insurance. Archaic acronym for SSA's original insurance programs. Also OASDI, Old-Age, Survivor, and Disability Insurance; and OASDHI, Old-Age, Survivor, Disability, and Health Insurance. See **RSDHI**.

P

PIA: Primary Insurance Amount. The 100% payment level yielded by a retirement, disability, or survivor computation. The PIA is the basis for payment computations for everyone entitled to benefits on a given earnings record (e.g. the worker, spouse, children, survivors, etc.). It is the amount of retirement benefits payable at **FRA** (Full Retirement Age). Often called "full payment amount" in this book.

Provider: As used by Medicare, a hospital, nursing facility, physician or other entity providing medical services.

Q

QC: Quarter of Coverage. Archaic term for a **Work Credit** on a worker's earnings record.

QMB Program: The Qualified Medicare Beneficiary program, which pays Medicare deductibles and premiums for low-income individuals.

R

Reconsideration: The first level of administrative **Appeal**, after an initial determination and before a **Hearing**.

Representative payment: Payment of Social Security benefits to a representative payee rather than directly to the beneficiary, because the beneficiary is incapable of managing money.

Restricted Application: a claiming strategy in which a **dualie** files for only one type of benefit rather than another, as in **spousal-only filing.**

Retirement Test: An appraisal to determine if a claimant or beneficiary of retirement, family, or survivor benefits is truly retired. Such benefits can be paid only if work activity is below the limits of the retirement test.

RIB: Retirement Insurance Benefit. A retirement payment from SSA on the work record of the **claimant**.

RRB: Railroad Retirement Board. The agency which processes claims and payments for railroad retirees.

RSDHI: Retirement, Survivor, Disability, and Health Insurance. Acronym describing SSA's insurance programs. Also RSI or RSDI, as appropriate. Archaic reference: **OASI**.

S

Service Representative: A Social Security representative skilled in processing changes to existing Social Security payment records, and with expertise in Medicare.

SGA: Substantial Gainful Activity. A specified threshold of work activity defining whether a medical impairment is a **disability**. SGA is usually measured by dollar earnings level, but can also be measured by work hours.

Skilled Nursing care: Nursing care providing at least 4 hours per day of highly skilled therapy such as injections or physical therapy.

SMI: Supplemental Medical Insurance. Same as **Medicare Part B**.

Spousal-only filing: A claiming strategy in which a **dualie** files only for spousal benefits, delaying his/her own benefits

SR: See **Service Representative**.

SSA: Social Security Administration. The government agency which administers the Social Security and **SSI** programs, and eligibility and premiums for the Medicare program.

SSB: Social Security Board. The original name for the Social Security Administration.

SSI: Supplemental Security Income. A public assistance (welfare) program, administered by **SSA**, providing **Medicaid** and cash payments to needy aged, blind, and disabled individuals.

SSN: Social Security Number.

Substantial services: Work limit used in the **monthly retirement test** for self-employed individuals.

Survivor benefits: Payments made to a living spouse, former spouse, child, or parent of a deceased worker.

Suspension: the ability to suspend one's own benefits from **FRA** to age 70.

T

Taxable earnings ceiling: The maximum amount of earnings subject to Social Security taxes.

TSR: TeleService Representative. A **Service Representative** specially trained in telephone interviews.

V

Voluntary suspension: see **Suspension**.

W

Work Credit: The basic unit of work used to establish eligibility for Social Security benefits. For example, 40 work credits are required for retirement benefits. One work credit is posted to a worker's earnings record for each $1,320 earned (2018), up to a maximum of 4 per year.

Workers' compensation: A program paying benefits to workers disabled by job-related injuries.

INDEX

Bold face indicates a figure/illustration

☆ NOTES ☆

☆ ABOUT THE AUTHOR ☆

Andy Landis is one of the nation's foremost authorities on Social Security and Medicare.

Andy has guided tens of thousands to abundant retirements while working at the Social Security Administration, AARP, multi-national corporations, and his own practice, Thinking Retirement.

Through Thinking Retirement, Andy educated both individuals and financial professionals with live workshops, books, articles, webinars, and professional education courses focused on Social Security and Medicare.

Andy's blogs appear on the *Wall Street Journal's* "MarketWatch" site. On TV, he has appeared on Fox Business News and PBS, and is a frequent guest on radio.

Andy's best-selling book *Social Security: The Inside Story* has been hailed as "the best" since the first edition debuted in 1993.

Andy is based in Seattle with Kay, Cody-dog, keyboards, camper, computers, cars, and sometimes kids. He's retiring in 2018 and hitting the road for full-time RV travel.

Link to Andy's vibrant blogs and YouTube videos at www.andylandis.biz.

CPSIA information can be obtained
at www.ICGtesting.com
Printed in the USA
LVOW09s1524150418
573560LV00002B/17/P